"This account of an Everest ascent effectively strips the journey of all sentiment. . . . Kodas forever dispels whatever romantic ideas readers may hold about the great Himalayan peak. A–." —*Entertainment Weekly*

"The perfect follow-up to Krakauer's riveting account of a perfect storm." —*Miami Herald*

"A disturbing account of stupidity and greed on the slopes of Mount Everest. . . . A thorough reporter, Kodas does an excellent job exposing the ways in which money and ego have corrupted the traditional cultures of both mountaineers and their Sherpa guides. He also brings a painful focus to the delusions, misunderstandings, and indifference that allow climbers to literally step over the bodies of dying people on their way to the top. . . . His narrative is as hard to turn away from as a slow-motion train wreck." —*Publishers Weekly*

"Climbing Mount Everest is usually seen as a noble, even spiritual experience. [Kodas] shatters that image by showing the impact of the climbers on the impoverished people that live there, the brutal and nasty in-fighting that plagues many teams, and the Wild West lawlessness that dominates." —*New York Daily News*

"Kodas has skillfully applied the investigative skills honed as a Pulitzer Prize–winning reporter for the *Hartford Courant* to recount [his story] in clear and unpretentious prose. . . . His absorbing description of the narrow moral compass governing human interaction at the top of the world is bound to shock both armchair adventurers and seasoned mountaineers." —*Chicago Tribune*

"In 2004, Kodas joined an expedition to scale Everest led by two veteran climbers. As if the constant threat of death weren't sufficiently terrifying, he discovered more deceit, thievery and double-crossing among his climbers than you find in a Martin Scorsese gangster film. *High Crimes* is both an adventure story and an exposé of a sport riddled with danger and corruption that has mostly gone unnoticed because so few can afford to play." —*Washington Post Book World*

"Kodas's cautionary tale paints a grim picture of Everest mountaineering today. . . . A clear-eyed, riveting narrative."

—*Kirkus Reviews* (starred review)

"There are plenty of books about the allure and danger of Everest, but this may be the first to explore the mountain's criminal element: the fraudulent commercial guides; the thieves and scoundrels who loot other climbers' camps, stealing vital supplies that can be sold at a profit; the violence among climbers. . . . A strongly written, passionate plea for sanity before it's too late." —*Booklist*

"[*High Crimes*] is hair-raising and lays bare the excitement and fear that face great explorers at the top of the world. . . . Sitting in the hot summer sun is not enough to keep the chills of fear from tearing down your spine while reading Kodas's chilling tale of greed, and ambition, atop Everest. Well written, and as deftly plotted as the finest mystery novel, Kodas brings to life a disturbing picture of society at high altitude."

—*Austin Chronicle*

"Kodas's remarkable book exposes the deceits, robberies and thefts, the drugs fueling some high-altitude expeditions, even the casual willingness of people paid to get climbers to the top to abandon stricken clients to almost certain death. . . . Kodas's descriptions of the struggles confronting even the best-prepared climbers leave the reader breathless."

—*Dallas Morning News*

"As his narrative unfolds, [Kodas] mixes the saga of his nearly disastrous climbing party with stories of other climbers led by other scheming organizers. . . . Compelling, and nightmarish, reading. . . . An important, brave and, yes, shocking book." —*Hartford Courant*

"A disturbing, fascinating book." —*Shelf Awareness*

"An absorbing and disturbing new book about the business of Everest."
—Veryshortlist.com

Michael Kodas

HIGH
CRIMES

*The Fate of Everest in
an Age of Greed*

HYPERION
New York

Library of Congress Cataloging-in-Publication Data
Kodas, Michael.
High crimes : the fate of Everest in an age of greed / Michael Kodas.
   p.   cm.
ISBN-13: 978-1-4013-0273-3
1. Mountaineering—Social aspects.   2. Mountaineering—Corrupt practices.   I. Title.
GV200.19.S63K63 2008
796.52'2–dc22   2007021477

Paperback ISBN: 978-1-4013-0984-8

Design by Michelle McMillian

FIRST PAPERBACK EDITION

1   3   5   7   9   10   8   6   4   2

Mount Everest

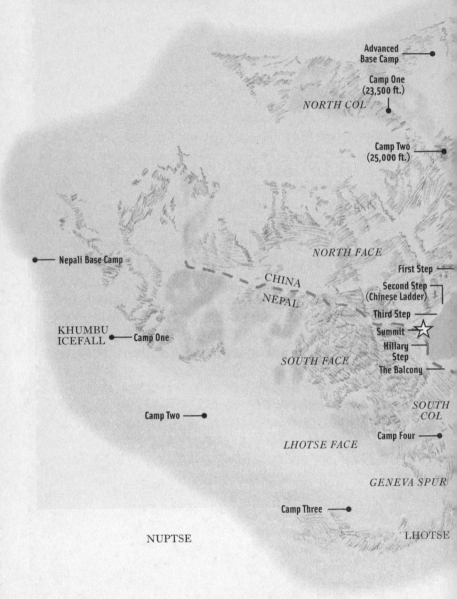

Advanced Base Camp

Camp One (23,500 ft.)

NORTH COL

Camp Two (25,000 ft.)

NORTH FACE

Nepali Base Camp

CHINA

NEPAL

First Step

Second Step (Chinese Ladder)

Third Step

KHUMBU ICEFALL — Camp One

Summit

Hillary Step

The Balcony

SOUTH FACE

SOUTH COL

Camp Two

Camp Four

LHOTSE FACE

GENEVA SPUR

Camp Three

NUPTSE

LHOTSE

Camp Three
(26,700 ft.)

EAST FACE

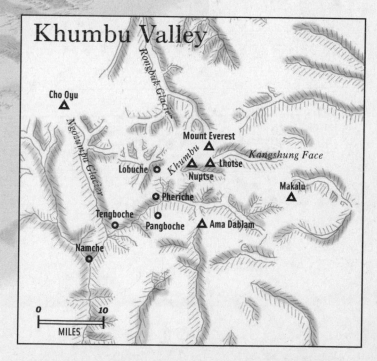

Khumbu Valley

Rongbuk Glacier

Cho Oyu △

Ngozumpa Glacier

Mount Everest △

Khumbu

Lobuche ⊙

△ △ Lhotse
Nuptse

Kangshung Face

Makalu △

⊙ Pheriche

Tengboche ⊙

⊙ Pangboche △ Ama Dablam

Namche ⊙

0   10
├────┼────┤
MILES

Preface

On May 8, 2008, a team of nineteen Chinese and Tibetan climbers carried the Olympic torch to the summit of Mount Everest, turning the peak into the first arena of China's games. By then, however, the flame was obscured by its own shadow.

To prevent activists promoting a free Tibet from disrupting the event, China imposed the climbing equivalent of martial law on Everest. It closed the peak to foreign mountaineers to allow its team exclusive access to the mountain. When violent protests erupted in Tibet, China closed the entire region to outsiders while they cracked down on the dissenters.

Ironically, a few weeks earlier, China had paved the road to Base Camp to facilitate the entry of the hundreds of climbers and tourists that they then wouldn't let in. With a hotel already built outside the camp, and a giant tower providing cellular phone service all the way to the summit, Everest's Tibetan Base Camp was like an Olympic village evacuated of athletes. Hundreds of perfectly regimented military tents replaced the global village of colorful nylon that normally sprawled beneath the mountain in the spring.

Activists for the Tibetan cause condemned the torch climb as a new way for China to plant its flag on the once sovereign country that it had occupied in 1950. China countered that criticism by including Tibetans in the climbing team and having one of them, a woman named Tsering Wangmo, bear the flame on the summit. But while China's climb put Tibetan mountaineers on a pedestal, it plunged the rest of Tibet deeper into poverty as tourism, a crucial part of the Tibetan economy, dropped some 80 percent.

"One world, one dream," the Chinese team shouted in English at the summit. "Welcome to Beijing." Their welcome, however, did not extend to the lands where the mountain they climbed rises. And to achieve its Olympic dream, China had deprived mountaineers from around the world of the chance to pursue their own.

Although Nepal allowed mountaineers on its side of Everest, it bowed to Chinese pressure and adopted draconian measures to keep order while the torch team was on the other side of the mountain. Nepali soldiers were posted in high camps with orders to shoot any mountaineer who tried to reach the summit while the Chinese were climbing. Officers locked down mountaineers' radios and satellite phones, and monitored all communications to the outside world. An American climber was expelled after authorities found a Tibetan banner amid his gear.

The situation was little safer after the soldiers left. The already crowded Nepali route got an influx of mountaineers who had initially planned to climb the Tibetan side of the mountain. Climbers waiting like racehorses to head up the mountain had little time to fix ropes, set camps, and reach the summit before the monsoon arrived in June. When the military restrictions and weather finally lifted, a photo taken by a mountaineer on a nearby peak showed a solid line of climbers queued up for thousands of feet below the summit of Everest.

Yet for all of the outrage over the militarization of Everest, many adventurers have long hoped that the governments of China and Nepal would impose some order on the ever-expanding frontier towns that, at least when the Olympics aren't there, spread farther up the world's highest mountain every spring.

Michael Kodas
JANUARY 22, 2009

Prologue

Most of the world came to know David Sharp because of how desperately late he was. I got acquainted with him because he was on time.

"Sam's Bar at seven." During the last days of March 2006, the words were a mantra among the group of climbers I would join on Mount Everest through the next two months. The small terrace bar in the Thamel section of Kathmandu was a warm refuge, both from our visions of the frozen mountain a hundred miles away and from the crazed, carnivalesque streets below. Most of us, wrapped up in our preparations for the climb, didn't get to Sam's until seven thirty or eight. But on the days that he joined us, David was there right on time, as was my wife, Carolyn, and on one occasion, me.

As we waited for the rest of our dinner crew, David said that once he knocked Everest off his list, he was probably going to give up mountaineering.

"I'm thirty-four years old. I want to go home, meet someone, settle down, and have children.

"I guess I might climb on weekends," he said, but he sounded doubtful.

It was David's third time on the mountain; my second. We were both more than familiar with the weeks of frigid suffering that lay before us, and I wondered how David could fire himself up for the long, cold climb with such a lukewarm attitude toward the sport he once loved.

He was six feet tall and thin, with wire-rimmed glasses, a big-toothed grin, and a barely there goatee that got scruffier on the mountain. The Guisborough, England, native had given up his job as an engineer to climb, but was starting a new career as a math teacher in the fall. He carried two books with him—a collection of Shakespeare in honor of George Mallory's readings of *King Lear* and *Hamlet* on the mountain eighty-two years before, and, although he claimed he was an atheist, a Bible. He brought only a disposable camera to record his trip.

"I've got all the photos I need," he told companions in Base Camp. "Except for the summit."

If he didn't make it to the top this time, he said, he wasn't coming back. He couldn't afford to. As it was, he had barely scraped up enough money for his current climb. He didn't have the cash to hire any Sherpa support, and had purchased only two bottles of oxygen for a climb on which most people use five or more. Two years earlier, on his second attempt, he had tried to climb without oxygen, but carried two tanks of gas with him just in case. He became so hypoxic, he told us, that he forgot to use them when it became apparent he wouldn't top out without them. Forced to retreat, he finally remembered the oxygen cylinders and took them out of his pack, put them down in the snow and, despite their value of nearly $900, walked down without them. His botched summit bid cost him more than the oxygen: He lost his left big toe and part of another to frostbite. But he laughed at the memory and said that he was willing to lose more digits to make his final attempt on the peak pay off.

Still, even though he was climbing solo, he had told his mother before he left England that if he got into real trouble, he could count on some help.

"On Everest you are never on your own," she would recall his telling her. "There are climbers everywhere."

The mountaineers I learned the ropes with would have honored David with the title "dirtbag," for bringing only what he thought he absolutely needed to survive, and part of me admired his bare-bones approach to the climb. But though I had once put together my climbs the same way, we now had little in common.

Instead of the scriptures, Shakespeare, and a cardboard camera, I had plenty of books—both for reference and entertainment—and six cameras, along with three laptops, a satellite modem and satellite phone, a DVD burner, external hard drives, two digital voice recorders, a minidisc recorder, an iPod, portable speakers, and dozens of notebooks. Carolyn brought three video cameras. All of that was on top of the ice axes, crampons, down clothes, Frankenstein-size boots, and the rest of the Everest climber's wardrobe.

I was loaded for bear, and I had been the last time we were in the Himalaya as well. In 2004, I reported live from the mountain for *The Hartford Courant* newspaper, covering the Connecticut Everest Expedition, a team with which I was also climbing. As I left for the Himalaya that March, I was convinced I was prepared for the endeavor ahead. But by the time I reached the mountain, I knew I was wrong. As it turned out, so was David.

On May 14, 2006, six weeks after our last dinner together, David Sharp came upon a corpse in a cave high on Everest and sat down beside it. It's believed, but not certain, that David had reached Everest's summit that afternoon, climbing on the mountain's northeast ridge in Tibet, the same route he had used to make his previous two attempts on the peak. It was quite late, in Everest climb time, and probably already dark when David, the last person out above the highest camp in the world, arrived at the tiny, jagged grotto. The dead man he sat next to, nicknamed "Green Boots," was an Indian climber who had resided for a decade inside the concrete-colored and crypt-shaped hole in a wall of overhanging limestone—Green Boots Cave. Orange, black, and blue oxygen tanks were strewn among the fractured stones at the entrance to the small room—scrap metal along a highway to the top of the world. David's two bottles of oxygen were almost certainly exhausted; he had been climbing for some twenty hours straight. He'd had no partner joining him on the ascent, or at any other time during his expedition. Instead he had signed on to the permit of an "international" team—a random group of climbers from around the world brought together only by their need to save money by sharing base camp facilities. David had no radio or satellite phone to communicate with the other independent climbers sharing his permit, or the more than thirty other teams in the lower camps. He was about as alone as a person can be on what has become a very crowded mountain. Still, it's hard to imagine that he didn't, at some time when he was approaching the cave, believe that he was in the homestretch to the rest of his life. He was less than 1,000 vertical feet away from Camp Three, where his own tent or other climbers could have provided everything he needed to survive the night—except the will to do it.

It wasn't until what high-altitude mountaineers call the morning, an hour or so after midnight on May 15, when some forty climbers headed up on their own summit bids, that anyone could have noted that David's struggle had turned dire. Some reported that he was still connected to the fixed rope, so most of the two scores of climbers would have had to unclip from that lifeline to get past him. Others saw him sitting up, fiddling with his oxygen equipment, or simply sitting with his pack between his legs as if he were taking a rest while making the same trip to the summit that they were. Most reported later that in the darkness, with their hooded faces gasping for breath through oxygen masks and staring with goggled eyes into the bubble of light from their headlamps, their own senses dulled from the lack of oxygen and the extreme cold, they either mistook David for the dead body that they knew was already there or didn't notice him at all. But on their way back down from the peak eight hours later, in the late-morning sun, it was impossible to miss him. The climbers who stopped to check on him found that his hands were wooden with frostbite. He was wearing only light liner gloves after removing his heavy mittens, hat, and oxygen mask (people suffering from hypothermia often remove clothes in the delusion that they are hot rather than cold). His feet were frozen to the knee, preventing him from standing, much less walking down the mountain on his own. The skin of his nose was already black, and his cheeks, at first bleached to a deathly white by the cold, were turning purple. The frostbite on his face kept him from speaking clearly, but when he was conscious, he at least tried to talk.

"My name is David Sharp," he reportedly said to a Sherpa who was wearing a video camera on his helmet to film a Discovery Channel documentary. "I'm with Asian Trekking, and I just want to sleep."

Nobody else who saw him in the cave had any idea who he was. Some glanced at his clothes for identification but noted nothing except that aside from his boots, his gear was old and worn. Descending climbers who had seen him earlier had reported he was comatose, but others later found him conscious, shivering with his teeth clenched. Their own assaults on the summit had left many of the descending climbers in little better shape: Several were badly frostbitten, and one was being rescued after falling unconscious. All were exhausted and running low on oxygen. A Sherpa for a Turkish team found a bottle of oxygen in David's pack, but it was empty. Other Sherpas rolled him into the sun to make him more comfortable. They put David's oxygen mask back on him and hooked him up to some of their own gas. A few tried to get David on his feet, but his legs buckled under his own weight. To everyone who saw him, it was clear that anything short of carrying him back to camp—a task that would have required perhaps a dozen fresh climbers—was only prolonging the inevitable.

By the next morning, there would be two dead bodies in the cave. Within a week, the whole world would learn about the dying man whom so many climbers stepped within arm's reach of but didn't notice, and the forty-some pairs of boots that walked away from him twice while his life was slowly frozen out of him.

Perhaps there was nothing that could have been done to save David Sharp. Nonetheless, to me and many of the other climbers following the news that trickled down the mountain and then spread around the planet, his failure to survive his descent represented the latest step in our sport's race to the bottom. Most notable of those outraged was the man who had been the first to reach the top of the mountain fifty-three years earlier.

"I think the whole attitude towards climbing Mt. Everest has become rather horrifying," Sir Edmund Hillary said when he heard of David Sharp's death. "People just want to get to the top. They don't give a damn for anybody else who may be in distress, and it doesn't impress me at all that they leave someone lying under a rock to die."

Three years earlier, during the 2003 party marking the fiftieth anniversary of Hillary's climb with Tenzing Norgay, many climbers had been shocked to find that the guest of honor was less than celebratory.

"I am not very happy about the future of Everest," Hillary, then eighty-three, told a press conference in Kathmandu. "At Base Camp there are 1,000 people and 500 tents, there are places for food, places for drinks and comforts that perhaps the young like these days . . . Just sitting around Base Camp knocking back cans of beer, I don't particularly regard as mountaineering."

But in David's death, Hillary saw the worst of his fears realized.

"Human life is far more important than just getting to the top of a mountain," he told the *Otago Daily Times* in New Zealand. "There have been a number of occasions when people have been neglected and left to die."

One of those left to die was Dr. Nils Antezana. Although Nils and I were on Everest at the same time in 2004, we never met. On the mountain, I knew of him only through a message from his daughter, Fabiola, that appeared on my laptop in Advanced Base Camp (ABC), and on other computers all over the planet.

"PLEASE I NEED HELP," she wrote, "my father is missing on Everest."

Fabiola never found out all the details of her father's fate. His body was never found. But she did learn that he died after begging for his life in suspicious and completely avoidable circumstances.

Despite the fact that his end was so similar to David Sharp's, Nils Antezana couldn't have been less of a "dirtbag." A wealthy doctor, he had had the means to put together as extravagant an expedition as he'd cared to—he had a guide, two Sherpas, and plenty of oxygen. And so, for his daughter, the mystery of what had happened in her father's final hours was soon matched by the mystery of how the previous months had led to them. A week after I read her note, I saw Fabiola in Kathmandu during her own expedition—not a journey to the top of the world but an investigation into the underworld that has spread beneath it. But there was little I could do to help her, even though my own Everest climb had led me to pursue a similar quest.

On the day that Nils Antezana vanished on the Nepal side of Everest, I was working my way toward the summit from Tibet with the Connecticut team. It had taken three months of planning, six weeks of trudging through the Himalaya, and ten days of climbing to reach a cluster of tents just two days' climb and 4,000 feet shy of the summit. But the high point of my ascent was the low point of my expedition. Gale-force winds blasted climbers from their feet, and the desperately thin air turned the hike up the snow covered north ridge into a grueling slog. It was not the elements, however, that made me decide to retreat from the summit, but some of my own teammates, who, in their efforts to stand on top of the world and make money doing it, behaved more like mobsters than mountaineers. In the end, some of my climbing partners threatened me more than the mountain did.

During the expedition, more than $10,000 worth of the tents, ropes, and bottled oxygen that my life depended on went missing, some of it turning up later, hidden amid other team members' equipment. Some of my climbing partners openly planned to help themselves to other teams' oxygen tanks and gear. They used the ropes and equipment other expeditions had fixed on the route but refused to contribute to the communal effort to make the climbing route safe. Sherpas hired to accompany us to the summit, whose assistance was crucial to our success and survival, extorted thousands of dollars to complete their work, then abandoned those of us who had paid them. Some mountaineers smuggled drugs across international borders and numbed themselves daily with hashish, beer, and whiskey more than 20,000 feet above sea level. Prostitutes and pimps propositioned climbers walking through Base Camp. Expedition members who tried to stand up against their teammates' thuggish behavior were physically threatened, cut off from the team's power supply, refused food, pelted with rocks and, in one instance, beaten. All of the members of our team survived, but looking back, I see I was little better prepared or less naïve than Nils Antezana—just lucky enough to realize the true nature of the peril I faced and turn back when he continued upward.

As Nils's and the Connecticut climbers' separate dramas played out, the largest of a score of film crews working on the mountain was making a feature-length movie about the 1996 Everest disaster in which eight climbers perished during a single ill-fated summit bid. Nils's death highlighted the changes that have occurred on the mountain in the years since that tragedy. In 1996, Rob Hall, whose repeated trips to the top of the mountain had made him the world's most respected mountain guide, perished on Everest because he refused to leave a dying client behind. In 2004, Nils Antezana died on the mountain after being abandoned by his guide, who Nils believed had climbed Everest before but was actually making his first trip to the summit.

The 1996 season exposed the peril that high-priced mountain guides and their often inexperienced clients brought to the top of the world during the 1990s. Today's story is darker and deeper. Much of the change is due to the tremendous boom in visitors to the world's highest mountains.

Those who thought Hillary's comments or the 1996 tragedies would diminish the traffic on Everest could not have been more wrong. During 2003's Golden Jubilee climbing season, a record 264 people reached the summit. The next year, that record was shattered, with 330 people standing on top of Everest. In 2006, at least 460 climbers stood atop the mountain, and in 2007, the number was nearly 600—six times the 98 climbers who had summited eleven years earlier. Along with that rush of visitors and the millions of dollars that they spend in a wilderness with virtually no legal oversight has come a new breed of parasitic and predatory adventurer.

Although most people recall the disaster on Everest in the spring of 1996, only the most die-hard mountaineering fans remember the exact human toll of the tragedy—twelve dead overall, with eight dying in a single storm. But the cash price the commercial clients paid to be there—$65,000 per person—became a benchmark fixed in minds the world over. Hundreds of foreign climbers and native workers arrived on the mountain in subsequent seasons looking to collect a paycheck from the new Everest industry. The greatest interest in exploiting the mountain of money came from the government of China, which loosened restrictions and began developing infrastructure to draw mountaineers to Tibet.

On May 10, 1996, when the Indian climber now known only as Green Boots (but presumed to be Tsewang Palijor) died in the killer storm, the Chinese side of Everest was a lonelier place. Just a handful of expeditions—a fraction of the number of climbers who visited the Nepal side of the mountain—climbed on the Northeast Ridge to the summit. Ten years later, when David Sharp joined Green Boots in his cave, the demographic had seesawed. With at least thirty organized expeditions, along with dozens of independent climbers, there were more mountaineers and more traffic jams on the north (Tibetan) side than the south. Some of the increase can be attributed to climbers avoiding the massive crevasses and collapsing ice cliffs of the Khumbu Icefall, the greatest peril on the southern route. There is no comparable objective danger on the north side. Ease of access can also account for some of the crowd: Instead of the weeklong walk to reach the Nepali Base Camp, a road runs all the way to Base Camp on the Chinese side, so visitors need only hitch a ride to get to the start of the climb. But most of the increase in climbing traffic is simply due to the fact that at between $3,000 and $5,000, the permit to climb the north side of the mountain costs a fraction of the one for the Nepali side. North side mountaineers pay as little as ten percent of the $65,000 charged by the best expeditions on the south side. And that price difference has made Tibet the Everest climber's Wal-Mart.

Although the government of China does much to put a clean and noble face on the Tibetan side of Everest—garbage collectors and giant trash bins have sprung up throughout Base Camp in recent seasons—it seems more than aware of a different and more insidious mess spreading at the base of their mountain. In 2007, when Chinese climbers arrived for a dry run of the expedition that would carry the Olympic torch up the mountain in the lead-up to the 2008 Beijing games, they brought along some pieces of equipment that have rarely appeared in the mountaineering arena—firearms to guard their equipment and keep the riffraff out of their camp. Although in the last few years a number of expeditions have posted guards to prevent burglaries of their tents, the soldiers who stood sentry over the Chinese camp were the mountain's first armed security workers.

The guns were just another in a long line of unusual accessories introduced on Everest. Every year, expedition leaders further tame the world's highest peaks with satellite weather forecasts, global positioning systems, bolted anchors, ladders fixed over the most difficult sections of the mountain, and thousands of bottles of oxygen that allow attempts at the summit by an ever-increasing number of climbers with an ever-decreasing average level of experience and skill. A growing army of Sherpas does almost all of the work, all but carrying many of the commercial clients to the summit. Those resources are in turn drawing a new kind of climber to the mountain—freeloaders and outlaws who plan to make it to the summit by exploiting the equipment, supplies, and legwork of better-resourced climbers and expeditions.

Many of the mountaineers putting together low-budget Everest expeditions are, either through intent or out of denial, bound to become burdens on the better-equipped and better-prepared. Climbers who arrive without the appropriate medications or medical equipment overwhelm doctors on well-resourced teams. One team I was on ordered its members not to mention that we had a doctor with us, to try to stem the flood of sick climbers from other camps. Some arrive without ropes, anchors, or high-altitude tents; watch hungrily as commercial operators equip the mountain; then crowd the guides and their clients from the lifelines and shelters they paid for. Oxygen tanks, stove fuel, and food vanish every year from the highest camps in the world, much of it appropriated by Western mountaineers who have shown up at the mountain with few of those resources. And when a boldly independent but woefully underequipped climber like David Sharp gets into trouble high on the mountain, everyone within range of helping will be faced with the same wrenching dilemma: give up on the dream they have spent thousands of dollars and months of suffering to achieve, to save someone who came underprepared—or leave him to his fate in order to stay focused on their own ambitions.

No other sport, perhaps no other human endeavor, has as bipolar a zenith as mountaineering. The very name of the game—climbing—promotes measuring success by the height attained. But the highest mountain in the world is far from being the world's most difficult to climb. In the way it is climbed now, according to many veteran mountaineers, Everest is actually the easiest of the world's 8,000-meter peaks. So it has become something of a wild card, the ultimate trump. With ladders and fixed ropes helping to overcome technical difficulties, neophytes who can barely tie their own knots need only the genetics that allow survival at high altitude and a good amount of fitness to put one foot in front of the other all the way to the planet's high point. Although many who reach the summit have climbed only a handful of peaks in their life, they descend with the title "World Class Mountaineer." Some, who were schoolteachers, car salesmen, or contractors when they started up, descend transformed into motivational speakers, authors, television personalities, sponsored athletes, mountain guides, or "life coaches." In other cases, the summit of Everest is simply a must-have entry at the top of a life's résumé—often that of doctors, business and government leaders, or athletes from other sports who would be among the world's most accomplished people even without the planet's high point on their curriculum vitae.

These trophy hunters pay their way to the top of the world and expect bottom-line results on that investment. Many of their guides and expedition leaders see the old rules of climbing—making one's way without artificial aids, carrying one's own gear, and leaving no sign of one's passage—as obstacles to their own financial success, and do whatever it takes to increase the odds for their clients. The ladders, expansion bolts, and tangles of fixed ropes that hang like spaghetti make some climbs seem more like construction sites than mountains. But those encroachments have begun to seem small. China announced, in the summer of 2007, its plans to pave a highway with "undulating guardrails" to Everest Base Camp in preparation for the Olympic torch climb. Although the government later backpedaled from that plan, an unpaved road to Base Camp has existed for decades. A multistory hotel has been open for a few years just an hour's walk from the camp, with soft beds, cold beer, and a telescope aimed at the summit. Nearby, a huge cellular phone tower constructed by China Telecom provided phone service all the way to the top of the mountain during much of the 2007 climbing season. And on May 5, 2005, astonished climbers reported watching a helicopter land on the summit.

It's not only climbers who are cashing in on the Everest brand. The Everest lectures, slideshows, documentaries, and reality television programs are only some of the ways that the mountain has become part of workaday life around the planet. In fact, the more people from developed nations make their way to the planet's highest mountain, the more Everest becomes part of the civilized world. The Chinese climbers' plan to carry the Olympic torch to the mountaintop for the 2008 Beijing Olympics is just one example. In 2007, the Ford Motor Company debuted its largest sport utility vehicle— the Everest—with a caravan of the trucks driving to their namesake mountain. In 2006, Disney's Animal Kingdom theme park opened Expedition Everest, a roller coaster, stalked by a Yeti on a man-made mountain that, at 200 feet tall, is the highest peak in Florida—as well as the company's most expensive and elaborate attraction. Yet even Everest's most wholesome reflections show the changes of recent years. It struck me as strangely appropriate that the greatest peril facing the tourists in Disney's fantasy of the mountain isn't getting to the top and back but a predator that attacks them while they are there.

Whether people walk to the top, cruise to Base Camp in a sport utility vehicle, land on its summit in a helicopter, or even ride a roller coaster over it in Florida, Everest is assured a continued boom of visitors and victims. And the pattern defined there is spreading to other mountains, other wildernesses, and other sports. Today thousands of sailors, climbers, paddlers, divers, and trekkers bring millions of dollars to isolated and lawless environments around the globe. That wealth and the daring lifestyle of the extreme athlete are in turn drawing a new peril to the mountains. Many adventurers are discovering that the most dangerous tests they face in the wild come not from nature but from neighboring tents, as greed and ambition conspire to draw corruption to the wilderness.

To plumb the figurative depths of the planet's high point, I have twice tried to stand on those few square feet of mountaintop by which much of the world measures all human accomplishment. In that goal, at least so far, I have failed. Nonetheless, the mountain has provided me with an excellent vantage point from which to look at the changing landscape of the world of adventure.

"I just want to get this Everest thing over with," David Sharp told me at Sam's, and I knew just how he felt.

But although before I first visited Everest I had no desire to climb it, I know that my time on the mountain has infected me with the same summit fever that David had. I can only hope that the contagion I've contracted isn't as virulent as the strain that took his life.

One

Along the highway of rope that leads above 8,000 meters on Mount Everest, the Balcony is probably the most accommodating rest stop, but Big Dorjee Sherpa and his teammates never planned on taking in the sunset from this perch. Climbers who see the end of the day here are often facing the end of their lives as well.

Most climbers on the south side of the peak, in fact, hope to see the dawn rather than the dusk of their summit day from the frigid overlook that hangs 27,600 feet above sea level. Even at daybreak, they have been climbing for four or five hours by the time they get to this ridge of snow that stretches out like a runway toward the climb ahead. The rising sun bloodies the sky behind Makalu, the fifth-tallest mountain in the world, but the jagged tooth would be hard to miss even if it weren't so massive and highlighted in crimson and saffron: The peak of the Balcony's triangular ridgeline points directly at it. Below and to the south, the lighted tents of Camp Four, the highest camp on the route, glow yellow in the still-dark desolation of Everest's South Col, the highest refuge on the route in all but the most desperate of circumstances. To the north, the remote, immense, and relentlessly steep wall of the Kangshung Face stretches nearly two miles beneath the mountaintop, blushing with first light as it plummets into Tibet. Even mountaineers focused only on their ascent do well to take in this vista anyway. If they can't see these things, they probably shouldn't be here at all; the most benign clouds that obscure this view can turn deadly higher on the mountain.

Those who continue up from the Balcony often take advantage of the wind break provided by a couple of large boulders at the edge of the ledge. They take off their backpacks for a few minutes, often sitting on them while they regroup. Virtually every face is hidden behind a mask connected to a tank of oxygen in their pack. At the Balcony, most climbers on oxygen take the bottle they are sucking on, unscrew it from the system's regulator, and spin a full bottle on in its place. There's often some gas left in that first tank, so they plant it in a carefully noted spot in the snow to retrieve on their return from the summit around midday. When they get back down, they'll switch their last bottle of oxygen, which is probably nearly empty, for the one they started with, using the dregs of that first tank's gas to get through the homestretch of their descent to the relative safety of the South Col. On a busy summit day, orange and blue oxygen bottles awaiting their owners' return poke up out of the snow like buoys bobbing in a wave. For mountaineers who arrive at the Balcony late, or exhausted or stormbound, that last bottle of oxygen can make the difference between survival and death. When Big Dorjee returned to the Balcony from the mountaintop that day, he and his teammates were all of these things. And sometimes, he knew, even a bottle of oxygen isn't enough to buoy a faltering climber.

It had been more than six hours since the four-man team stood on the summit, and they had been climbing in the mountain's notorious "death zone" for more than twenty. Their descent had run hours late, and the other climbers who had made it to the summit that morning had been back in the shelter of the high camp for hours. Help was impossibly distant. Mingma Sherpa, standing beside his friend and coworker Dorjee, had made his first ascent to the top of Everest that morning. He knew enough to be terrified, but lacked the experience to recognize the myriad ways in which the mountain was trying to kill them. Dorjee, however, was coming down from his tenth trip to the top, and could see death coming at them from every direction.

A cloud cap was dropping on top of the mountain, stirring up a fierce wind and threatening snow. Below them the dark shadows of night were climbing up the peak like frozen specters that would drop the temperature to 20 below zero or colder. Dorjee and Mingma's last oxygen tanks had run dry hours earlier. The man they would later say was dead when they left him grabbed at their legs like a zombie as they walked off the Balcony. But that was the least of their worries.

More than six feet tall, Big Dorjee Sherpa towers over almost all the other Sherpas, who are normally diminutive. Dorjee had grown up in Thame, a village some fifteen miles from Everest's south side Base Camp. For the people of the valley known as the Solu Khumbu, and residents of hamlets like Thame scattered about it, the big mountain had brought the highest standards of living in Nepal, and many villagers worked as porters or cooks for the mountaineers and trekkers who flooded the region. Others ran teahouses and lodges that catered to them. The Khumbu Valley's wealth shows in Dorjee's smile, which beams with a gold tooth from under his mustache—a product of the dental care that Sir Edmund Hillary and others had brought to the region, along with schools and medical clinics. Like a lot of Sherpas, Big Dorjee smiles a lot to compensate for his difficulty in speaking the languages of the climbers who hire him.

Big Dorjee, age forty, started his career in the mountains as a yak driver, prodding trains of pack animals that were sometimes more than fifty beasts long up the steep, rocky, and airless trails. But Dorjee's stature and strength assured him other opportunities in the same way that a cum laude from Harvard opens doors in the States. His brother had worked for climbing teams, and by the early '90s, Dorjee had an invitation to work from one of the ever-increasing number of Everest expeditions that head to the peak every April. On his second expedition, he stepped onto the summit and into mountaineering's major leagues: A Sherpa who had climbed Everest had the best paycheck in the Khumbu, and was assured of work during the climbing season. In two months, Dorjee earned more than he could in a full year of herding yaks. That income had allowed him to move his family to Kathmandu and send his two daughters to school, a path of economic and social advancement followed by dozens of other climbing Sherpas.

In the eyes of Manuel Lugli, the Italian expedition organizer who had arranged his current assignment, Big Dorjee was clearly an asset. Three months earlier, he had described him in an e-mail to his clients, Gustavo Lisi and Nils Antezana.

> *Dorjee Sherpa, 40 years old, very, very strong and experienced. He has climbed on Annapurna IV, Makalu, Cho Oyu, Kanchenjunga, and above all has been on Everest 15 times, arriving at the summit 9 times (!), the last in the past year with my expedition.*

The word "Sherpa" has so many uses, it's hard to grasp. The Sherpa are an ethnic group that migrated from Tibet to Nepal a few hundred years ago. The title is also the last name of most members of the tribe—which leads to confusion that is further exacerbated by the tribe's custom of naming children after the day of the week on which they are born. And in the last fifty years, Western mountaineers have appropriated the name Sherpa as a job description for mountaineering porters, who are often, but not always, members of the tribe. The word carries strong connotations of hard work, loyalty, and honesty, and most Sherpas still live up to that part of their name: Almost all Himalayan climbers readily admit that they would have little chance of success without the assistance of Sherpas.

From the beginning, the Bolivian-American doctor and the Argentine guide who had hired Dorjee and Mingma seemed an unlikely couple. Nils Antezana, a slender physician with salt-and-pepper hair, was reserved and polite, even to the most ragged of the porters who hauled their hundreds of pounds of equipment to the mountain. To Dorjee, as well as to most of the other climbers Nils met on Everest that spring, he looked like he was a few years beyond fifty. He didn't boast of the fact that, at sixty-nine, he would be the oldest American to reach the top of the world, or that he wore the same pants size that he had when he was forty years younger. His pride in his fitness was something he kept to himself. Each year higher-profile climbers set youth and age records, broadcasting the news around the world from the summit, but it would be a week before even Nils's teammates learned his actual age.

His guide, an Argentinean named Gustavo Lisi, however, didn't mind boasting. The thirty-three-year-old seemed to step right from the mold of the rock-star mountaineer, turning his thumb up for photos, throwing his arm around campmates, and recounting his climbs in South America and his previous climb to the top of Everest four years earlier, in 2000. Other climbers on the mountain knew the story behind Gustavo's previous trip to Everest and some of his climbs in the Andes, but they didn't like to talk about them. Big Dorjee and Mingma would have heard few of his tales—Gustavo didn't speak English; Dorjee and Mingma spoke no Spanish. Nils had to translate all but the simplest of instructions between his guide and the two assistants. Although Gustavo was the guide, Big Dorjee and Mingma quickly figured out that Nils was the man who was paying for everything, and that made him the boss—even if he rarely gave them any orders of his own. The two Sherpas didn't mind that Gustavo spent little time with his client, Nils, often leaving them to lead the doctor up the mountain. The soft-spoken doctor was easy to get along with and put far fewer demands on them than the Argentinean. It was Nils's first time on Everest, so he would have had little idea what to ask of them, even if he had been more demanding by nature. Hanging out with him was not only more amicable, but might entitle the Sherpas to the kind of hefty tips and bonuses—$2,000 or more each—that they knew Nils's guide couldn't afford.

But as soon as the team had stepped on top of Mount Everest, Big Dorjee realized that it was unlikely they would see a tip at all.

Witnesses and team members say the group reached the summit of Everest just after ten a.m. on May 18, 2004. They agree on little else. Dorjee claims they had been climbing for only ten hours, meaning the team would have started their summit bid at midnight, but other climbers saw the group leave camp on the South Col a little after eight o'clock the night before.

"I have finished equipping myself, it's eight at night and we are ready to leave for the summit," Gustavo reported by satellite telephone to his Web site before heading out.

Although ten a.m. is a reasonable time to summit, with an eight p.m. start, they had been climbing nonstop for fourteen hours when they reached the top—the halfway point of any summit day. They would need nearly half that amount of time to climb back down to their tents . . . if everything went well. The team had planned to make their round trip to the summit from Camp Four the previous day, when forecasts sent to the mountain by satellite predicted sunny skies and calm winds. They chose instead to spend that day resting. By the time they headed out from Camp Four on the evening of May 17, the weather report that had called for favorable conditions for several days had deteriorated. But at the summit, Big Dorjee didn't have time to worry about the turn in the weather, only the storm that seemed to be descending on his client's brain.

The doctor had been slow climbing up, but Dorjee says he didn't notice anything in his client's behavior to indicate that he was suffering from altitude sickness. Nonetheless Dorjee had repeatedly tried to turn the team around, complaining to both the doctor and his guide that they were climbing too slowly to make it to the summit and back down safely. Neither was willing to retreat.

But on top, Dorjee says, the doctor stumbled toward the edge of the summit and looked as if he were going to jump off. Then Nils pulled off his oxygen mask and lay down on his back on the snow.

During the more than forty-five minutes that Nils, Gustavo, and their Sherpa assistants stayed on the summit—an unusually long time for a team that arrived there late in the morning on a day with unstable weather—Dorjee says he could hardly get the doctor to stay on his feet.

"He's going mad," Dorjee recalls thinking.

Gustavo, however, says he saw none of this.

The guide was busy making photographs and videos of the vistas from the summit and of himself standing amid them, but says he would have noticed a climbing partner in such obvious distress. The only indications that Nils was in trouble, Gustavo says, were that Nils asked him why he had his headlamp turned on when the guide wasn't wearing one and that the doctor took several seconds to wave to the video camera after Gustavo asked him to. The video, which passes over Nils for just those few seconds, is the only record Gustavo made of his client on the summit, although members of another team that also made it to the summit that morning took a photo of Nils kneeling and waving to them from the top. He doesn't appear mad or sick in any of the images.

Once the team began its descent, however, it was clear that Nils would need assistance from all three of his teammates to make it back down.

The doctor was disoriented, had difficulty seeing, and staggered drunkenly as he walked, wobbling and stumbling down the narrow ridge of snow. Dorjee and Mingma stayed on either side of him, steering him downhill, clipping him into the ropes that were anchored to the route home and holding his arms to support him when his legs seemed ready to buckle. Gustavo joined them to help with the most difficult sections, but Dorjee says the guide was usually a few steps in front of them. By the time the team had descended two hundred feet below the summit, wherein lies the most difficult section of the climb—the forty-foot bluff of snow, ice, and rock known as the Hillary Step—Nils had collapsed. Dorjee pulled a rope from his pack, and the Sherpas lowered the doctor down the headwall. But three hours later the team had made it only another hundred feet down the mountain to the South Summit, where Nils nearly tumbled off the ridgeline. In the meantime, the weather had begun to turn in earnest, and the wind often knocked the climbers off balance. Gustavo's last bottle of oxygen—he and the Sherpas planned on using only two bottles each, but brought five for their client—ran dry.

As the Sherpas held tight to their struggling client, they looked up to see Gustavo stepping away from them, pointing at Mingma and waving for him to come down the mountain with him. But Mingma stayed put, and the two Sherpas watched as the guide turned and began walking down the mountain without them. Dorjee had become accustomed to Gustavo racing ahead of his teammates, but he was shocked that the guide would leave them when the life of the man who had paid his way to Everest was hanging by a thread.

Gustavo claimed later that Dorjee told him to move ahead to clear the ropes of ice and snow, but Dorjee says he told him nothing—they don't speak the same languages. Dorjee says Gustavo was soon out of sight a few hundred meters in front of them. Gustavo would claim, at different times, that he was only forty meters or fifteen meters away. But with the entire team debilitated by hypoxia and exhaustion, he might as well have been on another planet.

When Dorjee, Mingma, and Nils made it back to the Balcony, 1,500 feet below the summit, Dorjee says the doctor collapsed again. Nils was unconscious much of the time now, the Sherpa said, and when he came to, he spoke gibberish. They tried to give him water, but it just dribbled down his chin. Now, they realized, all three of their lives were at stake. It would take most of the night for the Sherpas to drag an incoherent climber down to camp and, by then, all of them might succumb to the cold, the wind, and the lack of something to breathe.

On the Balcony, Dorjee and Mingma found a bit of shelter behind a block of snow and leaned Nils against it. Then Dorjee says he took the team's last two oxygen bottles from his pack. Although he, Mingma, and Gustavo had all run out of oxygen, they say they did not consider using their employer's remaining two bottles of gas themselves and, although it was almost certain he wouldn't use them, they left them with him. If Nils came to, if by some miracle he got back on his feet, he would have plenty of oxygen to get himself down. If someone could mount a rescue, it was that much bottled gas they wouldn't have to carry up the mountain. As he planted the oxygen tanks into the snow, plainly within the doctor's sight and reach, Dorjee saw a flicker of recognition in Nils's dazed and goggled eyes. Even if he couldn't pick up the bottles that would save his life, he already grasped what they signified. They were leaving him. Mingma took off the down jacket he was wearing and wrapped it tightly around the delirious doctor. But as they prepared to go, Nils protested.

"I'm going to stay here, and you stay here with me," Dorjee recalls Nils insisting. "The mountain is my home. Don't leave me. We should all die together."

As they backed away, the doctor made one last appeal. He clutched at the Sherpas' legs and held on, literally, for dear life. Mingma stepped out of his grasp and the two Sherpas turned their backs to him to follow the ropes down to the shelter of Camp Four. It's impossible to know when Nils Antezana died, and not much easier to determine when the Sherpas decided to say that, despite the eyes and arms their employer laid on them as they walked away, he was dead when they left him.

About an hour after they stepped away from the grasp of Nils Antezana on the Balcony, Big Dorjee and Mingma Sherpa stumbled onto another man lying in the snow. Gustavo Lisi, the doctor's guide, had left his teammates behind hours earlier, but didn't make it far below the Balcony before he dug a hole in the snow and climbed into a nylon bivouac bag. The Sherpas were shocked to realize that the man they had assumed had already made it back to camp was asleep at their feet. Here, they knew, Gustavo's nap was likely to last forever—hypothermia or hypoxia would probably kill him while he dozed—so they shook the bag to rouse him and helped him to his feet. Before they started down, the guide asked what happened to his client.

" 'Let's go down because Nils cannot anymore. He is dead,' " the guide would insist that the Sherpas told him when he first recounted the tragedy. But that story would change repeatedly. Later he would report, in a taped interview, that the Sherpas told him the doctor was unconscious, but still alive. Still later, Gustavo would tell me that he saw the doctor die when he himself was with him on the Balcony. At the moment of their reunion, neither Gustavo nor the Sherpas would live to tell any tale if they didn't get down fast.

To Dorjee and Mingma, it seemed that as soon as they put down one body, they had another to hold up. In the darkness Gustavo caught a crampon and tripped, tumbling several dozen meters down a snowy slope known as the Triangle Face and tearing his down suit on the rocks he slid past. As the Sherpas helped him up, they could see his headlamp shining on the mountain above them where it had come off during his fall. Below them, other lamps were just beginning to make the tents of Camp Four glow as another team of climbers prepared to head up the mountain.

In Camp Four, Victor Saunders, a British architect turned mountain guide, along with the team of three clients and three Sherpas he was leading, crawled from his tent. They began tying on their crampons and adjusting the flow of their oxygen regulators. As Victor gazed at the slope above them, he immediately saw things that weren't supposed to be part of the architecture—lights on the Balcony. Somebody was seriously late getting back to camp. It was nearly two hours later when Victor and his team passed the three descending climbers marked by the headlamps—Big Dorjee, Mingma, and Gustavo Lisi.

"We were quite astonished to see lights high up there at nine o'clock, but we were even more surprised that we didn't actually cross them until we were nearly at the same height," he said. "So they were going very slowly."

Victor's team had just climbed into the cloud cap that was descending on the mountain when he ran into the Argentinean and his Sherpas. Neither the mountaineers climbing up into the deteriorating weather, nor Gustavo's ragged team, had time to chat. Big Dorjee and Mingma, descending faster and a few steps ahead of Gustavo, huddled together with Victor's Sherpas when they met on the ropes. The Argentinean looked at Victor and grunted, but they never spoke. Still, Victor could see that Gustavo was in bad shape—hunched over, staggering, and with a gash in his down suit that was bleeding out clumps of feathers.

"Something's odd here," Victor recalls thinking. "Something's going wrong."

When his Sherpas walked away from Dorjee and Mingma, they were shaking their heads. Victor avoids making judgments that can affect someone's ability to make a living in the mountains, but his Sherpas weren't so generous.

"Bad Sherpas," they said when Victor asked what had upset them. "Bad Sherpas."

Victor's *sirdar*—the head Sherpa—mumbled that Big Dorjee and Mingma had moved on while one of their climbers was still up on the Balcony. But he didn't say that the man was sick or stranded, only that he was straggling.

"It wasn't clear to me from my Sherpas, who were talking to [Gustavo's] Sherpas, that [someone] had actually been abandoned," Victor recalls. "If I had realized that there had been somebody up there still alive, I would have seriously considered pushing on to look for him."

Victor can't say for sure that he could have rescued a climber at night in a blizzard above 8,000 meters—he had three clients of his own to look after and a storm moving in that would eventually turn his team back. But since Sherpas are the strongest men on the mountain and they get hefty bonuses for getting their clients to the top, it's rare that they are the first to retreat. So it struck Victor as strange that, after meeting with Big Dorjee and Mingma, his Sherpas were reluctant to climb any higher.

"In hindsight, I think it's clear that they had been told there was a dead man sitting up there," he says. "It's also clear that he wasn't dead."

Victor and his team turned back just below the Balcony, within a few hundred meters of the spot where Nils Antezana spent his last hours alive.

Soon after the two teams passed, Big Dorjee and Mingma left Gustavo behind as well. Mingma, without the down coat he'd left with Nils, was shivering and hypothermic. All three men had run out of bottled oxygen hours earlier, somewhere around the South Summit. The only tanks of gas that they hadn't used, according to Big Dorjee and Gustavo, were stuck in the snow of the Balcony next to their client. As the oxygen supply in their bloodstream plummeted, the brutal, subzero cold stabbed right to their bones. Death was a real risk for all of them now. Big Dorjee and Mingma raced down as fast as they could. Other Sherpas helped them into camp, but they made their way to their tent without letting anyone know about either of the climbers they had left behind.

The Sherpas who assisted Dorjee and Mingma returned to their own tent but soon heard a wailing in the night and went back out. It was half an hour later, nearly midnight, when they found Gustavo, about 200 meters from camp, delirious, disoriented, and screaming in the stormy darkness. He was close to shelter, but climbers have frozen to death within steps of their tents. The Sherpas led Gustavo down to their tent, gave him two bottles of oxygen, and then sent him on to his own shelter, where he passed out. Gustavo said nothing of his client still stranded on the Balcony.

Neither did he sound the alert the next morning, when he called his mother and his webmaster with a satellite telephone. By that afternoon, people around the world knew of his previous day's accomplishment from his Web site, which boasted in Spanish, SUMMIT! GUSTAVO LISI HAS CONQUERED EVEREST.

"We reached the summit with Nils at 10 in the morning," Gustavo said on his blog.

He did not mention that Nils had not come back down, or the fact that although by then he was probably already dead, the doctor was sure to perish if someone didn't go up to get him. The man who had paid for the entire expedition, in fact, wasn't mentioned again in the posting.

"He is very tired, Gustavo took long pauses before speaking, but you can hear the happiness in his voice," the webmaster wrote after posting the update Gustavo had phoned in. "He has rested in the South Col and will commence the descent to Camp Two in a few minutes."

Nearly twenty hours after he left Nils Antezana, as Gustavo packed up his gear to begin his trip home, he had still not made any effort to mount a rescue for his client or let anybody know he had abandoned a man on the mountain.

CAMP TWO, MOUNT EVEREST, TIBET

Sometime during Big Dorjee and Mingma's struggle to drag Nils Antezana down to the Balcony, I arrived at a similar platform of snow on the opposite side of the mountain.

At a handful of tents staked some 25,000 feet above sea level, I plopped down on my pack, gasping. Below me, a 2,000-foot ramp of snow ran like a ski slope down to Camp One, where more than sixty tents spread into a nylon subdivision atop the mountain's North Col. It had taken me six hours to climb the slope, queued up in a line of more than thirty-five climbers from around the world, placing my feet into the exact same steps that had been kicked into the hardened snow by hundreds of boots. Occasionally stronger climbers would step out of the line onto Styrofoam-like snow to forge a new path long enough to pass, but most of us just followed one another up the staircase. A few of the climbers had already donned oxygen masks to help fuel their ascent, but most wouldn't start using bottled gas until they reached the next camp or, in a few cases, wouldn't use it at all.

With or without supplemental oxygen, most of the climbers moved with underwater slowness, hunching into the slope to rally a few steps, then raising their heads to fight for breath as though they were trying not to drown. Fifteen minutes behind me, Anne Parmenter, my climbing partner, was finishing the punishing slog.

Above us lay another 1,500 feet of scrambling over jagged, loose rock to reach our own Camp Two tents. The clouds that had haunted Big Dorjee, Nils, Gustavo, and Mingma on the south side of the mountain were blowing over the peak's flanks and falling onto the camp, driven by gusts strong enough to knock climbers from their feet. Nearby, one climber made his way on his hands and knees to the ropes that led to the higher camps.

But like Big Dorjee, I was struggling with different problems from the one building in the sky. This tempest had been growing within my climbing team for the past month. The four teammates who had accompanied Anne and me from the United States, along with the four Sherpas we had hired to assist the group, had already left us behind. But unlike Nils Antezana, we were thankful that they had. Conspiracies, thefts, threats, and extortions had marked our time together. Sitting on my pack, wishing that one of the tents lashed to that icy, wind-scoured terrace was my own shelter for the night, I recalled overhearing something in the days leading up to the summit bid. George Dijmarescu, the man who had invited me onto the climb, had sat in a nearby tent listing the ways that he could ensure that I didn't come down—sabotaging my oxygen system, setting my tent on fire . . .

For me, the climax of that expedition would come not on top of Mount Everest but on the balcony of a Kathmandu trekking agency a little more than a week later. Anne, co-leader of the Connecticut team, was too busy settling the team's accounts to notice the workers hanging a bright red banner honoring our group.

CONGRATULATIONS TO MR. GEORGE DIJMARESCU FOR YOUR SIXTH CONSECUTIVE SUMMIT, TO MS. LHAKPA SHERPA FOR HER FOURTH WORLD RECORD SUCCESSFUL SUMMIT AND TO THE MEMBERS OF THE CONNECTCUT [sic] MT. EVEREST EXPEDITION, read the ten-foot-wide flag.

By mountaineering measures, it had been a successful expedition—four of the team's seven members reached the Earth's high point. But when Anne stepped onto the balcony of the fourth-floor office of Asian Trekking on May 27 and saw the banner, she responded with anything but pride.

"Take it down," the Trinity College field hockey coach told Dawa Sherpa, the company's business manager. "If you're going to recognize him," she said, her voice rising in anger, "I'm not paying my bill."

Dawa got scissors to help Anne slice out George Dijmarescu's name. When he found the edited version too ugly to display, Anne offered to pay for a new one. But in the end, the tribute was never hung again.

Nothing in the e-mail signed by George that I received five days later indicated he knew about the edited flag. Still, the note boiled with rage toward Anne.

"From now on, I will do all I can to hunt this bitch down, like a hiena [sic]," he wrote.

In another e-mail, sent to the entire team a week later, he cautioned Anne against commenting about him to a corporate sponsor.

"I am warning you and yes I am threatening you, you will be very sorry," he wrote. "I promise I will give you the opportunity to see worst [sic] in your life."

Two weeks later, in Bristol, Connecticut, a neighbor noticed a truck that matched the description of George's parked in front of Anne's house while she was away. Anne notified the local police and showed them a copy of the e-mail he had sent the team. They, in turn, contacted George. He denied visiting her home and promised to send no more e-mails.

Six months earlier, just after Thanksgiving 2003, I had introduced the two mountaineers at a pub between Anne's Trinity College office and the walkup George shares with his wife, Lhakpa Sherpa, in the West End of Hartford. Earlier in the fall, I had run into George and Lhakpa, who live a few blocks from me, pushing their daughter in a stroller near my house. George told me his dream of organizing an Everest team from Connecticut. But he didn't know many climbers here, he said, and asked if I might make some introductions.

Anne and I had made our first Himalayan climb together four years earlier and she had since become close with both my wife and me. I knew she was interested in Everest and I was happy to introduce her to George. At the time, I was proud to plant the seeds that might grow into an Everest expedition.

I had never yearned to climb Everest. Hundreds of other peaks have more graceful lines and more technical challenges. Everest's reputation as one of the world's costliest adventures was as daunting as its death toll. But the mountain Tibetans call Chomolungma—the Goddess Mother of the World—has many seductions: fame, riches, bragging rights. For me, the mountain was a big character in an epic drama—but not the biggest. I was enchanted by the opportunity to tell George's story: swimming the Danube River to escape communism and then climbing Everest five years straight. Lhakpa, too, was fascinating: an illiterate single mother who came of age in the shadow of the mountain before climbing it, believing it would provide a better life.

I was surprised when my editors at the newspaper where I worked fell under the same spell; shocked when they agreed to pay my way. The idea was to climb Everest with the expedition, transmit photos and stories to the paper, and then follow George and Lhakpa to the world's second-highest peak, K2, a far more challenging climb on the other side of the Himalaya. There I would report from base camp in Pakistan as the couple attempted a jaw-dropping feat: summiting Everest and K2 in the same season. Carolyn Moreau, my wife and a *Courant* reporter, would accompany the team, write a freelance blog for the newspaper's Web site, and videotape the expedition as far as its summit push on Everest.

I told George's story in a front-page profile that ran on March 29, 2004—the day we left for the Himalaya. Lhakpa's story landed on Page 1 three weeks later. Before the expedition got under way, our relationship was warm. But although George beamed and slapped me on the back when he read his profile, I sensed him growing hostile as the days passed and we neared the frigid peril of Everest. By the time we reached the mountain, he and Lhakpa were hardly speaking to Carolyn or me.

I felt obligated to cover the tensions, even when I didn't understand what had brought them on. And the more my wife and I wrote about the crumbling team, the faster it fell apart. My enthusiasm, both as a climber and as a journalist, helped bring seven mountaineers together and get us to Tibet. My efforts also were part of the team's undoing.

I sent my last dispatch from Kathmandu in late May, after nearly two months on the mountain. It took me twice that long to figure out how a group of one-time friends collapsed in an avalanche of intimidation, abuse, and recrimination.

Three of us failed to climb to the top of the world. But my disappointment as a mountaineer paled beside the guilt and embarrassment I felt for my part in an adventure that brought threats to a close friend, suffering to my wife, and a burden to dozens of people chasing their dreams in one of the most inhospitable environments on Earth. Seven climbers perished on the mountain during the week our party headed to the summit. Any one of us could have been among them.

In that winter of 2004, when George and Lhakpa, two of the most experienced Everest climbers, invited me to join them in Tibet, the world's highest summit seemed to shine like a beacon through my New England neighborhood. By the summer, when I returned from the Himalaya suspicious enough of them to install a home security system, I realized the mountain on the other side of the world cast a shadow long enough to fall on my house. Still, the gloom fell far darker in some other quarters.

Two

One day, the year before his trip to the Himalaya, Nils Antezana stepped out of the shower in the master bathroom of his Washington, D.C., home. He wrapped a towel around his waist and sat down on the polished, brown marble of his Jacuzzi with his hands pressed together as if he were praying. He stared at the floor and then at his wife, Gladys. It had been forty years since Gladys, as a favor to a friend in the community of Bolivian expatriates living in Washington, had picked up Nils at the airport when he first arrived from South America. It wasn't love at first sight, but the two Bolivian immigrants quickly realized they were excellent companions for each other. Nils, who had studied medicine in his native Bolivia, soon passed the exam to practice in the United States. After they married, Gladys went back to school, earned degrees in economics and finance, and started her own contracting company. Together they had constructed a life of culture and comfort. The vacation home they were building in Annapolis was nearly complete, and a two-story apartment filled with art and antiques at the top of a Cochabamba,

Bolivia, high-rise awaited their visits to their homeland. But despite all they had and all they had accomplished, Nils told Gladys, his life still felt incomplete. She had heard this complaint from him before and had learned to live with his secret ambitions.

"With you I am very happy," he had told her a few years earlier. "But I seem to be missing something."

"Gladys, I want to go to Everest," he now told his wife as he sat on the edge of the bath.

Since retiring, mountaineering was a growing part of Nils's life, and Gladys and their children, David and Fabiola, had heard about his Everest fascination for years. But the ever-confident doctor seemed to realize that this dream might be out of his reach, so this time he wasn't just looking for her blessing, but for some encouragement as well.

"God bless you," she said, placing her hand on his forehead to slide his wet hair back and look into his eyes. It was the best she could do. "God bless you."

When Nils was chosen to head the pathology department of a military hospital in Wilmington, Delaware, in 1969, Gladys couldn't imagine leaving Washington. Both she and Nils had looked forward to raising their children in their adopted country's capital. Nils took the job, along with an apartment near the hospital. His family stayed in Washington and he visited on weekends. But during the week he had a bit of what was fast becoming the most precious resource in his life: free time.

Gladys had asked a few times if he was lonely, and wondered what he was doing to pass the nights without his family; but it wasn't until he had been in the post for more than a year that she found out. He was learning to fly. His wife was neither concerned about the safety of his new hobby nor surprised he had taken it up. But when Nils was named head of the pathology department at Jefferson Memorial in Alexandria, Virginia, and moved back with the family, she put her foot down. They had two young children, she explained. He couldn't just go risking his life in some little airplane for fun.

Nils not only agreed to stop flying but expressed his own concern that their children would be orphaned if both their parents died in an air disaster. The family would travel extensively until Nils's death, but Gladys and her husband would never fly together again to ensure that, if the unthinkable happened, one of them would be around to take care of David and Fabiola. Nils returned to his adventures aloft after David's graduation from medical school, Fabiola's start in her first job in finance, and his own semi-retirement. But despite the hundreds of hours Nils spent in the cockpit, his wife never rode in a plane he piloted.

After his death, Gladys would thumb through the pages of Nils's flight log as reverently as she did his journals and poems, imagining what it would have been like to sit beside him as he flew. The detailed entries jump seamlessly from 1972 to 1997, when Nils again signed up for flying lessons.

As a teenager in Bolivia, Nils had once dreamed of being an aerospace engineer, but his father insisted he study medicine. With his children grown, he was intent on having some of the adventures he had passed up for his career as doctor. He started ground school at Freeway Airport in Bowie, Maryland, where a few dozen planes tied onto the grass surrounded a small office, a barbecue grill, and a single runway. At the small airport, Nils found a group of largely blue-collar pilots who didn't take themselves as seriously as the doctors he was used to—more jeans and T-shirts than coats and ties. He wasn't about to roughen any of the polish of his own wardrobe, but he found it easy to relax among the crowd that hung out around the airstrip.

Ground school, however, was another matter. All but one of the half dozen students were in their early twenties or younger. Nils gravitated to the only other student who seemed anywhere near his own age, a Maryland electrician named Bob Metler. The young students pursued flying with bravado, like players on a football team, but Bob and Nils were happy to push their noses into their books. Other students sometimes joked about the questions that Nils asked, but Bob found that he was often puzzling over the same details.

Nils and Bob soloed within two weeks of each other, in December 1997. As far as they could tell, they were the only two students from their class to actually get their pilots' licenses, which they celebrated with an ecstatically nervous ride over Chesapeake Bay.

Not long after that, Bob approached Nils. "It would be a real neat idea if we could get together and buy an airplane," he told him.

A few weeks later Bob met two other electricians who were interested in buying a plane. One was Eddie Pickens, whose father owned a 1973 Piper Cherokee but had lost his pilot's license after a heart attack. Mike Roberts was doing odd jobs around the airport. The Piper had been serving as a training plane and was pretty beat-up, but the foursome bought it anyway. Other pilots warned them that four partners going in on an airplane was a recipe for disaster. But they never had an argument over the plane, perhaps because of how often they flew together.

"I think we found every airport we could possibly find in Maryland, Virginia, and Pennsylvania," Bob said, "just for the sake of flying that direction to see what it looked like on the other side."

He called Nils almost every week to go flying, and if his new friend couldn't go on Saturday, Bob would wait until Sunday.

"Flying, we were brothers," he recalls.

Neither Bob nor Mike had met anyone named Nils before, and they often called him "Niles" by mistake. "It's *Neels*," he would say, politely correcting their pronunciation, but they kept falling back into the familiar error. Eventually Nils gave up, smiling at Bob's embarrassment when he lapsed into his habitual mispronunciation.

"Go ahead and call me Niles," Nils said.

Bob and Mike were surprised when they started to get calls from Nils, inviting them to parties or wishing them happy birthday, and even more surprised at how Nils and Gladys could make a couple working stiffs feel at home in the middle of a room full of wealthy professionals and expatriates.

"He befriended us more than we befriended him," Bob recalls.

One day when they waited for some fog to clear, Nils knelt in the grass behind the plane to pick mushrooms—another hobby he had picked up—and then showed them how to tell the ones they could eat from the ones that would kill them. But when his flying partners washed the plane, Nils found a way to stay as far from the soap and scrub brushes as he could. The others would crawl beneath the plane to scrub, and shake their heads when they found Nils manning the hose, filling a bucket, or folding rags—whatever it took to keep his dapper clothes clean and dry. They ribbed him for being too precious to get dirty, and he made up for his aversion to grime by bringing a dozen doughnuts.

Bob had been flying with Nils for more than eight months when he first heard someone at the airport address his copilot as "doctor," and although he was surprised that Nils had never mentioned he was in medicine, it made a lot of sense. Nils often asked after the health of his partners in the plane.

In September of 2000, Mike was flying with Nils and mentioned that he had some abdominal pain and had recently had a mild fever. When Mike told Nils what the doctors he had seen had told him, the semiretired pathologist had a bad feeling and pressed his friend.

"No, you've got something wrong with you and you have to take care of it," Nils said. "They've misdiagnosed you."

Nils called Mike's wife, Andrea, to tell her that her husband was sick and she needed to get him to a hospital. Mike refused to put down the job he was on and lose yet another half-day's pay. Nils called Andrea back repeatedly, insisting that she get her husband to a doctor. Mike finally broke down and visited a hospital, where they took some blood and gave him a CAT scan. He came home exhausted.

"I'm so tired, I feel like I'm going to die," he told his wife, and went straight to bed.

But as soon as he lay down, the phone rang. His wife ran into the bedroom weeping.

"You have to go to the hospital right now for emergency surgery," she told him. "Your appendix has ruptured."

In the hospital, Mike didn't know what to say when his dapper friend came to check on him.

"If I hadn't gotten up that night and gone into the hospital," he said, "I probably wouldn't have woken up in the morning."

Nils shrugged, smiled, and said he was glad Mike was feeling better. Then he asked when he could go flying again.

Nils went away for two or three months at a time, and when the pilots asked where he went, Nils told them he was visiting family in Bolivia and climbing mountains.

When he told the stories of his climbs, Nils became animated in a way they had only seen a hint of when he was flying. To Bob it was clear that walking up into the sky did something for Nils that riding there on a pair of wings didn't. The other pilots were captivated by Nils's tales of adventure in the mountains and, much the way he had done with the mushrooms he picked off the airport lawn, Nils was inspired to teach them about this new hobby.

About two years before Nils's final expedition, he was out flying with Bob and mentioned that he was working up to climb Mount Everest. Bob couldn't fathom that he was serious.

"Yeah, Nils, that's a great, great aspiration," Bob said, though it seemed like a pipe dream. "I hope you do it."

Nils kept his flying friends filled in as he climbed to incrementally higher elevations, but by 2004, Bob wasn't seeing much of his friend at all. Nils didn't have a lot of time to fly. Now when they spoke over the phone around the holidays, he said he was training hard for mountaineering. He called Bob on a Friday night in March to say he was leaving for Everest the next day and wouldn't be back until June.

"When I get back, we're going to celebrate," Nils said. "You, me, Mike, and Ed are going to go out and have a terrific dinner."

Nils told Bob how to follow the climb on the Internet, but Bob couldn't find any news of his friend. Not until he saw the note about the accident.

After Nils called Bob, he and Gladys went out for dinner with their friends Nick and Diana Ellyn. Nick, an ophthalmologist, got to know Nils when he started working at Jefferson Memorial Hospital in 1979. The two doctors had hiked a few times together, but they didn't really become close until 1997, when Nils called Nick and Diana and asked them to a restaurant to celebrate Gladys's birthday. At a nearby table, Placido Domingo sang to his own wife during her own birthday dinner.

Nils's and Nick's hikes in Shenandoah National Park, along the

Billy Goat Trail and over Old Rag Mountain, became a bit more regular after that, and although Nick often had trouble keeping up with the man who scampered up craggy trails, he enjoyed their conversations and the way his friend pointed out various species of trees and flowers to him.

After what would be their last dinner together, Nick invited Nils and Gladys back to their house for the nightcap that had become a tradition with the couples, but this time Nils begged off. He had a flight to catch in the morning, he said. His friends asked where he was headed.

"I'm leaving to climb Mount Everest," Nils said.

It was the first they had heard of Nils's upcoming expedition, and Nick was shocked that Nils had never mentioned that he was planning such an epic adventure, that he hadn't even brought it up during the dinner conversation. On the other hand, Nils had also never mentioned that he was a pilot and owned part of a plane. Nils's adventures were often surprises even to his family. A few months earlier, while in Bolivia, he had vanished for a few days, and it wasn't until family members in Bolivia told her that Gladys learned where he had been: climbing in the Andes to train for the Himalaya. Diana immediately wished Nils had told them about Everest earlier—her husband might have had enough time to coax his friend out of this crazy dream.

"I guess this is our last supper," Nick kidded Nils, unaware of how prophetic his joke was.

Later that night Nils called Dave Okonsky, another close friend, to let him know that he was leaving for the Himalaya the next day and to apologize for missing the trip that Dave had planned for them in Belize. Although the doctor was more than twenty-five years his senior, Dave had quickly realized that he and Nils shared an appetite for adrenaline. When Dave told Nils that he was taking his daughters to a climbing gym, Nils joined them and was just as eager to take his turns climbing the walls as the children. A few months later Dave mentioned scuba diving in Bonaire, an arid island off the coast of Venezuela, and Nils had jumped at the opportunity to get certified as a diver. Dave had gotten used to nagging friends to get them to commit to a trip, but this time it was Nils who was calling him, asking dozens of questions, one of which he kept repeating.

"When are we going?"

Nils completed the confined water portion of his scuba certification—dives in a swimming pool—in Virginia, so he just needed to finish the open water portion of the program. Dave, his wife, Terry, Nils, and another friend, Morrie Wolfe, arrived in Bonaire for six days of diving in 2002.

They stayed in a basic condominium, rode around the island in a pickup truck, and picked up their air tanks at a drive-thru window on their way to dive sites marked by rocks splashed with gold paint. When they first arrived, Dave worried that a wealthy doctor who was used to five-star hotels and fine dining would be disappointed in such a simple life on a desert island. He anticipated an older diver's slow, step-by-step preparations and expected Nils to take his time getting under the water. Instead, he looked up to find Nils suited up, hoisting his tank, and walking into the sea where a reef terrace teemed with parrot fish and damselfish.

"It's just like you said," Nils said to Dave as they walked back onto the beach.

Nils told Dave about how as a child in Bolivia, he had ridden in the back of a pickup truck with railroad workers and seen the mountains as they crested a hill, how the beauty of that vista had drawn him to mountaineering. He said he was going to remember that first dive the way he remembered that first time he really saw the mountains of Bolivia.

Scuba diving led to skydiving when Dave invited Nils to his lake house in 2003 and they took lessons at a nearby airport. And Nils was as eager to share the mountains with Dave as Dave had been with the sea and sky. They made a deal: Dave would take Nils diving in Belize, and Nils would take Dave mountaineering in Bolivia.

Dave had planned a trip with Nils and Gladys for the spring of 2004 in Central America, but his friend was calling to say he was going to climb Mount Everest instead.

"More power to you," Dave said.

Nils promised that when he got back, he and Gladys were going to join the Okonskys in Bonaire to celebrate. Then he and Dave would take that trip to Bolivia.

HARTFORD, CONNECTICUT—NOVEMBER 2003

The second-floor walkup in Hartford where George Dijmarescu lives with his wife, daughter, father, and occasionally his mother is a distant world from the grand house in Washington, the Annapolis vacation home, and the Bolivian penthouse where Nils Antezana lived.

The first thing I noticed walking into George's home four months before we would head to the Himalaya together was the brightly colored rubber mat displaying the alphabet that covers almost the entire living room floor of the apartment. The letters spoke when I stepped on them.

" 'A' is for apple. 'T' is for turtle."

Nils had sent his daughter, Fabiola, to France and Russia to learn languages. George's daughter, Sunny, and her mother, Lhakpa, who can speak four languages but read none of them, learned their ABCs together by walking on the talking floor.

The only obvious similarity between George's and Nils's homes is the collection of photos of mountains that hangs on their walls. Each corner of George's living room holds a certificate or photo from one of his climbs to the summit of Everest. As different as their worlds were, there were some similarities: Both were immigrants to America, although one came as a doctor and the other as a defector, and both took a fast track to the world's highest peak.

George and Nils, in fact, began climbing in the mid-1990s—around the time of the *Into Thin Air* Everest disaster. Each climbed only a handful of mountains before heading to Everest. While Nils made his first climbs up Bolivian peaks, George said his first was a January attempt on New Hampshire's Mount Washington (6,288 feet), fabled as home to the "Worst Weather in the World." He made his way up the snow-choked Lion's Head Trail with sneakers and a

Snickers bar—the kind of poorly prepared character who makes experienced mountaineers cringe—and was forced to retreat only a few hundred feet shy of the summit. Two hours after his descent, he stomped into a North Conway outfitter and spent $1,000 on plastic mountaineering boots, an ice ax, crampons, and Gore-Tex clothes. He was standing on the summit by noon the next day.

"When I saw that I could do this on Mount Washington, that was it," George told me. Although that first peak was just 6,288 feet tall—four miles shorter than Everest—it fueled an appetite that would be sated by only the highest mountains and inspired an audacious plan for indulging that craving. George wouldn't waste his time on smaller mountains, relationships with climbing partners, or learning the ropes down low. Within a few months he was making his way, alone and out of season, up Aconcagua, the Argentine peak that at 22,840 feet is the highest mountain in the Americas.

His mountaineering résumé is as dramatic as it is short. Aconcagua in 1996 and 1997; Alaska's Denali—20,320 feet—in 1997; and then his first attempt on Everest in 1998.

In late May 1999, at Ragged Mountain in Southington, Connecticut, half a dozen climbers moaned when my cell phone broke the solitude with a call from the *Courant*.

"Hey, some guy named George from Hartford just made it to the summit of Everest," I said. "Anybody heard of him?"

Nobody had.

My only adventure in the mountains with George before heading to Everest with him in 2004 had been a trip to the Presidential Range in New Hampshire's White Mountains. On the northern flank of Mount Adams, 80 mph winds took turns throwing five of us onto the rocky, ice-caked slope. It was January 2004, and the wind chill above the tree line fell to a record 103 degrees below zero. A meteorologist at the Mount Washington Weather Observatory four miles away stepped outside to throw a bucket of water in the air; the water crystallized and blew away before a drop hit the ground. An off-duty ranger, who himself had once vowed to climb Mount Everest, froze to death on South Twin Mountain, ten miles away.

The brutal weather set an appropriate mood for George's tales of his family's suffering in Romania under one of the world's most repressive communist regimes, and the peaks named for the founders of American democracy seemed an appropriate backdrop for his story of risking his life to gain his freedom from the Eastern Bloc. When we were forced to retreat, George folded the hood of my coat to cover my cheek where frostnip had bleached the skin white. He held up my wife, Carolyn, after she took a fall during the desperate descent to tree line. Neither of us needed the help, but the attention inspired confidence.

"If it had been like this on Everest," he said, "I never would have gone back a second time."

We chuckled at his comment, but with what we had learned about George during our days in the White Mountains, I don't think any of us believed him. In fact, the more I learned about George, the less I knew what to believe.

It had been two a.m. on July 13, 1985, George told me, when he stepped into the Danube River just below the Iron Gates hydroelectric plant in communist Romania. He was twenty-three and had been planning his swim to freedom ever since his discharge from the military more than two years earlier. George, who claimed he had been a member of the elite Mountain Hunters infantry, said he had guarded a mountain pass above Transylvania with horses and artillery.

"The Romanian army was a test of life," he said.

He had learned to ski, shoot, and survive in the cold starvation of a rusting and threadbare communist military. Near the end of his service, he was assigned to Drobeta-Turnu Severin, a city on the Danube.

"I ate in the same place as the border patrol," he recalled. "I would buy them a couple beers and they'd get drunk and then tell me everything. Where they change guards. How long the shifts are. What is their path."

He also learned the consequences for a failed escape.

"What do you do to these guys if you catch them?" he had asked. Beat them on the shins, the guards replied. Prisoners with battered legs spared guards the inconvenience of chasing down runaways. After his military service, George returned to the city as a laborer. At night, he used binoculars to search for a route past the border guards. Before and after work, he swam laps in the city pool.

"I'm a far better swimmer than climber, I'll tell you that."

The night of his escape, George selected clothes to make him look like a tourist—an Adidas tracksuit and a thin leather jacket—and put them into a plastic bag, along with binoculars, maps, food, and money. He sealed the bag by melting the plastic with a clothes iron, and towed it behind him in the river with a telephone cord tied around his waist. He wore his army bayonet in case he needed to cut it loose.

"I tried to cross where people wouldn't look," he said. "The thinner parts of the river are better guarded."

The river is about a mile and a half wide below the Iron Gates dam. As he swam toward the lights in Yugoslavia, black currents tumbling from the dam pushed him back in the inky blue Danube—back to the dark tyranny of communist Romania.

"My arm would twist in the current as I swam. I was just shaking. . . ."

Seventy minutes after he stepped into the Danube, George reached Yugoslavia. Too tired to walk, he crawled up the bank and slept. A little more than a week later, he was on a hill overlooking the Italian border. He scoped out the border crossing with his binoculars, but when he got close, guards appeared and drew their guns. They interrogated him at their barracks, jailed him for eight days, and then put him on a train headed back to Belgrade, where a tribunal would decide whether to return him to Romania.

This time, the man whose life would later depend on his lungs said he saved himself by asking for a smoke.

"You deny me a cigarette?" he shouted when his escort said he didn't smoke. When the guard went to find one for him, George jumped from the train.

The first time he reached the Italian border, the path of least resistance had led him to captivity. He wouldn't make that mistake again. This time, George headed for the Alps. On the horizon,

George could see the lights of Trieste. He headed straight for the city through the mountains.

"I was just standing there stunned," he said of his arrival in the Italian city. "I almost got run over by cars, looking at the lights of the city."

He spent nearly a year in a refugee camp before U.S. authorities granted his request for political asylum. George offered up everything he knew about the Romanian military, but it was the tales of his family's suffering—his mother's time in jail for refusing to sell her cherries at the price fixed by authorities, the older brother who was run to death at school and autopsied in the front yard of the family home—that he said opened the door to the United States.

Since the fall of communism, coming to America from Romania has become a bit easier. George's mother, Elena, comes to Hartford each year to care for her granddaughter while George and Lhakpa are away on expeditions that can last for months. Their plans to climb Everest and K2 back to back would keep them away from their daughter for five months. In 2004, to celebrate her arrival from Romania, Elena poured glasses of home-brewed cherry brandy. In the fridge were sausages and ribs from the pig she had slaughtered for Christmas. George's brother, Claudio, whom George told me he helped sneak into the United States but who is now a citizen, dropped by with his wife and their four-year-old daughter.

George walked through the cramped apartment with his own daughter, Sunny, in his arms, pointing to the photos on the wall. "And what's this?" he asked.

"North Col!" Sunny responded, pointing at the glacier on the mountain that draws her parents away from her every April and May.

In the weeks leading up to his departure, George and Sunny spent every moment they could together. She climbed into his lap when he worked at his laptop, sat on his shoulders as he ate dinner.

"I've had people accuse me of child abuse when they hear how long I will be away from my daughter," he said.

George was eager to tell his stories. He'd told them on Connecticut Public Television and in visits to schools in Hebron, and also in South Windsor, where teachers used George's climbs as the anchor for an entire Everest curriculum. In the auditorium, two months before our 2004 expedition, more than four hundred students and teachers sat in quiet awe as George showed his slides and video.

"I am not a professional climber. I'm not even a semiprofessional climber," he said. "I am a vacation climber."

"What's your greatest accomplishment?" one student asked.

"My greatest accomplishment is not climbing Mount Everest," he replied. "My greatest accomplishment was escaping Romania. I could climb Mount Everest a hundred times, [but] it won't mean as much to me or my family as escaping communism."

After the presentation, George and Lhakpa visited classrooms and the school's lunchroom, where students swarmed the couple who once called the school from a satellite phone from Everest. For the 2004 climb, the one I would join him on, George would take another satellite phone, purchased with money that Timothy Edwards Middle School's PTO paid him for his visit; to that point, George said, it was the only money he'd ever made from mountaineering.

School assemblies won't pay for much Himalayan climbing. I wondered why George hadn't turned his success on Everest into greater financial reward. Climbers with less impressive résumés make thousands of dollars at corporate speaking gigs.

By then, the Connecticut Everest team was holding weekly meetings, and at one of them George recited a list of flags and photographs he had carried up Everest. Chuck Boyd, a mountain guide and ski patroller who was considering joining the team, asked how much he was paid to do it.

"I don't ask for anything," George responded.

Chuck put his chin on his hands to keep it from hitting the table. "Five hundred dollars, George," he said, citing the figure he would charge people to take things to the summit. "That's the minimum to carry something up Everest."

"I won't ask for money," George said resolutely. "It is my honor."

George has never refused to carry an item up Everest and never asked for any compensation for the task.

In 2003, George had stood atop Everest at four thirty a.m. He took photographs of the sun rising on the horizon, then handed his camera to a Sherpa, pulled a white plastic grocery bag from his pack and, one by one, held up flags for the camera. One was from the Hartford Canoe Club, a prestigious men's organization.

Months later, at the club's lodge on the Connecticut River, George spent five hours mingling, signing T-shirts and photos, and presenting a slideshow he hoped would bring in some real money. He had Lhakpa, Sunny, and his mother with him, as well as a few members of the Connecticut Everest Expedition to help out. He returned the club flag, along with photos of him holding it atop Everest. But his pride wouldn't let him ask for money. An executive he had hoped would pony up a few thousand dollars after George carried his company's flag up the mountain offered $50, on top of $300 from the company, and George was insulted.

"He could offer me ten thousand dollars and I wouldn't take it now," he blustered.

But when the moment came, Lhakpa stepped in and took the money with a gracious smile. As her husband stepped away with a grumble, Lhakpa showed me the money in her pocket and giggled. In the end, they left the event with less than $400.

"Congratulations," George said darkly. "We made enough money for one bottle of oxygen." Actually the oxygen tanks cost a bit more than $400 each. And the Connecticut expedition would need about sixty of them.

While his bare-bones expeditions cost a fraction of the $65,000 that the highest-end commercial guides charge for a climb up the Nepal side of Everest, it's still a hefty chunk of change. Members of the 2004 Connecticut expedition paid $5,200 apiece—a price that included the permit, Base Camp facilities, three cooks, food, and transportation to the Tibet side of Everest. Once he factored in airline tickets, time in Kathmandu, and supplies for the high camps, George estimated he paid about $12,000 for each of his annual Everest climbs. But his mountaineering dream—with the additional expense of an expedition to K2—had grown beyond the capital from his home-improvement business to fund it.

Though he had trouble raising money, George said he had no problem sharing the wealth with the people he shared the mountains with. Since his first visit to Tibet, he had brought a half dozen Sherpas stateside to work for him in the off season. Apa Sherpa, who holds the record of sixteen summits on Everest, wielded a paintbrush and a hammer working for George during the winter of 1999–2000.

But as we prepared for our expedition, George told me his relationship with the Sherpa was deeper than that. On his expeditions, George said, he ate not in the dining tent, but in the kitchen with the Sherpas. The good-natured loyalty, work ethic, and strength of the Sherpa were qualities he said he sought to cultivate in himself. To some degree, the communist control of their ancestral homeland in Tibet was a flashback to his own youth in Romania. But mostly, he said, it was that, as climbers, he had more in common with the Sherpa than with his mountaineering peers. Like George, the Sherpa went straight to the highest mountain in the world because that was where their horizons were the broadest, their future the brightest. In the end, George married a Sherpani because, although they knew only a handful of words in common when they met, one of them was "Everest."

Ever since the Texas oilman and ski resort developer Dick Bass became, in 1985, the first person guided to the top of Everest, as well as the first to climb the "Seven Summits," complaints about amateurs in mountaineering's biggest game have echoed through the hills. At first glance George Dijmarescu, and later Nils Antezana, struck me as just two more greenhorns who managed to slip into climbing's World Cup. Not that my climbing résumé is particularly impressive, but in more than twenty-five years in the mountains I had worked my way from local rock climbs to mountains throughout the United States, Europe, and New Zealand. And unlike George or Nils, I had reached the summit of another high Himalayan peak—Ama Dablam—before attempting Everest.

But Everest, like the rest of the world's highest mountains, has always attracted wealthy dilettantes and can-do dreamers. In 1933, Maurice Wilson, with no mountaineering experience and only a few flying lessons, flew an open cockpit Gipsy Moth airplane from Britain with the intention of crashing the plane on Everest and bagging the first ascent of the mountain using faith and prayer but little climbing equipment. Wilson was forced to sell his plane in India, so he walked to the Himalaya, snuck into Tibet, and climbed as far as Everest's North Col before perishing. Rumors that Wilson had women's clothes in his rucksack, coupled with the discovery of a woman's shoe at 21,000 feet by a Chinese expedition in 1960, not only made Wilson one of the earliest rookies to make it to the mountain, but put him at the top of a long list of colorful and determined characters who visited the peak.

During my trip in 2004, two female climbers raced each other up the mountain to become the first Norwegian woman to summit. Two others hoped to drive the first golf ball off the peak, only to have their dreams spoiled when a perennial Everest guide announced that he had already clubbed a shot from the top, without fanfare, a few years earlier. When I returned in 2006, two teams of climbers from the Philippines competed to become the first from their nation to reach the summit. The first British couple to summit climbed from the north, and another couple was attempting to achieve the same feat for Australians from the south. In 2007 a climber attempted to reach the summit wearing shorts and a T-shirt while members of Stray Cats, Squeeze, The Fixx, and The Alarm announced plans for a rock concert in Base Camp. Other climbers carried their maladies up the mountain, which has played host to diabetics, asthmatics, a sufferer of high blood pressure sponsored by the maker of his medication, three blind mountaineers, the first climber with one arm, with one foot, with one leg, with no legs, and two climbers with Adult Attention Deficit Disorder attempting to set the youth record for the Seven Summits. A schizophrenic planned an ascent in 2007, as did a man with no arms, and another who had recently had the aortic valve of his heart replaced. A black South African woman was recruited onto a team only because she had AIDS. One hundred cancer survivors planned a trek to Base

48

Camp in a program organized by a survivor of both Hodgkin's disease and Askin's sarcoma who, when he summited Everest in 2002, boasted that he was the "least-experienced Everest climber." But there's a lot of competition for that title. So much, in fact, that when a portly eighty-five-year-old Englishwoman named Mary Woodbridge announced on her Web site that she was going to forge a new route up Everest in 2006 with her dachshund, Daisy, without using supplemental oxygen, Sherpa support, or fixed camps, news sites around the world bought into the spoof as just another goofball headed for the top of the world. "The hoax of the 85-year-old British woman climbing Everest from the South side has finally been figured out by the 'press,'" reported EverestNews.com about what was actually a marketing campaign for an equipment manufacturer, "but a 74-year-old Japanese woman is planning to attempt Everest, as we reported earlier here."

Everest: No Experience Required was the working title of the six-part documentary the Discovery Channel was producing when Sherpas videotaped David Sharp as he was dying on Everest's Northeast Ridge in 2006. The title was changed, but it proved an accurate description: During both of our trips to Everest together, Anne Parmenter learned high on the mountain that teammates touting impressive mountaineering credentials didn't know how to rappel—one of the sport's most basic skills.

When Nils Antezana and George Dijmarescu first arrived at their respective Base Camps on either side of Everest, their short mountaineering résumés were no longer the exception, but the rule.

Three

If anyone understood what drove Nils Antezana up to the highest mountain in the world, it was his daughter, Fabiola. Her mother and brother had always been amazed at how, even when she was a child, Fabiola and her father could occupy each other's heads and share jokes that nobody else understood. Fabiola and Nils often had the same dreams when they slept. They were always nightmares. Their secret, shared language was just one of many that Nils wanted his daughter to know, so he encouraged her to study and work throughout Europe and in South America. She earned a diploma in French and art at the University of Paris, others in Russian and Journalism in Moscow, where she also worked as a translator for the Bolivian Embassy. In Washington, D.C., she earned her BA at Catholic University and MBA at George Washington University, then studied finance in Madrid. In New York and later in London, she worked at Lehman Brothers, then at ABN AMRO in the capital markets of Argentina, Brazil, Chile, Mexico, Israel, Germany, France, and Spain. At thirty-four, she speaks five languages with an accent that is equal parts British, Latino, and American. It's impossible to tell from listening to her where she is from, except to say that it is an educated, cultured, and comfortable place. Her voice and manner make her classic Bolivian beauty—almond-shaped eyes and almond-colored skin—seem as likely to come from the Middle East as South America. In 2002, during a weeklong celebration in Italy, Fabiola married Davide Percipalle, a Sicilian stock trader whose fastidiousness is a solid anchor for Fabiola's adventurous enthusiasm.

Fabiola was the family member who most shared Nils's appetite for adventure, the only one he would press to keep his pace. Several years before his Everest expedition, he treated Fabiola to a birthday safari in Africa, with the finale being a hot-air-balloon ride over the Serengeti at dawn and a champagne brunch in the wilderness. They spent that night tracking a leopard and then flew to London, where they had an overnight layover. Fabiola was thankful that it was cold and rainy and they were in an airport hotel. She finally had an excuse to get some sleep. But after they washed up, her father gave her a nudge.

"Come on, let's get up and go out into the city."

It was natural that Fabiola was Nils's confidante while he was on the mountain, even though he needed a satellite to share his whispers. Although Nils had often held the plans for his previous climbs close to his vest, this time he seemed to want to share them, to reach out for some kind of reassurance. He called Gladys once or twice a day throughout his expedition, and she wired money for him several times, at least $10,000 of which he said he planned to carry as cash with him during the climb to use for tips, bonuses, and emergencies. He called Fabiola every few days as well, apprising her not only of the stunning landscape and colorful people he encountered, but also of the intestinal illnesses he struggled with and the difficulties of the trek to Base Camp as well.

Still, it wasn't until her father stopped speaking Spanish, the language their family was most comfortable conversing in, that she really got worried.

"Why are you talking in English? What's wrong?" Fabiola

snapped when her father, calling her from Base Camp, switched languages. His voice was hoarse and he sounded weak.

"I don't want him to hear me," Nils replied.

Nils's reports of his persistent intestinal illnesses and diminishing weight had his family concerned, but sickness comes with the territory and was something they were prepared to hear about. Suspicion about his guide, the man he was sharing a tent with, was not.

"What's wrong?" Fabiola persisted.

"It isn't going so well," Nils said. "I don't trust him."

Gustavo was volatile and unpredictable, Nils said. They had argued. Fabiola had heard enough to urge her father to come home, but Nils headed off the plea that he knew was coming.

"I can rely on the Sherpas. . . . They are good."

When Fabiola joined her mother in Washington as the days of her father's summit bid approached, she spoke with him more often. Each of Nils's calls made his wife more nervous, so Gladys usually handed the phone off to her daughter after a few minutes.

On May 17, as he was resting and making the final preparations for his summit bid, Nils called his wife and daughter. Depending on the weather, he said, he would be heading for the top of the mountain that night or the next, starting upward in the dark of night, his face covered by an oxygen mask and goggles. The image terrified Gladys.

"No, I don't want to hear any more," she blurted into the phone as he tried to explain what he expected the summit bid to be like. "It makes me nervous. It makes me sick."

Nils pleaded with her to keep talking to him, but she couldn't bear to listen to him.

"I love you," he said.

"Don't tell me any more. I don't want to hear any more," she said, passing the phone to Fabiola, who would have to send enough luck and love for both of them.

Meanwhile, Nils's son, David Antezana, was racing to tie up loose ends at his neurosurgical practice in Portland, Oregon, before flying to Minnesota for the ten-year reunion of his medical school class.

When he was growing up, David Antezana had never felt as close with his father as his younger sister did. Even as a teenager, Fabiola had been away from her D.C. home for months at a time, but it just seemed to bring her closer to her father.

David's relationship with his father, on the other hand, was defined by the fact that he had always known that he wanted to be a doctor too, so his career path kept him closer to home. The difference still shows when they chat. Fabiola's voice flows with a refined and worldly accent as she switches without hesitation between English, Spanish, and Italian depending on whether she is talking with American friends, her family, or her husband. David's voice is just as polished, but every bit American and, while his sister talks of world events, David would just as soon talk about the Redskins or, perhaps, the Vikings.

"Fabiola was my father's fantasy," David says. "I was his reality."

When others in the family admired how Nils's hair was still more black than gray, David was the one who would point out that his father had been dyeing it for years.

But David's relationship with his father warmed when he moved farther away from home. Although the trappings of his life at the University of Minnesota weren't nearly as exotic as his sister's in Europe and South America, tales of his son's medical studies were just as exciting to Nils as Fabiola's were when she worked in the Bolivian embassy in Moscow. Healing was the language that would bring David closer to his father. Watching his son make the same journey through medical school that he had made forty years earlier had the same effect on Nils as scuba diving, skydiving, and mountaineering. He seemed younger. Nils called David often and, at times, the veteran physician seemed more fascinated by the studies than the student.

As David began seeming less an apprentice and more a doctor, he and his father found another interest in common: Bolivia. Nils Antezana had always been involved with the Bolivian-American Medical Association, but when he went to South America with David, he stopped in at their annual conference only long enough to show off the latest physician in the Antezana clan. There was far too much for them to catch up on in his homeland for him to spend much time in a convention hall. David had never felt closer to his father than he did chatting about medicine as they rambled through Cochabamba and La Paz.

David knew that his father had always had a private world that balanced the social demands that his life as a doctor, father, and friend put on him. Although nobody in the family had been to the mountains with Nils, now that David was also practicing medicine, he recognized that the solitude and beauty of mountaineering was an important part of his father's life.

"He kept a few things close to himself," David recalled. "It was the only thing he had that was his own."

Nils had slowly begun to talk about introducing his children to the sport he loved, and he and David had chatted about what David's first mountain should be. It would, of course, have to be a Bolivian peak.

"After medicine, after Bolivia, this was now going to be area number three where I was permitted to enter into his world," David said. "I was very much looking forward to it."

Nils climbed Aconcagua in Argentina in early 2000. But when his father recounted the climb for his son during a visit later that year, David recognized that his father was looking ahead to a different peak.

"Well, you've done Aconcagua now," David said. "I suspect I know what you're thinking the next step is."

"Yeah," his father responded with slow thoughtfulness. "Yeah."

"It's a calculated risk," David said, digging into the conversation.

"Yes, yes it is," his father responded quietly.

"Emphasis on *risk*," David said, pressing the point without the emotional reaction that he knew would close his father's mind to him.

Nils Antezana looked into space and waited a few moments to respond to his son.

"Yes," he said slowly.

That was all they said, and although neither of them ever uttered the word "Everest," David knew where his father was headed. And he knew not to press it any further. That part of the conversation was over.

It was more than three years before the issue resurfaced. Six months before he would head into the death zone, Nils began calling David in Oregon, where the younger Dr. Antezana now worked, to talk about medicine. But this time it wasn't fascination with his son's studies or practice that drew him to the phone. He was looking for advice.

"I'm not worried about getting up," Nils confided. "I'm worried about getting down."

Nils had never surfed the Internet, but his son was more than happy to sit at a computer investigating things that might help his father make it to the top of the world—or, more important, come home safely. But when the topic he was called on to research was mountaineering equipment, David knew he was getting drawn out of his depth. Still, he was thrilled to be helping and charmed that his father was including him in some small way in such a grand adventure.

David and Nils agreed to rendezvous in San Francisco, which they both claimed as their favorite American city but had never visited together, for a shopping trip to Marmot Mountain Works. A domed spire marks the entrance to the store, which fills a vacant church. The first thing David noticed was that despite its size, the store was so crammed with clothes and equipment that only a few customers could make it feel crowded. Nylon and Gore-Tex of every possible color filled racks, and ropes woven with contrasting threads hung from the walls and the rafters. Spools of colored webbing, like holiday ribbons, filled walls next to the glinting, medieval menace of ice-climbing tools.

David watched his father try on a variety of down clothes—Michelin Man suits in massive pillows of red and yellow that make it easier to see climbers on vast snowy peaks. David provided what advice he could.

"Papa, it might be easier to urinate out of that suit," David said, pointing one out, knowing that while this comment might sound funny amid racks of clothes on a sunny California morning, high on

Mount Everest, difficulty in going to the bathroom is the kind of thing that can cause real problems.

David spent hours watching his father collect a couple thousand dollars' worth of clothes and equipment, but his fascination never waned. Still, although their weekend together was very much about the mountain and they spoke mostly of Nils's upcoming expedition, David can't remember many details from those conversations. Instead he recalls strolling with his father through a sunny and unseasonably warm winter weekend in San Francisco, sitting in the bar on top of the Hilton hotel to take in the view, and long dinners at the Colonade and Aqua, where his father, as was his custom, critiqued each course.

After their weekend in California, Nils's calls came more often. At first he rang his son every week or so, but as the expedition neared, he was on the phone with David nearly every day, sometimes twice, to ask about neurological reactions to altitude, how his age might affect his performance, and what his son thought he could expect from his body as he fought off the ravages brought by six weeks of oxygen starvation on Everest. David sat at his computer to research each topic that came up, then passed his findings on to his father during their next conversation. Within a few weeks, he, too, was an expert on the many ways high mountains can destroy human bodies long before they have the chance to reach the summit. He began suggesting some medications that might give his father an advantage, or at least make up for the fact that he was so much older than just about anybody on the mountain.

"Nothing can make you stronger at the summit," David told his father, "but if you can keep yourself healthy and strong low on the mountain, maybe you'll have a little more strength left on top."

David passed on to his father whatever he could find on the high-altitude benefits of everything from antibiotics to steroids. Then he sent him a ream of prescriptions.

"If you get sick, start taking the antibiotics and turn around. Papa . . . don't wait. If you start feeling tired or you start feeling like you're not thinking right . . . you need to take your Decadron and start turning around. . . . You're a physician. You've got some insight into this."

David knew that there was one disease that he could not provide medication for: summit fever.

"You're not going to want to turn around, because you've got that desire," he told his father with the same dispassion that he used with his patients. "The point of the medications is not to help you get to the top of the mountain. The point of the medications is to take them and then turn around so that you still have the strength and the means by which to get down the mountain."

But soon, David recognized that his father's interest in the medications was like the gratuitous smiles and nods he got from patients who had no intention of changing their lifestyle. Nils, he realized, knew from the beginning that he wasn't going to enhance his performance with drugs. It wasn't his style. But he loved the way talking about the medicine brought him closer to his son.

David asked his father about his guide, but, in the end, never even learned the man's last name.

"Who is this 'Gustavo'?" David asked, but Nils shared little about the man who would soon hold his life in his hands, other than the fact he had climbed Everest before.

Just a few weeks before Nils was scheduled to depart, the calls stopped. By this point, any climber headed to Everest would be flat-out packing, training, and making last-minute preparations. But with barely a week left before his flight out of the country, Nils called to say he wanted to buy a satellite phone. Today it's rare to find an expedition that doesn't have satellite communications, and sat phones, not much larger or heavier than a cell phone, often accompany climbers all the way to the summit.

The next day David ordered an Iridium satellite telephone. When it arrived, he rushed through the thick manual to learn how it worked and programmed his family's phone numbers into it before he sent it on to his father.

But after the hours they had spent on the phone in the months leading up to the expedition and their magical weekend in San Francisco, David found the phone calls from his father once he was in Nepal to be superficial. The more than thirteen-hour time difference made connecting difficult, and the time delay in the calls, even when the connections were good, emphasized how far apart they now were rather than bringing them closer together. David was rarely available when his father called. When he returned the calls, he usually got the phone's voice mail, where he listened to his own voice recite the outgoing message he had recorded for his father and then left messages that he knew Nils wasn't getting.

In the few conversations they had, it was obvious that things weren't going well. David knew that if his father was willing to admit that he was sick at all, it was a lot worse than he was saying. David felt he pulled the trigger early, and worried that the one moment where his concern for his father overcame his physician's dispassion kept Nils from being as open about his troubles as he otherwise might have been.

"If you have a bit of a G.I. bug, these are the things that weaken you and soften you up for the final blow. If you're having these kind of issues, you need to turn around and get off of that mountain," David implored.

His father promised to look after his health and to monitor his condition closely, but said he felt OK to continue upward.

It was nearly a week before they spoke again, and the connection was bad. When David could hear his father, his voice was weak, both from the bad connection and his exhaustion. When he asked Nils where he was, either the question or the answer was lost in the ether.

"He must be in Camp Three," David thought, knowing that climbers in Camp Four used oxygen, and the mask made it difficult to put their mouths to a telephone receiver.

The phone couldn't hold the connection long enough for father and son to have a real conversation. But the lonely, gasping fear of a high mountain camp breaks down even the strongest climber's defenses, and David still felt better connected with his father than in the previous calls from the hill. Nils hinted that he still was having problems with his health and his guide. David realized that this was his last, best chance to get through to his father, both as his son and as a doctor.

"Turn around," David urged. "Get off that mountain."

The line was silent.

"Papa?" David asked, afraid that he might have lost the connection.

The breathless voice that came back through the receiver seemed farther away than before, heavy with disappointment and melancholy. David still hears it like a recording in his head.

"Oh, David," his father sighed through the silence. "I cannot hear you."

HARTFORD, CONNECTICUT—JANUARY 2004

On the weekend that David Antezana was in San Francisco helping his father equip for Everest, my expedition was barely a dream. Everest expeditions used to take a year or more to plan. We had three months to raise money, equip the team, and arrange our flights, permits, Sherpas, and cooks. We called it the Connecticut Everest Expedition because we didn't have time to think of anything better.

As a coach of women's sports at Trinity College in Hartford, Anne Parmenter knows how to organize athletes and raise money. As a guide, she had stood atop the highest peaks in North and South America, as well as Ama Dablam, a 22,494-foot mountain just twelve miles from Everest's summit—a climb we made together. She had grown up in England dreaming of Everest, but considered the top of the world out of reach until George Dijmarescu, who had completed successful ascents of Everest in each of the previous five seasons, proposed that she and I join him to create the Connecticut Everest Expedition.

At six feet two, George was nearly nine inches taller than the petite coach. Anne thought that George, in his Adidas shoes, warm-up jacket, ponytail, and mustache, looked more like a soccer fan than a mountaineer. She was surprised that a man who had climbed Everest five times could live nearly in her backyard without her hearing about him. Nevertheless, as soon as he dangled Everest in front of her, she was mesmerized.

"It's not that hard," he commented over a round of beer, leaning toward Anne. "I can see it in your eyes. You are strong enough. You can climb this mountain."

His $12,000-a-person budget—plus another $3,200 for each climber who hired a Sherpa—was cheap by Everest standards. With the companionship of George and his wife, who had herself climbed Everest three times, the price seemed to buy excellent odds of success. And, if George's plans came off, we would be part of something historic: George and Lhakpa's Everest/K2 doubleheader. Although none of their Connecticut Everest teammates would climb K2 with them, we all felt part of the endeavor.

Early support proved promising. Once on board, Anne was consumed by the project, garnering a team invitation to the state capital, finding someone to make a batch of free promotional T-shirts for the climbers to hawk, and printing additional shirts at a discount when sales exceeded expectations. She ran off posters and postcards, coaxed her college to host an expedition Web site, and arranged for a slideshow by George that packed a hall at Trinity, raising team spirits. Colleagues at the college cut checks to the expedition. The players on her lacrosse team gave part of their meal money.

The CEO of Eastern Mountain Sports heard about the expedition and offered sponsorship: about $20,000 worth of equipment and $1,600 in cash to buy boots. A few hours after I heard about the support from EMS, my cell phone rang. It was Chuck Boyd, the climber from Suffield, Connecticut. Chuck had the most impressive climbing résumé of any of the mountaineers considering joining the team. He had been a part of acclaimed first ascents of mountains in Pakistan and Peru and had climbed extensively in the Alps when his wife's corporate job had relocated them to France. Now in his fifties, his dark ponytail and beard going gray, the spectacled climber was nevertheless showing a fresh determination to become Connecticut's leading mountain guide. Chuck had bowed out of the expedition a week earlier, claiming it was too expensive, but, upon hearing of the EMS sponsorship, had changed his mind.

"This is just the kind of support I need," he said.

Chuck was not only back in, he was insisting on bringing a friend, Dave Watson. Dave had grown up in Connecticut, taken his first climbing classes from Chuck, and was now working as a climbing guide and ski patroller in Vermont. He wouldn't be around to attend any of the team's meetings, would participate in few fundraising events, and raised no money for the group. In fact, no members of the team spoke with Dave for weeks after Chuck announced his friend was coming.

"He's too busy ski patrolling and guiding snowmobilers to come to Connecticut," Chuck snapped when team members questioned Dave's commitment.

Bill Driggs, on the other hand, dove into the expedition the same way he had for the swims of the five Ironman triathlons he had competed in. He called me as soon as he heard about the expedition. His wrist was still in a cast from a skiing accident when he met the team at one of our weekly gatherings.

"This is the kind of team I want to be a part of," he said.

Bill worked for a printing company during the week and built houses on the side, but within a couple weeks, he had arranged the expedition's most successful fund-raiser—a $20-a-person reception at a Land Rover dealership, capped by a $1,000 donation from the owner. Bill recruited a local vineyard to donate wine and paid for the wineglasses himself.

Three months after meeting her, George recommended Anne as co-leader of the expedition. "As a woman, as a coach, she will be able to keep us working as a team," he said.

"George, you have the climbing experience on Everest," she responded.

"I'm a laborer, not a leader," he said. "Because of that English accent, people listen to you."

In the Himalaya, he said, people listen to Lhakpa, who, although she cannot read or write, speaks both Tibetan and Nepali and had led an Everest expedition before. She would lead there. Struck by the irony of an illiterate woman leading an expedition because of her language skills, I suggested we teach Lhakpa to read during the trip. Anne suggested the team could also help Lhakpa pursue U.S. citizenship.

"She doesn't need that," George responded.

Despite her misgivings, Anne agreed to share the leadership duties with Lhakpa. The entire team, however, knew that George, although neither our leader nor our guide, would be our man on the mountain, using his experience to negotiate with the trekking agency, select Sherpas, and plan the ascent. But that experience, we all realized even at the time, was as narrow as it was deep. Although his six trips to the north side of Everest gave him an encyclopedic knowledge of our climbing route, he had climbed only a handful of mountains. He had little experience with crevasses, no avalanche training, and few navigational skills. He laughed when I spoke of practicing to "self-arrest"—the basic skill of using an ice ax to keep from sliding off a mountain. I puzzled over the same question that most climbers who met George asked: "Why do you climb the same route on the same mountain every year?" George said he loved the place and the Sherpa people, but his yearly climb up Everest seemed to involve as much thought as an annual vacation to Aruba.

Even Lhakpa said she would rather climb one of the other Himalayan giants: Cho Oyu or Shishipangma.

The team held its last U.S. meeting at George and Lhakpa's apartment a week before departing. We had a daunting to-do list, but celebrated nonetheless with berry wine that George's mother had made in Romania.

During the days that followed, as the team raced between

banks, the EMS store, the state capital, and the *Courant*, the good feelings began to evaporate.

George held a second fund-raising slideshow at Yale University four days before our departure, but it was poorly attended. I was one of the no-shows, and George blamed me, not only for the weak turnout by other climbers, but for the team's generally meager finances. He had dreamed of the kind of well-heeled expedition that created legend on Everest. If I pushed the *Courant*, he said, the newspaper would not only pay for Carolyn and me but also sponsor the other climbers. My explanations of the ethics that prevent a newspaper, at least the one I worked for, from paying its subjects' way up Everest just made him suspect that we were exploiting him.

My ambition was an elaborate, multimedia telling of the expedition's story. In addition to weekly stories and photographs in the paper, satellite technology made daily blogging from the mountain possible, complete with audio, video, and interactive maps. I also proposed that the Newspaper in Education (NIE) program at the *Courant* run first-person stories from each of the climbers. For the mountain guides on the team, who could introduce themselves to thousands of potential clients, the NIE component seemed like a no-brainer. And George, who already had a long-term relationship with the middle school in South Windsor, could now tell his story in schools across the state.

It was uncharted territory for everyone. None of the mountaineers had climbed with such a heavy intrusion of media, and although they eagerly courted the publicity that could draw some financing to their endeavors, several expressed suspicion of the scrutiny that would come along with it. Newspapers rarely allow staff members to be both storytellers and subjects, and my editors worried that by literally tying myself to my subjects I would find it difficult to report objectively on them. And I had never covered people on whom my life depended so completely. Like anyone walking new ground, our first steps were awkward.

The week before our departure, Carolyn and I brought the entire team in to the *Courant* offices for video interviews, portrait sessions, and planning meetings. *Courant* editors sought the team's permission to use the video Carolyn would shoot, along with footage they took themselves, for TV news coverage and, perhaps, a documentary. The proposal wasn't well received.

All the attention, in fact, convinced George that the newspaper, Carolyn, and I would make thousands of dollars covering the expedition, and that we were planning to cut the rest of the climbers out of those profits. He spent $4,000 on his own professional-grade video camera just days before we left, and announced plans to produce his own documentary. When we were waiting for our flight to Asia at JFK Airport, George approached Carolyn with his new camera and asked her to show him how to turn it on.

Chuck Boyd also was wary of our plans to chronicle the expedition. Computers, satellite phones, and e-mail were not things he liked bringing on a climb.

"I go to the mountains to get away from that stuff," he said during a team meeting. "Dave and I are going to climb a mountain, not play on computers."

He was also upset with George for inviting three climbers who were not members of the expedition to share our permit—a pair of novice climbers named Dan Lochner and Dan Meggitt, and a young Mexican named Guillermo Carro Blaizac, who had befriended George on Everest in 2002 but failed to summit. George was in turn furious that Chuck's protégé, Dave Watson, was taking as much of the team's support as he could get but doing nothing to help organize or raise funds for anyone but himself.

The expedition members who didn't work for the *Courant* made plans to share equally the money the team raised, after they returned. Until then, they committed to paying their own way. Nonetheless, a couple of members demanded payments from the team's account on their last weekend in Connecticut. The group agreed to cut checks only to George and Lhakpa because they were the only parents on the team. They received $4,000, as well as two airline tickets to Bangkok from donations of frequent flyer miles from workers at the printing company where our teammate Bill Driggs worked.

It was easy to dismiss these last-minute disputes as pre-expedition stress. Even the mellowest climbers are tense in the days before a big expedition, and this, after all, was Everest.

"It will get better when we get to Kathmandu," Anne predicted.

Lhakpa was also eager to get to Kathmandu, but she wasn't sure things would get better for her. Just thirty-six hours before we departed for the Himalaya, Carolyn visited Lhakpa at her apartment. George was at work. "My heart, it is so heavy," Lhakpa said.

George was hitting her, she told Carolyn. "This man, oh, I cannot live with this man."

Carolyn came home shaken, worried that our adventure was causing suffering to another woman. Maybe Lhakpa was exaggerating, I told her.

But Lhakpa also spoke with Bill about her husband's volatility and told Anne that George had threatened to take Sunny away from her if she didn't go along with his plan to climb K2. The next day, when George answered my phone call to their apartment, Lhakpa asked to speak to me. "Michael?" she asked, and then burst into tears.

"What did you say to her?" George demanded when he got back on the phone.

After I hung up with George, Carolyn and I sat amid our piles of gear and stared at each other. George, Lhakpa, Carolyn, and I were scheduled to head to the airport at four thirty the next morning to fly to Nepal, but if what Lhakpa had told us was true, and given the increasing tensions on the team, I wondered if we should be going at all. I already felt as though I was barely holding on. Long days at the paper, planning the coverage with editors, finishing stories, and preparing the electronics that would turn a camp 21,000 feet above sea level into a bureau of a New England newspaper tumbled into sleepless nights of packing for the climb. I couldn't see how we could scuttle it now. We had already spent thousands of dollars on permits and plane tickets and gear. The team had been honored by the state, received a proclamation from Senator Chris Dodd, and accepted thousands of dollars in support from local businesses and individuals. The *Courant* and local television outlets had promoted us throughout the state. What would we say if, after all that, we just didn't get on the plane in the morning?

Carolyn and I called Anne to talk about it. We decided that the best thing for all of us was to stay the course. If what Lhakpa said was true, Anne, Carolyn, and I rationalized that she would have family to help her when she got to Kathmandu. And Lhakpa had said that her family would be there for us, too.

"In Nepal the Sherpa listen to me," she said. "Not George."

But in the end, perhaps none of us was willing to let other team members' troubles get between us and our dreams.

Four

At the moment Gustavo Lisi was contacting his mother and his Web site to let them know he had reached the summit of Everest, Gladys Antezana was awaiting the news of her husband's climb from a Baltimore hospital bed. It was as if her husband's worrisome calls actually had made her sick.

She had undergone surgery in early April, and Nils had waited to start his trek to Everest until he was sure everything had gone well. But six weeks later, just as Nils was heading for the summit, an infection had set in. While Fabiola was with her awaiting news of the climb, Gladys managed to keep the illness at bay. But as soon as she took her daughter to the airport for her flight back home to London, Gladys visited her doctor, who checked her into the hospital. Nils's son, David, was on the other side of the continent, in Oregon, packing for his medical school reunion. Alone in her hospital room, Gladys lamented that the family wasn't together to offer Nils their support during his climb. Who could he call if he was in trouble?

Her family's scattering around the globe seemed a symbol of how her husband's adventure was falling apart.

"Everything is against him," she thought to herself, crying softly.

Nils planned to stand on top of the world the morning of Tuesday, May 18, or Wednesday, May 19, and be back in his tent in the early afternoon, which would have been one in the morning in Washington and seven a.m. London time. But by Thursday morning, his family still hadn't heard from him. Fabiola comforted her mother from the other side of the Atlantic. They rang each other every hour or so through the day Thursday, puzzling about why the man who had so diligently called each member of his family as he prepared to go up the mountain would take so long to let them know when he made it back down. Fabiola tried to keep her mother calm, but with each passing hour and every call they shared, worry turned to dread and then to desperation.

"Didn't he tell you which day he was going to summit?" Gladys kept asking her daughter, who in turn repeated that Nils wasn't certain during his last call. He was waiting to see how he felt and what the weather was predicted to do.

It was 11:30 a.m. in Washington on May 20, more than two days after Nils collapsed on the Balcony, when Gladys's cell phone rang. "It's Gustavo," a ragged voice said over the phone, and she immediately knew something had gone terribly wrong.

"Nils and I summited," Gustavo continued before Gladys could get a word in.

"Where is my husband?" she barked into the phone. "Put my husband on the phone!"

"He's been in a terrible accident," Gustavo said. "There's been a disaster."

Gladys was speechless as her husband's guide raced through his story. Nils didn't make it down, he explained, but had stayed on the mountain because that's where he wanted to finish his life. Nils, in fact, was ecstatic when he lay down in the snow to die, Gustavo said.

"Estaba cho cho!" Gustavo said. "He was bursting with happiness."

When she regained her voice, Gladys asked about a rescue. It would have been futile, Gustavo replied. There was no way he could have survived up there.

"Why didn't you send somebody up!" Gladys shouted. "How could you just leave him up there?"

"Because I was sick myself," Gustavo responded.

Then Gustavo told Gladys what he said were her husband's last words to him.

"Nils said, 'I want to stay here,'" Gustavo told her. "'The mountain is my home.'"

Her husband had become a terrific friend, Gustavo said, and he had tried to revive Nils as if he were his own father, begging him to get back on his feet, to keep fighting for his life, when he reclined in the snow high on Everest.

"Nils, you have a family," Gustavo said, recalling his pleas to his client. "Come on!"

Nils didn't answer; he just lay stock-still in the snow.

Just before Gustavo hung up, Gladys asked about Nils's belongings. Gustavo said he would bring them with him to Argentina. She could retrieve them there.

Fabiola had spent the night and day after she got back to London with her hand on the telephone. Davide, her husband, was desperate to get his wife out of their apartment, and, as futile as it seemed, as far away from her worries about her father as he could. He called her from work to say he wanted to get a haircut at Harrods that evening.

"Why don't you leave the house?" he said. "Come with me."

At the department store, Fabiola and Davide walked through the sporting-goods section, past hacking jackets and jodhpurs for horsemen and ropes and carabiners for rock climbers, to the men's spa. Davide had just checked in with the receptionist when he got a voice-mail message on his phone from his mother-in-law. Fabiola called Gladys right back.

"Your father hasn't come down," Gladys said, her voice weak with sedation and shock.

Nearby a group of men in business suits was touring the store. Fabiola took a few steps toward the counter in the spa to have as much privacy and quiet as she could.

"What do you mean he hasn't come down?" she said, trying to stay calm.

"He's still on the mountain," her mother replied, as though she didn't completely understand what that meant.

"Where is the guide?" Fabiola asked, her voice rising in spite of herself as her husband stepped closer to her and cocked his head toward the phone.

Gustavo had called to say that they had summited, Gladys explained. He made it down.

"When did he summit?" Fabiola asked of her father, no longer trying to control the tenor of her voice. "You have to tell me, what was the day that they summited?"

The businessmen turned their gaze from the staid opulence of the department store to the woman growing slowly hysterical inside the spa.

"Tuesday," her mother replied. "They summited on Tuesday."

Fabiola's legs buckled and she fell into her husband's arms, sobbing. If he had reached the summit Wednesday, perhaps there was a chance someone could still mount a rescue. She knew there was no way her father could have survived two nights out above 8,000 meters on Mount Everest, but she still tried to hold on to a thread of hope. She wailed into the phone.

"Have they sent somebody up? Who's going up just to try to save him?"

Gustavo had said there was no way they could have rescued him, Gladys said, weeping on the other end of the phone. Nils couldn't have survived the night.

"When did he stop and call you?" Fabiola asked.

"Just now," her mother replied.

"And he summited two days ago?" Why would Gustavo take so long to let them know what had happened to Nils?

"No, no, no, no, no, no, no, it can't be," Fabiola wailed. "My father, my father."

Davide apologized to the receptionist, who looked happy to have the drama leave when he said they would have to go. He could barely keep up with his wife as she ran sobbing down the escalators to the ground floor, her legs shaking and her cell phone still clutched in her hands.

Outside, Fabiola leaned, weeping, on her husband's shoulder as they made their way to Davide's car. Diners taking in the sun at a sidewalk café stared at the sobbing woman staggering down the street.

Back at the apartment, Fabiola headed straight for her computer and turned it on to check Everest sites and send e-mails in hopes of finding some information about her father. But after a few minutes she stopped and ran to a bookshelf in another room and began tearing through the shelves to find a magazine. Within the pages she found two pieces of cardboard pressed together with a plastic sleeve between them. The photograph inside had come to her in a frame, but it had been cracked in a move. She had put it in the magazine to keep it from getting torn or creased. It showed her father standing atop Illimani, a mountain in Bolivia that Nils had summited within days of Fabiola's birthday a few years earlier. He was holding up a large piece of paper on which he had drawn a homemade sign. It read SAPO VERDE FABIOLA— "green toad Fabiola" in English. Since her childhood mispronunciation of "happy birthday" as *sapo verde*, Fabiola's family had embraced calling each other green toads to mark the anniversaries of their births.

Fabiola stared at the photo that, only a few moments before, she had been terrified was lost. Her father had thought of her at the top of a mountain and gone to the trouble of writing a birthday message when merely breathing was tough. Now Fabiola wondered what he was thinking when he stood on the summit of Everest and, most of all, what he was thinking when he couldn't make it down. She took the photo and put it in her date book, where it would travel halfway around the world with her as she looked for the answers to her questions. Then she sat back down at the computer and sent e-mails to EverestNews.com and ExplorersWeb, rival Web sites that follow the Everest climbing season. George Martin, who operates EverestNews.com, responded with a promise to put Fabiola's plea for information on the site. He also sent e-mail addresses for several of the expeditions on the mountain, and Fabiola sent notes to all of them:

I am Dr. Nils Antezana's daughter. We have received word from my father's guide that he reached the summit sometime today or yesterday . . . and stopped short . . . on the way back to Camp 4. THERE MUST BE A SEARCH PARTY SENT OUT FOR HIM!!!

PLEASE CAN SOMEONE RESPOND!! . . .

Nobody in her family had ever known Gustavo's last name, but on EverestNews.com, Fabiola found lists of that year's Everest climbers that included her father and his guide. She searched under Gustavo Lisi's name and found his Web site and the announcement, from two days earlier, that he had reached the summit with her father, but no note of any problems. Then she found the reports about his previous trip to Everest.

"How could my father not know about this?" she thought to herself.

Five

Nils had told his family little about his guide for the Everest climb—only that Gustavo had been to the top of Mount Everest before, and that they had met while climbing in Bolivia. But when Fabiola tracked Gustavo online, she found his deepest tracks not in the Himalaya or the Andes, but in the Basque Country of Spain—a place where he had never set foot.

The gothic towers and walls fortifying the medieval quarter of Vitoria, Spain, date back to the ninth century, defining the center of the almond-shaped city. But it's the Plaza de la Virgen Blanca, just outside the ancient walls, where the heart of the capital of Spain's fiercely independent Basque Country beats the strongest. The monument to the battle of Vitoria, at the center of the square, is the starting point for many of the demonstrations that mark political anniversaries in the city, when colored chalk is applied like makeup to the easiest to reach of the bronze soldiers' faces, and mobs of chanting punks march by crowds with graying hair waving banners in the street. The architecture that surrounds the square is 1,000 years younger than the relics nearby, and it seems more representative of the city, which really found its voice in the last century and began shouting with it a few decades ago after Vitoria was named the autonomous region's capital.

In a tavern on a corner of the square, locals chat and munch on tapas. Although animated political discussions are unavoidable, a sign in front of the bottles of spirits jokingly prohibits talk of soccer, the most popular sport in the country. But amid the magazines stacked on a whiskey barrel in the corner, where there is only one edition of every other publication, there are four copies of *Desnivel*, the Spanish climbing magazine. The Basques take mountaineering, and their mountaineers, almost as seriously as they take their politics.

Juan Carlos Gonzalez didn't realize how much mountaineering was a part of the Basque culture until he started making plans for an expedition to Everest in 2000. Gonzalez, a postman in Vitoria, found himself standing on the stoops of homes where he was delivering mail to answer questions about the upcoming climb, his first Himalayan expedition. People from his routes waved and shouted encouragement to him on the street. They still do, although the hands that he waves back with are a few knuckles shorter than they were then.

Juan Carlos headed for Everest as part of a team of Basque mountaineers sponsored by local companies and municipalities. A crew from a Spanish television program, *Al Filo de lo Imposible (To the Edge of the Impossible)*, would document the climb. As the expedition came together, the team's leader, Josu Feijoo, heard from the trekking agency in Kathmandu that some other climbers—from Italy and Argentina—were interested in sharing the team's permit and facilities.

Silvio "Gnaro" Mondinelli, an Italian mountaineer, needed no introduction at all. Whippet-thin, with a hairless head and friendly baritone voice, Silvio looked a bit like Popeye, and was renowned for speed at altitude. Even without his reputation for strength, skill, and "simpatico," Silvio would have been welcome on the team. He was a friend of Edurne Pasaban, a rising star among the Basque climbers and the only woman on the team.

Nobody on the team had ever heard of Gustavo Lisi, the Argentine mountain guide the trekking agency was adding to the permit, but when he saw the résumé that Gustavo sent, Josu was surprised that they hadn't. He recalls that Gustavo listed impressive guiding qualifications as well as ascents of the 8,000-meter giants Cho Oyu and Manaslu. Gustavo's accomplishments had prompted his hometown of Salta, Argentina, to sponsor his climb.

"He could be the strongest guy on the team," Josu thought to himself.

Months later, in May, Juan Carlos found himself with Gustavo on the way to the summit. A sudden storm had turned the Basque team back from their first summit bid. Juan Carlos and Gustavo regrouped at Camp Two, at about 7,700 meters or 25,000 feet, while the rest of their team descended to Advanced Base Camp at 21,000 feet. Juan Carlos had responded well to the altitude, and a weather report held out hope that the storm might clear from the summit during the coming two days. Although Juan Carlos hadn't planned on climbing with Gustavo, they had gotten along all right during the expedition and were ready to head for the top at the same time. They moved up to Camp Three, at 26,700 feet, through blowing snow.

During the early morning, the weather cleared and Juan Carlos, Gustavo, and a Sherpa headed for the summit together. But at a feature of Everest known as the Yellow Band, Gustavo worried that they were running late and the weather could change suddenly. He retreated to Camp Three while the Spaniard and his Sherpa continued to the summit. Clear skies made Juan Carlos's time on top of the world transcendent, but it was late—after one p.m.—when he arrived there, and things weren't where they should have been. He couldn't find the tripod that marked the summit, although the piles of prayer flags and memorabilia, as well as the lack of anywhere else to climb, left little doubt that he was in the right place. As he hunted for the landmark, he tripped and slid some fifty feet down the slope, tearing the pants of his down suit. His Sherpa, Lakpa, who had been slowed by sickness, arrived as Juan Carlos climbed back up. This was indeed the top, he said. Juan Carlos took some snaps of the panorama that surrounded them and a picture of him and Lakpa together. Lakpa used the same camera to take a photograph of Juan Carlos standing on the summit.

By then it was after two in the afternoon and it would be a race to get to camp before dark. A quick thought of his wife and kids was enough to get Juan Carlos started down fast, but above the Second Step, an area where many climbers lose their way on the descent, freezing fog and snow began blowing across the peak. As darkness began to fall, Lakpa raced ahead. The Basque climber could no longer see his Sherpa or find the way down.

Abandoned, Juan Carlos stopped to think before he took any steps that he might regret. He still felt strong. If he dug into a bivouac and spent the night out in the storm, he would suffer, but he was confident that he would survive. But if he got lost in the dark, he would never make it down alive. Juan Carlos burrowed into the snow and hunkered down for the night. Surviving an unsheltered night out above 8,000 meters on Everest, however, is far more rare a feat than climbing it. From their tent at Camp Three, Gustavo and Lakpa watched for a headlamp in the night as Juan Carlos's teammates back in ABC pressed their ears to radios for news of the climber who, at least by the numbers, was almost certainly dead.

Juan Carlos crawled back out of his hole at about four thirty a.m., and for a few hours he thought he'd gotten away with his night out at 28,215 feet above sea level. It wasn't until he neared camp that he realized that he couldn't open his hands. His fingers were badly frostbitten, and he had trouble holding on to the ropes.

Gustavo and Lakpa were packed up and leaving the camp when Juan Carlos stumbled in as if he were crawling from the grave.

Gustavo claims he went out to search for Juan Carlos during the morning, but neither he nor Lakpa had helped Juan Carlos get into camp. Before he collapsed in a tent, Juan Carlos remembers Gustavo promising to get him food and water and that he would wait for him in Camp Two, the next campsite down the route, to help him get down the mountain. But, in the end, Gustavo provided no assistance to his stricken partner.

Juan Carlos struggled to continue his descent. His hands seemed to be turning into wood, and he couldn't find his camera, which he usually left hanging around his neck. He finally found it stuffed inside the tear of his down suit, settling into the leg of his pants. Perhaps he could have mistaken the tear for a pocket, he thought, but he didn't remember taking his camera off his neck and never carried it in his pants pocket. Strange.

In Advanced Base Camp, Silvio Mondinelli and the rest of the team had kept their ears to their radios and their eyes to a telescope to follow Juan Carlos's climb, his failure to return from the summit the night before, and his miraculous arrival at high camp that morning. Silvio works in mountain rescue for the Italian military, and as soon as he heard that Juan Carlos was badly frostbitten after a bivouac high on Everest, he and two other climbers headed up the mountain fast.

Silvio hadn't become very friendly with Gustavo during the expedition. He remembers that the Argentinean wore a gold ice ax on a chain around his neck—the Piolet d'Or—an annual award that is something akin to an Olympic Gold Medal for mountaineers. The other climbers thought it must be a joke. They would have heard of Gustavo if he had won that coveted prize. The Italian and Basque climbers, who enjoy bringing their proud culinary traditions to the most remote environments and sharing them with mountaineers from around the world, kept the dining tent filled with treats from the Alps and the Basque country. But the Argentinean brought nothing to the table. Although Gustavo was quick to latch on to strong or well-known climbers when they were in lodges or dining tents, he rarely managed to keep up with them on the mountain.

During the rescue of Juan Carlos, Silvio raced through fog and wind, bypassing Camps One and Two altogether on his way to Camp Three. One hundred meters below the high camp he ran into Gustavo, who was exhausted and having difficulty descending himself. Silvio took Gustavo's backpack and helped the climber back down to Camp One, and then turned around and headed back up. He found Juan Carlos, crippled with frostbite and staggering along the rope at about 7,900 meters. His Sherpa was a ways farther back, sick and providing little help. Silvio assisted Juan Carlos down to Camp One, then down to Advanced Base Camp, while other climbers assisted Gustavo.

Once they were down, the team noticed that Lakpa, the Sherpa who summited with Juan Carlos, seemed unusually attached to Gustavo. That seemed strange to Silvio. Gustavo had been unfriendly with the Sherpas before the climb, and his rude demeanor toward them had troubled his teammates. Now he rarely let Juan Carlos's Sherpa out of his sight. Juan Carlos, on the other hand, was so elated about summiting and so worried about his fingers that he thought little about the fact that the Sherpa who had abandoned him and the climbing partner who had promised and failed to help him were now inseparable. When Gustavo did break away to chat with Juan Carlos, he was open in his envy, his coveting of Juan Carlos's few minutes atop Everest.

A week after summiting, Juan Carlos was in a hospital in Zaragoza, Spain, where a mountain medicine specialist cut three frostbitten fingers on Juan Carlos's right hand down to the first knuckle, and four fingers of his left hand down to the second. He would be in the hospital for more than two months. While he was recovering, he asked his brother to take the camera he wore around his neck on the summit to a photo lab for processing. But there was nothing in the camera when the lab opened it. That just couldn't be, Juan Carlos told his brother. For mountaineers, having your camera prepared to prove that you reached the summit is second only to having your ice ax and crampons ready to get you there. He had lost not only his fingers but also the last thing of significance that he did with them—pushing the shutter release on his camera.

"Losing the photos hurts much more than losing my fingers," he said.

Juan Carlos contacted the agency that had made the arrangements for the expedition and asked them to investigate what had happened to his photos. They in turn spoke with the expedition's cooks, porters, and Sherpas. But when he called Josu to tell him what had happened, the expedition leader quickly came to his own conclusion.

Silvio Mondinelli, the man who rescued Juan Carlos, was in Italy, driving home from work, when his cell phone rang. His job in search and rescue kept him in the mountains more than most of his friends, but like the majority of full-time climbers in the new millennium, he still spent more time with a cell phone in his hand than a carabiner or an ice ax. This call was from Edurne Pasaban, and he was happy to hear the voice of his climbing partner from Everest until he recognized the distress in it.

"Do you know what happened to Juan Carlos's photos?" she asked.

Silvio was baffled at the question. He had visited the badly frostbitten climber in the hospital in Zaragoza. But he had never seen Juan Carlos Gonzalez's summit photos, never seen the film, and never seen the camera. Edurne was in tears. The expedition leader thought that Silvio had taken his friend's photos.

Silvio hung up the phone and thought back. He and Gustavo had had a few extra days in Kathmandu after Juan Carlos and the Basque climbers headed home. While they were visiting an Internet café, Silvio overheard Gustavo talking excitedly into the phone.

"I have photos from the summit," he remembered Gustavo saying.

Silvio had watched the summit with a spotting scope from Advanced Base Camp the day that Juan Carlos had reached the top, and he was certain he had seen every climber who had topped out. He never saw Gustavo.

After overhearing the phone call, Silvio had asked to see Gustavo's photos. The Argentinean said his pictures weren't any good and refused to show them. Silvio had shrugged and assumed he'd just misunderstood what Gustavo had claimed in his phone call to Argentina. But now it was all starting to add up.

"I've seen people stealing from each other, and fighting each other," he recalled, thinking about his years in mountain rescue. "But I've never heard of anyone who would steal something from a dying man."

He pulled his car over to call Edurne back. Perhaps she should contact the television producers who were with them on the mountain to help them look into whether Gustavo Lisi was showing a photo from the top of Mount Everest to the media in Argentina. A photo that he was claiming showed him on the summit.

Back in the Basque Country, the team's leader, Josu, was at home raving about the theft when his mother explained it to him.

"Gustavo has the photos," she told her son.

She had never met the Argentine guide, but she had heard enough about Gustavo leaving Juan Carlos behind, his bluster during the expedition, and his strange behavior when he returned to Kathmandu.

Josu stood dumbfounded.

It didn't take long for the news to make it back to Spain from Nepal and Argentina. Gustavo had indeed shown a Sherpa in Kathmandu a photo from the top of Everest. The photo was also seen on Argentinean television and had shown up in newspapers there. Each appearance was marked by the claim that the man hidden behind the oxygen mask, cap, and goggles was Gustavo Lisi, not Juan Carlos Gonzalez. One article reported that Gustavo had not only summited but had rescued Juan Carlos. Online were the minutes of a meeting of the city council in Salta, Argentina, where the city leaders honored Gustavo for his climb to the top of Everest.

Gustavo Lisi was no longer just a mountain guide. He was a mountain guide who claimed to have conquered the highest mountain in the world and had photos to prove it. But while Gustavo had everything he needed to take his career in the mountains to the highest level, back in Spain, Juan Carlos hadn't lost just his fingers and photos but his job, as well. He couldn't handle mail anymore. But he was determined to get back the pictures he had sacrificed so much for.

Dialing a phone wasn't too difficult, but with the amputations to his fingers still fresh, hooking it up to the recorder made this call a bit more challenging.

"*Hola,*" a voice said on the other end of the line.

"Gustavo? . . . *¿Qué pasó con mis fotos?*"

The conversation went on for thirty minutes, but, for the answers Juan Carlos got, it shouldn't have lasted more than five. Gustavo, however, readily admitted that he had stolen the photos.

"I'm very bad, I'm going to a psychologist," Gustavo said. "My mother is really bad too, and I've asked your forgiveness. I committed a huge error with you. . . . I've told you the situation with the photos I stole . . ."

Juan Carlos had called Gustavo once before to ask about his photos and sent several e-mails. Gustavo had returned a dozen pictures, but none of the most valuable ones—those from the summit.

"I took the roll of photos from you . . . and for fear that you would ask for the photos and embarrass me for what I had done, I destroyed these photos [from the summit] . . . I'm being totally sincere with you, Juan Carlos, totally sincere," Gustavo said. "I have nothing more to hide."

Juan Carlos told Gustavo of the telephone call Silvio had overheard in Kathmandu, in which Gustavo said he had photos from the summit. Gustavo denied making the call. Juan Carlos said he would call the police, bring in Interpol, hire a lawyer, and notify the embassy. Gustavo kept repeating that he was sick and seeing a psychologist, and that his mother was ill as well.

"The pain you're causing me and my family," Gustavo said. "I don't know why."

"And the pain *I've* suffered?" Juan Carlos said. "That doesn't count, eh?"

The letter arrived at a Salta government building a few weeks later.

I am Juan Carlos Gonzalez, a Spaniard . . .

In the Spring of this year, 2000, and more concretely the 27th of May at 1:15 p.m. (Nepal time) I succeeded in reaching the summit of Mount Everest in the company only of my Sherpa. Well, after suffering severe frostbite in both my hands, I discovered that the slides that I had made on the summit had disappeared . . . It was discovered that the person responsible for such an abominable theft was an Argentine citizen with residence in Salta, don Gustavo Lisi.

After contacting Mr. Gustavo, I succeeded in getting him to send me 12 positives from that roll, but I am still missing more and three in particular, one in which my Sherpa appears and two in which I am standing on the summit with my flags from Castro Urdiales and from Cantabria. Mr. Lisi assures me that he has destroyed them, something that is beyond belief, so I think that he is committed to using them to say that he made it to the summit, SOMETHING THAT IS TOTALLY FALSE.

I request that you please show interest in this subject because . . . it was the Government of Salta that sponsored and covered the economic cost of his trip to Everest . . .

"He robbed me out of envy, that's what Lisi told me," Juan Carlos told *Desnivel*. "It frightens me a little, because for the same reason, one day instead of robbing photos, it could make him do things more dangerous that could put alpinists that ascend with him in danger.

"I have spoken various times with him and he told me that he was jealous that I made it to the summit and he did not. . . . What he didn't explain very well is why he sent me 12 slides, some of which I made just before arriving up high. The ones from the summit, of me and the Sherpa, he says that he has destroyed, but I can't come to believe it."

Juan Carlos wouldn't speculate further, but others worried that Gustavo's theft of Juan Carlos's photos didn't just show that his envy would drive him to put climbers at risk, but that the photos themselves could be deadly. Like a lot of crimes that are petty at sea level but lethal at high altitude, the photos stolen from the top of the world could convince an unsuspecting mountaineer that Gustavo was an experienced Everest climber with the top qualification to lead them up the mountain, namely that of having been there before.

Climbing hoaxes with misappropriated visuals supporting them go back at least a hundred years, to Dr. Frederick Cook's claim that he had made the first ascent of Mount McKinley in 1906. For proof of his accomplishment, Cook provided a summit photo that, after repeated investigations by skeptical mountaineers and photographers over a period of ninety years, was proven to have been taken from the top of a small peak nineteen miles away that is now known as Fake Peak. Cook's descriptions of the summit of McKinley—aka Denali—bore no resemblance to the top of the mountain seen by thousands of subsequent mountaineers. Two years later Cook claimed to be the first to reach the North Pole, a claim that is also almost universally seen as a hoax. The man once honored with parades in New York was convicted of stock fraud in 1922, imprisoned until 1930, and eventually pardoned by President Franklin D. Roosevelt. The Frederick A. Cook Society and the doctor's family continue to defend his accomplishments, as he did himself with books, articles, and lawsuits until his death in 1940.

With entrepreneurs in the new business of mountaineering earning thousands of dollars in guiding wages, speaking fees, book contracts, and business ventures from their accomplishments on top of mountains, climbing hoaxes have become so common that every climbing season now has some disputed summits. These days on Everest, sometimes there's not even a week between them.

In 2000, Byron Smith made his bid to reach the summit of Everest from the Nepal side six days prior to Juan Carlos Gonzalez's attempt with Gustavo Lisi from the north. The Canadian car dealer

MICHAEL KODAS

put half a million dollars into what he describes on his Web site as making "television history by organizing and leading the most extensively televised Everest expedition—ever." Byron spoke with Canadian Prime Minister Jean Cretién from Base Camp and held a half-hour question-and-answer session with schoolchildren in a Toronto television studio. Eventually his Web site, promoting him as a motivational speaker, carried a video of a climber in a red down coat, leaning over to speak into a radio. "I can't go any further," the climber says. "I am on top of the world." A caption superimposed over the image states BYRON SMITH SUCCESSFUL SUMMIT, MAY 21, 2000.

But a climber working with Everest historian and journalist Elizabeth Hawley noted that the clothes on the climber on top of the mountain were different from those that Byron was wearing earlier in his summit bid. Eventually it came out that the climber in the video was not Byron, but Mads Granlien, a Danish climber who had made the summit the day before Byron's attempt, and whose own Web site shows a frame grabbed from the video with the caption, in Danish, I CAN'T GO ANY HIGHER. Byron, admitting that the climber in the image isn't him, says the cold and wind prevented him from using his thousands of dollars of photographic and video equipment when he was on the summit. He paid Granlien $4,000 for the use of the image, he said, so that viewers of his Web site and slideshows would have an image from the top of the mountain. He combined that video with a recording of his own radio call.

Byron claims it was obvious that the climber in the image wasn't him; however, dozens of Everest veterans had seen his video without ever realizing it. Although the criticism prompted him to add a disclaimer to his Web site, it indicates only that some of his summit video was not recorded by his expedition, not that the climber in it isn't him. Byron provided sworn statements from eleven climbers defending his character and his claim of reaching the top. Six Sherpas, all of whom were working for Byron, confirmed that he was on the summit. Michael Down, a well-regarded Canadian climber with a different expedition, had planned to climb to the summit with Byron, but a malfunctioning oxygen regulator had forced him to retreat. He saw Byron approaching the Hillary Step and has consistently expressed certainty that Byron made it all the way up. However, there were no witnesses to Byron's time on the summit who weren't on the climber's payroll. Tim Ripple, cameraman for the expedition, also turned back from the summit bid but was in Camp Four when Byron returned—just three and a half hours after he says he reached the summit. After the expedition, Tim told Elizabeth Hawley that he doubted Byron could have made it to the summit and back to Camp Four that quickly. Other members of his team said they were forbidden to talk to the media by contracts Byron had required them to sign before the expedition. Byron's relationship with his teammates was so acrimonious, in fact, that all of them had quit the expedition by the time he returned to Base Camp from the summit. The team's doctor, the last to leave, waited just long enough to patch Byron's radio call from the summit through to Canada before heading home.

Climbers who contacted mountaineering Web sites questioning Byron's accomplishments were threatened with lawsuits, as were the sites themselves. Then, in April of 2006, Byron filed a lawsuit against the American Alpine Club for defamation because they listed Byron's summit as "disputed" in the Himalayan Database they published of Elizabeth Hawley's forty years of records. Byron's suit alleged that disputing his summit claim was costing his car dealership business. "I had to shut one car dealership down," Byron told me, justifying his outrage and legal actions against those who have called his summit of Everest into question. "I had customers say they wouldn't buy from me because I'm a liar."

In August of 2007 Byron's suit against the AAC was dismissed.

Byron also claimed his detractors' skepticism of the Sherpas who verified his ascent would hurt the locals' careers. But according to his detractors, a 2003 climb that Byron made of Carstensz Pyramid, the Indonesian mountain that is the highest in Australasia, seems to belie Byron's concern for the local people who assist him. This adventure had even more skullduggery than his climb of

Everest. Carstensz overlooks the controversial Grasberg Mine, the largest gold and copper mine in the world and part of New Orleans–based Freeport-McMoRan Copper & Gold. The mine is aggressively guarded by both the Indonesian military and private security. Criticism of Grasberg for human-rights violations, environmental degradation, and the suspected involvement of the military protecting the mine in the murder of three educators prompted the government to stop issuing permits to climb Carstensz. Officials, however, announced that they would continue to honor permits issued before the ban. But in a long trip report on EverestNews.com, Byron described sneaking past military checkpoints, disguising himself as a soldier, and bribing his way to the mountain to complete his climb without a permit. His report angered the government enough for them to cancel all the permits already given to climb the mountain. Ramon Blanco, one of the climbers whose permit was pulled, had officials brandish Byron's report when they denied him access. No permit is ever sure to be honored at Carstensz. Ramon nonetheless chastened Byron in an open letter, quoting Byron's own guide from the climb:

> *... even though he doesn't mention any names it was so clear that all of the ARMY guys who helped him are easily recognized from the article as he mentions ranges, positions, posts and their unit ... Freeport [Mines] is smart enough to find out all of the actors behind this project. Because of this, now there is very little chance left for me to run the [Carstensz Pyramid] Climb with such arrangements in the future.*

Byron responded to Ramon by having his lawyers contact the Web site where the letter was published. In the meantime Byron's speaking engagements and television appearances feature a summit image from Everest that actually shows another climber.

Six months before Byron's visit to Carstensz Pyramid, in the first weeks of Operation Iraqi Freedom, I was filling in as a picture editor at the *Courant* when we selected a striking photo of an Iraqi man carrying a child being ordered to take cover by a soldier. We ran the photo, taken by an internationally renowned photographer at the *Los Angeles Times*, across the entire width of the front page of the newspaper. The following day I watched as another employee in my department circled people who seemed to appear more than once in the photo. It struck me as strangely appropriate that it was April Fools' Day—the day after the photo was published—that the photographer was fired for making a digital composite of two photographs to increase the drama of the image. In the years since, I've seen a number of other news photographers lose their jobs for excessively manipulating images in computers and presenting them as the truth. Now I see that as digital sophistication increasingly makes its way to the top of Mount Everest—where scrutiny of the scene in which the image is made is unlikely—hoaxes like those of Dr. Cook may be impossible to recognize.

I have little reason to doubt that Byron Smith made it to the top of Everest. But after nearly twenty years working as a photojournalist, I know that if I misrepresented myself as being the subject of a photo that actually showed someone else, I'd be out of a job.

Six

It was the busiest week of the Everest season, so Tom and Tina Sjogren hadn't been sleeping much. Scores of e-mails and dispatches from dozens of climbers and expeditions arrived at all hours to their Web site, MountEverest.net, and the Sjogrens got the posts up onto their site as fast as they could. Several climbers were unaccounted for, and a few were already confirmed dead. Nonetheless, the notes from Fabiola Antezana were bound to stick out.

PLEASE I NEED HELP . . . my father is missing on Everest.

Tom and Tina dropped the rest of their work and read the note together.

Gustavo Lisi, my father's guide only called my mother . . . 2½ days after he and Nils summited . . . WHY WOULD HE WAIT SO LONG TO CONTACT US?? Does anyone know the whereabouts of Gustavo Lisi . . . ?

DOES ANYONE KNOW IF THERE IS A RESCUE TEAM BE-ING SENT FOR MY FATHER????

Nineteen years earlier, Tom and Tina had realized that the Himalaya was going to change their lives when, on their second or third day in Lhasa, Tibet, they saw a man in a vintage tuxedo cleaning a human skull with a toothbrush at a public well. The man, a British citizen and, like Tom and Tina, among the first sightseers to visit Tibet when China opened the region to tourism in 1985, said he retrieved the skull from the site of a "sky burial," the traditional Tibetan undertaking in which monks hack apart the bodies of the dead to leave as carrion for vultures. The tux, a remnant of the closed but strangely cosmopolitan Lhasa that had existed before the Chinese invasion of the country, he bought at a shop in town.

Tom and Tina had not been dressed much more practically. Tom had worn a trenchcoat for much of their trip across China. Tina had high heels, a bikini, and a couple of skirts and shirts. They were outfitted better for a nightclub than the rugged, arid emptiness of Tibet. But they got directions from the man in the tux anyway and hitched a ride to the site of the hours-long ceremony.

"He takes the skin off everything and he cuts the head and he puts the head beside him," Tina recalled as she thumbed through the photos years later in the office of ExplorersWeb, the company she and Tom founded to provide news coverage and technology for expeditions. "So now the head with eyes and everything is sitting facing us on the rock. And he takes the big slab of skin and—*slap*—he puts it beside him here on the rock. Now he takes the meat and he starts to chop up all the meat. . . . He crushes the bone until it's only powder left. . . . And then he takes all of this and he makes this giant meatball."

While the monk worked, Tina and Tom noticed vultures landing on the hilltops above him.

"He raises his arms and he says something to [the vultures] in Tibetan and they come down in a flock and within like two minutes, everything is done."

During the coming decades, Tom and Tina would see a lot more death in the Himalaya.

Tina Sjogren is blond, buxom, and big-eyed, with wild hair that floats around her head like yellow smoke. In her eyes you can see the drive that took her to the summit of Mount Everest, and partway up the mountain each of the three years before she stood on top. She converses with that same determination—pushing and challenging, her face beaming with wonder one moment, seething with outrage the next.

Tina, her mother, and her brother had defected to Sweden to escape communist Czechoslovakia. She had met Tom during their first year at university in Stockholm. But she had had little use for the Swede until she needed help moving. Tom was the only person she knew with a car. When it ran out of gas at Tina's new apartment, he never left.

Tina fell for Tom, at the time a competitive figure skater, when she saw him on the ice. But even off the rink, his calm pragmatism and dry sense of humor seemed a cool counterpoint to Tina's smoldering—ice to her fire. And in the abuse Tom had received as a boy on figure skates and the oppression Tina had overcome in the Eastern Bloc and as a refugee in Sweden, they discovered one thing they had in common: They hated bullies.

After they graduated from college, the couple married and traveled through Asia, the first of dozens of adventures they would take, literally to the ends of the Earth. On their way overland across China, they learned that Tibet had recently been opened to tourists, and on a whim decided that they wanted to see Mount Everest, which was then an unusual attraction for sightseers. It took weeks to get to the mountain, and as they neared it and the roads gave way to rugged trails through glacial moraine, Tina realized her sexy shoes and skirts weren't going to get her through the Himalaya. She bought lug-soled boots, rugged nylon pants, and shirts in a Tibetan village, then dug a hole beside the trail to Mount Everest and buried her slinky wardrobe, Walkman, and cassette tapes. From the moment she saw the mountain that Tibetans and Sherpa call Chomolungma, the Goddess Mother of the Universe, she wanted to know her intimately.

Eleven years after that first look at the mountain, they made their first attempt to climb it, an achievement they had vowed to complete as a couple, during the infamously disastrous 1996 climbing season. In the intervening years, they had sold vacuum cleaners in Australia and bankrupted the first company they founded in Sweden, but finally hit their stride with a toilet-paper-delivery service. When they arrived at Everest Base Camp in Nepal for that first expedition, they approached the climb the same way they had their business endeavors—ready for a few failures. They had taken a mountaineering course in Norway, climbed a bit in Europe, made unsuccessful attempts on Denali and Mont Blanc, then set their sights on Everest, where they showed up carrying a pair of guitars. The couple was a textbook example of the new breed of mountaineers who began arriving on Everest in the 1990s, who focused on the top of the world without wasting a lot of time on shorter peaks.

Technology was also changing things on Everest. In 1996, the world was stunned when Rob Hall, dying on the South Summit, was patched through a satellite to his wife in New Zealand to name their unborn child and say good-bye. When Tom and Tina finally stood on top of Everest, in their fourth attempt in as many years, they made it look as much like a high-tech office as a mountaintop, with wireless communications transmitting live photos, videos, and commentary to the watching world. It was a giant step into the new century of adventure, in which athletes around the world can update their Web sites and blogs daily from the most remote environments on the planet, and in which many expeditions carry more laptops than stoves.

Although they had minimal mountaineering experience, Tom and Tina's business skills served them well on the mountain. When they were foiled climbing the mountain in 1998 because ropes didn't get fixed on time, they came back prepared to oversee the process. When they were iced out of the weather reports that other teams had, they arranged for forecasts from Europe for everyone on the mountain to share. When Babu Chiri Sherpa, a famously strong Sherpa working for the Sjogrens, expressed his dream of spending a night on top of Everest, some climbers saw it as a death wish, but Tom and Tina supported it. Babu spent twenty-one hours on the summit without supplemental oxygen, a record that is unlikely to be broken.

After Everest, which is often referred to as the "Third Pole," the Sjogrens focused their attention on the other two. Although Tina had never skied, she arrived in Antarctica and headed for the South Pole with her husband. They were turned back on their first attempt, but the following year they made it to both the South Pole and the North Pole unsupported. The North Pole journey, they said, was far and away the most challenging, uncomfortable, and dangerous of their adventures. With only enough food to supply them on the most direct route to the pole, they didn't have time to ski around the frigid ocean water that blocked their way across the Arctic ice. So they swam, in drysuits, across the watery gaps in the ice in order to stay on the straightest line. At camp, in temperatures well below zero, they would strip naked outside their tent before climbing inside and starting their stoves in order to avoid filling the shelter with moist air that would saturate dry gear. It was important to keep their electronics dry so they could keep the world updated about each day's suffering and success with palmtop computers, satellite phones, custom-made programming, and homemade cables.

Tom and Tina's stories struck me as tall tales, and with the amount of scrutiny they give others on their Web sites, they have made plenty of enemies who would like to prove they are frauds. But the ample technology they bring along with them on their adventures has provided them with plenty of documentation—photos, videos, and witnesses. Each time I thought a story was simply too outrageous to believe, they showed me photos or I found journal entries from other adventurers confirming the account.

Four years after their trip to the North Pole, in the spacious, L-shaped office of their company, ExplorersWeb, the Sjogrens brought the most remote mountains, the oceans, the poles of the Earth, and even outer space, to downtown Manhattan. Photos of the expeditions up Everest and to the North and South Poles lined the walls. The expedition communications equipment they sold and rented, along with the software that they had developed, sat in cases along one wall. Computers received blog updates and news from Everest teams, ocean rowers, and polar explorers, which were then added to the ExplorersWeb collection of Web sites, among them

MountEverest.net, K2Climb.net, and ThePoles.com. Autographed oxygen bottles decorated the windows that looked out onto Soho, Little Italy, Chinatown, and NoLita. A six-foot-wide blowup of a photo from the summit of Everest showed the couple, gloves off, with their cameras, batteries, and sat phones. A sled that they dragged on a polar expedition hung from the ceiling.

In the five years since they had stood on top of it, Everest had turned into a mountain of media. During Nils Antezana's and my time there in 2004, climbers and journalists filed live to more than 100 Web sites, blogs, newspapers, television outlets, and radio stations. My own expedition filed photos, stories, and video to four Web sites, two television stations, and a newspaper. But in the cloud of information coming off the mountain describing heroism, tragedy, and the workaday suffering of life at high altitude, Tom and Tina were concerned that some information was still hard to find. Most dispatches came from climbers hoping to lure funding to their adventures or commercial operators hoping to drum up business and keep their clients' families calm. For them it wasn't profitable to present Everest as anything but wholesome. But during their time on Everest, Tom and Tina had seen the corruption that was spreading beneath the peak, and wondered why so few climbers would speak of it.

When Fabiola's first e-mail arrived in May of 2004, Tom and Tina were already digging for information about a Bulgarian climber who had perished on the north side of the mountain and a British climber who had been missing for more than a day. But the desperate plea from the doctor's daughter made them recall another notorious accident on Everest that had occurred the year that they reached the summit. In 1999, when Tom and Tina first turned the Everest drama into a live performance that climbers would broadcast annually around the world, they'd camped beside a commercial expedition with two ultrawealthy clients, Michael Matthews and Constantine Niarchos, whose deaths became a dark backdrop that would hang behind the Everest show for years. Tom Sjogren got in touch with Fabiola as soon as he saw her note and told her what little he knew about her father's disappearance. Then he told her of another climber who had vanished on Everest whom he knew plenty about.

On the surface, the similarities between the deaths of Nils Antezana and Michael Matthews were striking. Nils, the oldest American to reach the top of Everest, and Michael, who five years earlier became the youngest Brit to summit, both perished near the Balcony in sudden afternoon storms. Both their guides descended below them, claiming they were clearing the ropes of snow. Both Nils and Michael climbed slowly and continued upward despite the suggestions of other climbers that they should turn around. They were the last people descending from the summit on the days of their deaths. Neither of their bodies were found. And as with Nils, climbers on the mountain with Michael fueled suspicions when they contacted the victim's family. Tom and Tina were among those witnesses, and more than anything, what they saw on Everest in 1999 sparked the outrage that burns in their Web sites' reporting of crime and corruption in the wilderness. When Nils Antezana perished on Everest, Michael Matthews had been dead for half a decade. But the controversy surrounding his expedition was very much alive, a storm spreading from the high Himalaya to the high courts of England.

As she sat in her London flat, begging for information about her father's fate on Everest, Fabiola Antezana was within a few miles of the places where Michael Matthews and Constantine Niarchos had lived, and the courts that continued to adjudicate their deaths.

MOUNT EVEREST, NEPAL—1999

Michael Matthews was handsome and charismatic, the son of a self-made millionaire. He had inherited so much of his father's ambition that he skipped college and, by the time he was twenty, was making his own fortune as a stock trader in London. He decided to climb Everest after a friend dropped a magazine story about the mountain on his desk. He signed on with Sheffield-based OTT Expeditions, which had put twenty-nine climbers on the summit during the previous three seasons without any significant accidents. OTT was charging about $40,000 for spots on its 1999 Everest trip.

The OTT expedition was huge and, at least on the surface, elaborately provisioned, filling two full climbing permits with more than a dozen clients, six experienced guides, and thirty-some Sherpas. Several clients, however, complained that the expedition was disorganized, didn't plan appropriately for the summit bids, didn't explain how the clients would be supported by guides and Sherpas, and did little to build team cohesion. Some equipment, such as radios, was old and in ill repair. Most worrisome, however, were the team's problems with its oxygen equipment. On April 30, weeks before the team's summit bids, Dave Rodney, a Canadian climber who became Michael's closest friend on the expedition, wrote in his diary

Big O2 problems. I'll let them sort it out—if they can't figure it out after the money we're paying them, they're in serious shit!

The oxygen troubles haunted a number of expeditions that year. At different times Rodney and the Sjogrens discussed the problems with Jon Tinker, leader of the OTT expedition, and Henry Todd, the man who provided their oxygen. Jon and Henry were old friends—Henry was the best man at Jon's wedding—and to some degree, they collaborated in purchasing and reselling the equipment.

The clients' oxygen masks and regulators were from the Russian company Poisk, which manufactures the most reliable oxygen equipment for mountaineering. Most of their oxygen tanks, however, came from a British company called LSE. When the team tested the oxygen equipment, they discovered that the Russian regulators did not couple properly with the British bottles, and failed to release oxygen into the system. In Camp Two, and again at Camp Four, where most climbers should already be using oxygen, OTT guides and Sherpas ground down the valves atop the oxygen bottles with files and a Leatherman tool in hopes of making them function properly during the climb to the summit planned for the following day. But expedition leader Jon Tinker suffered a minor stroke in the high camp, and the first summit bid was scrubbed. He handed off leadership of the expedition to guide Nick Kekus and returned to England.

The troubles with the team's oxygen supply persisted. A client detailed the problems in a letter to OTT after the trip:

I was not alone in encountering oxygen problems. In fact, most of the climbers had these problems when cylinders were connected to the regulators, which cut out when climbing on summit day.

In Camp Four, on the eve of the expedition's next attempt on the summit, Dave Rodney and the team's head Sherpa went through six bottles of oxygen before they found one that worked. Dave roused Nick Kekus to come and see the malfunctioning cylinders. The leader of the team, according to Dave, responded by chasing him through camp trying to hit him over the head with one of the tanks.

The team's tensions and equipment problems were further complicated by a bit of intrigue—a mountaineer identified before the expedition only as "Mr. X" on the OTT permit. Constantine Niarchos, the real name behind the "X," seemed to have been born into a Greek tragedy. He brought the last chapter to Everest with him.

Constantine was also the son of a self-made man. His father, Stavros Niarchos, was both the archrival and the brother-in-law of Aristotle Onassis. Among the wealthiest men in the world, Stavros owned paintings by Van Gogh and Renoir; homes in Paris, London, the Bahamas, Cote d'Azur, and St. Moritz; a private island with imported sand; the world's largest private yacht; and a private jet that whisked him among the casinos of Monaco, Swiss ski slopes, and the tracks where his Thoroughbreds raced. By the time Constantine was born in 1962, his father had filled the covers of both *Time* and *Sports Illustrated* magazines. But the family's troubles matched its lavish lifestyle.

On May 4, 1970, Constantine's mother, Eugenie, died after taking twenty-five Seconal pills while vacationing on their island. A physician examining the body found severe bruising on Eugenie's neck and body, which resulted in Stavros's arrest for manslaughter—charges that were dropped after he committed $200 million to Greece's shipyards and oil refineries. During the inquiry into his mother's death, Constantine Niarchos lived in England with his aunt, Tina, ex-wife of both Aristotle Onassis and the Duke of Marlborough. Eventually Tina married Constantine's father, the man suspected of killing her sister. Three years later, she also died, engulfing Stavros in another cloud of suspicion, this one stirred up by the overdose of barbiturates in Tina's system and her husband's delay in announcing the death. In three years Constantine had lost his mother and the woman who was both his stepmother and his aunt. His own infamy would soon match his father's.

In 1977, he was expelled from Gordonstoun, an elite private school in the north of Scotland, after a bodyguard for Prince Andrew, who was one of Constantine's classmates, found marijuana in a hollowed-out chair leg in Constantine's study. After college, he pursued the Studio 54 version of his father's socialite legacy. Champagne became cocaine, and the "jet set" turned into "Eurotrash."

One Christmas morning, Constantine broke into the hotel suite of the Muslim spiritual leader Aga Khan, who had wooed a model away from his brother, Spyros. "Here, take this if you love money so much," Constantine was reported to scream while throwing banknotes. In 1987, he married an Italian aristocrat, but she divorced him seven months later, telling a horror story of rage and violence.

But ten years after that, Constantine appeared to calm down. He moved to London, dug into managing the family's shipping empire, and married a New York artist. He also discovered mountaineering.

He climbed the highest peaks of Europe, Africa, and South America, and then Tibet's Cho Oyu, the most common practice peak for Everest. Before each expedition Constantine would abstain from drink and drugs to get fit. But afterward he was known to party hard to celebrate his achievement.

In the spring of 1999, journalists reported that despite repeated requests, they were unable to get a complete list of the members on OTT's commercial expedition to Everest. Few climbers on the mountain knew that one of the wealthiest men in the world was there with them, although in reality the OTT expedition that Michael Matthews had joined had been put together specifically to get Constantine Niarchos to the summit. Constantine, in fact, was the first client on the expedition to reach the top of Mount Everest in 1999. Michael Matthews was the last.

Around ten p.m. on May 12, Michael Matthews and Constantine Niarchos headed up from the South Col with four other clients, three guides, and several Sherpas in OTT's second attempt to put climbers on top of the mountain. Michael was noticeably weaker than he had been during the earlier, aborted summit bid. The team's *sirdar* told Michael he was climbing too slowly and he should turn back. However, as Michael neared the Hillary Step, he met up with OTT guide Mike Smith, who agreed to accompany him to the top. They summited by themselves, just before noon. But on descent, Michael slowed and struggled to negotiate the terrain as a cloud came down over the summit, bringing strong winds and a snowstorm.

By two p.m., the weather was deteriorating fast. On the way down from the South Summit, Smith moved ahead of Michael to clear the ropes of drifting snow. Just after three p.m., Smith arrived at the Balcony, where he waited for his client. After an hour he tried to climb back up to look for Michael, but the fresh snow and gusting winds pushed him back.

"I had to make a decision," Smith wrote later in a note. "Do I stay there and wait ad infinitum and fall asleep and never wake up, or go down?"

Smith left the Balcony at around 4:40 p.m. and later lost a toe to frostbite. Michael Matthews was never seen again.

Tom and Tina had watched the unraveling of the OTT expedition. A few days after Michael vanished, they received an e-mail in Base Camp, asking about the status of the search-and-rescue operation that the Matthews family had been informed by OTT was under way. The Sjogrens responded that they could hear a party in the OTT camp, and they were not aware of any rescue attempt. The only person they had noted climbing high enough to search for Michael was Henry Todd, the man who had provided his oxygen. This also struck them as strange, since Henry had never summited Everest and rarely climbed very high on the mountain. When he came down, Henry, who also oversaw the rope-fixing operation through the treacherous Khumbu Icefall, announced he was removing his gear from the glacier, effectively closing the south side of Everest. It was still early in the season, with many climbers waiting to attempt the summit. Tom and Tina demanded that Henry leave the icefall equipped, and he relented, but his strange behavior, and their belief that OTT had made no real attempt to find Michael Matthews, would trouble them for years to come.

Constantine Niarchos also vanished after reaching the summit of Everest, although not until after he had safely descended. He left the mountain in a helicopter, after which reports placed him in a Kathmandu hospital, at the Arizona camp where he had trained for his expedition, in New York with his wife, and in Hawaii. On Monday, May 30, Baroness Michelle von Lutken de Massy, a close friend and former lover of Constantine's, was at a dinner party in London, where she was surprised by a call from him. He was now in London. He sounded agitated and was wheezing, she said in a statement released during the subsequent inquest. Constantine was ill at ease when he answered her knock on his door later that evening but then gave her a hug and a smile and showed her his pictures from Everest.

Constantine had a large bag of coke, Michelle reported.

"He was complaining the cocaine was wet and he could not snort it. He put some into a microwave and became impatient and started to eat some of it out of the bag."

Most of the powder had hardened, and it shattered when Constantine tried to cut it into lines.

"He reached into the plastic bag, got a handful about the size of a 50p piece, put it into his mouth, and ate it," Michelle said. "It looked to me like more than one gram."

As the drug rushed through him, Constantine became agitated

and paranoid, pacing through his apartment with Michelle trailing him, trying to calm him down. He headed into a bedroom and asked her to leave him alone. After forty-five minutes, she went to look in on him.

"The bathroom light was on," Michelle stated. "I saw him lying on the floor."

Constantine's eyes were open. There was blood running from his nose. A bottle of sleeping pills lay on the floor beside him.

"I shouted at him and he gargled in his throat," she said.

He was admitted to St. Mary's hospital at 7:33 a.m. on Tuesday, June 1, and pronounced dead twenty-one minutes later.

Three years after finding Constantine, the baroness herself was found slumped beside a bloodied syringe and a blackened spoon in her apartment in London's West End. Before her fatal overdose, she had undergone addiction treatment at thirteen clinics and admitted spending more than $350,000 on drugs.

In the days after Constantine's death, the Niarchos family speculated that the rapid descent from Everest had killed him, apparently confusing mountaineering, where going down is always healthy, with scuba diving, in which surfacing too rapidly brings on the deadly bends. Friends said he had complained of chest pains and guessed that he had died of a heart attack.

But on July 7, Dr. Paul Knapman, the coroner, pointed out that just seventeen days after becoming the first Greek to reach the summit of Mount Everest, Constantine Niarchos had set another record.

"The amount of cocaine [in his blood] was at a very high level. An amount exceeding this has only been found in somebody who had swallowed it in the course of an attempt to smuggle cocaine in packets into this country."

The postmortem examination showed that Constantine died with enough cocaine in his system to kill twenty-five people.

Expedition leader Mike Trueman, a former commandant of the British Army Mountain Training Centre, commented on Constantine's death in an article he wrote for the *Sunday Times* of London, titled "Drugs and Money Conquer Everest."

> *In 1999 I reached the summit at the same time as Constantine Niarchos, a wealthy Greek with a history at the Betty Ford clinic. He was in a bad way and was close to collapse. Then suddenly he revived, descending the mountain very quickly. His climb was soon proclaimed a great achievement. Two weeks later he died of a drug overdose. It is no secret among the mountaineering community that Niarchos must have used drugs to reach the top.*

Mike said that although he can't be certain that Constantine took drugs during his climb, there is a growing tendency to use drugs to reach the summit of Everest.

> *A number of Sherpas report this trend, including one who told me in the presence of a government liaison officer that he had climbed with an American who had used drugs. The American had collapsed and almost died when he descended but had claimed to have made the summit from the South Col in just six hours—faster than the Sherpas he was climbing with. Those same Sherpas reported that he was swallowing tablets all the way to the top.*

Virtually every banned, performance-enhancing substance that has driven sponsors and fans away from two of the world's most wholesome sports—cycling and baseball—has made its way into mountaineering. And while no rules ban taking performance-enhancing drugs in mountaineering, the consequences of their use in a frigid, oxygen-poor environment can be far graver.

"It is immoral and dangerous—both to the users and those who have to rescue them," Trueman wrote in his *Sunday Times* article.

He speculated that climbers are abusing dexamethasone, the steroid injected to revive climbers crippled by altitude sickness long enough to descend to safety. Climbers, instead of using a shot of the drug in an emergency descent, were taking several doses to help them reach the summit, Trueman wrote. During my own trips to Everest, climbers have admitted to doing just that.

Tom Sjogren contacted Fabiola Antezana as soon as he read her desperate e-mail. Then he and Tina sent electronic messages to all the expeditions that they knew had climbers high on the mountain.

> *Guys, we need some action here. The . . . doctor was left on the Balcony with two bottles of oxygen and a blanket. He summited May 18. The family is devastated. They don't know what's going on, or what happened to Nils . . . Do you have any information? Is there a search/rescue going on?*

They made a satellite phone call to a climber on the north side of Everest who had once worked for them. He relayed the message to a guide on the south side, who agreed to see what he could find out as he climbed higher, which, in the end, was nothing.

"Everybody just went dumb, silent," Tina said. "We need someone on the mountain to talk to people face-to-face, or this is going to turn into another Matthews thing."

In the end, their break came with a call from Salt Lake City rather than Mount Everest. Damian Benegas, a mountain guide in Utah, was looking for information about a climber who was missing on Everest. Damian's twin brother, Willie, was guiding on Everest and saw Gustavo Lisi and his client during their ascent. He had just learned that only one of them made it down. He didn't yet know the missing climber's name—Nils Antezana—but he wanted to make sure the climber's family was notified about the situation before the media got word of it. Something wasn't right, Damian said.

During their phone call, Tom and Damian realized the answers they brought each other—the name of the missing climber—posed a dozen more questions that would not be answered for weeks, or months, or ever.

"Look, I'm in touch with Base Camp every day," Damian said. "Willie is taking care of things there. If the Antezana family wants to get to the bottom of this, I'll help them."

Seven

Fabiola's fingers moved frantically over the keyboards on her laptop and her phone, exchanging e-mails and calls with Explorers-Web in New York, EverestNews.com in Ohio, Gustavo Lisi's webmaster in Argentina, and Manuel Lugli, the man who had made the arrangements for her father's expedition, in Italy. But none of them knew what had happened to Nils, and nobody in the Himalaya was responding to her pleas for information, or for a party to head up Everest in search of him.

"When Gustavo spoke to my mother this morning," she wrote to Tom and Tina Sjogren, "he said that on the way back to Camp 4, my father refused to go on, which is completely out of character for him. Gustavo also said to my mother that it was too late to send a rescue team as Nils would not have survived the night, but that he could send her the pictures and video of their summit. I am outraged by this!!!!!! . . ."

Fabiola included Gustavo's announcement of summiting Everest with Nils, along with a translation into English.

"Gustavo does not even mention that he had to be helped down by a Sherpa. How is it that he was helped back by a Sherpa but my father was left? . . . This story conflicts with other information I have received and read on Everest news . . .

"I WOULD BE ETERNALLY GRATEFUL IF SOMEONE FROM BASE CAMP COULD CALL ME . . . PLEASE!!!!!"

Late that night her phone rang.

"I'm Damian Benegas," the caller said in Spanish. "My brother's Willie Benegas. He's on Everest guiding for Mountain Madness. I'm very, very sorry for what happened to your father. We know Lisi, we're Argentine."

It was the first real news that Fabiola had heard about her father's climb.

The Benegas twins were born in 1968 to an Argentine businessman and his American wife. The wealthy family lived in a massive home in Buenos Aires with a sprawling lawn and a playground. Damian and Guillermo, who today is known throughout the climbing world as Willie, attended a private school. In 1976, when they were eight years old, armed men in uniforms came to their home. The twins ran through the house laughing, thrilled at the chance to play army with real soldiers—until they saw their mother's sobs. La Guerra Sucia—the Dirty War—had begun.

"We lost everything," Willie says. "One day we lived in a huge house. The next we were out in the street."

By the time Willie and Damian were eleven, they were living on the Patagonian coast where their father had bought a boat to lead fishing trips and started a scalloping business. The family lived in a trailer with no beds for the twins, so they slept in the cab of their father's pickup truck. The boys quickly took to life without school uniforms and, with nobody around to see them, sometimes wore no clothes at all. They constructed rafts out of worn-out tires and discarded planking, with old sheets for sails, living off clams and mussels they gathered on the beach when they were blown off course. They swam with southern right whales often enough to name one. An injured Magellan penguin that they rehabilitated became a pet named Pengui, in whose honor Willie carries a plush toy version on his expeditions.

During the long, frigid Patagonian winters, their father's stories of climbing in the Andes mesmerized the twins. They learned to read largely from his mountaineering books and learned to rappel on the metal frame where he dry-docked his boat. They cobbled their climbing shoes out of sneakers and the rubber of blown-out tires from the local racetrack.

Although they lived in Patagonia, legendary for its skyscraping granite spires, their coastal town had little to climb other than crumbling clay sea cliffs and the chimneys of their friends' houses. They made scores of climbs up the mud bluffs using ropes from their father's boat and giant wooden screws to anchor them.

By the time they were twenty, they had climbed Fitzroy, Patagonia's most daunting spire, and put up a new route on Aconcagua. They started driving mule trains for climbing teams, took jobs carrying gear and pitching tents for other climbers, and were soon guiding climbs in the Andes.

By 2004 they had guided climbs in Bolivia, Peru, Ecuador, Chile, Africa, Khirgirstan, and the United States. Damian had made one hundred ascents of El Capitan and Half Dome, the giant cliffs of Yosemite; and multiple ascents of Nepal's Ama Dablam and Tibet's Cho Oyu—the sixth-tallest mountain in the world. Willie has been up Cho Oyu several times; set a speed record up Aconcagua; put up a new route on Pakistan's massive Nameless Tower; run the Leadville 100, a hundred-mile footrace over 13,000-foot peaks in the Colorado Rockies; and, as of 2007, made six trips to the top of Everest. They both hold spots on the team of athletes sponsored by The North Face, the outdoor clothing and equipment manufacturer.

But the Benegas twins' intense productivity posed some unusual risks. Aside from the odds of injury or death, which increased in direct proportion to the amount of time they spent in the mountains, the Patagonian brothers realized that anything that befell the reputation of one would hurt them both equally. They had a shared face to protect, and agreed early about how to do that. Helping people would come first, they said; climbing second.

When Willie Benegas came down from his fourth visit to the summit of Everest on May 17, 2004, he felt pretty good. He had puked his way up the mountain, vomited on the summit, and sometime during the climb had shat his pants, but he had taken a client to the top of the world and got him back to camp safely, and that was what he was getting paid for.

When he made it back to Camp Four in the South Col, he was surprised to find Gustavo Lisi and his client, Nils Antezana, still in camp, resting for a day before making their attempt on the summit. They had arrived in the camp on the same day he had, so he had assumed they would be making their attempt on the summit on his schedule as well. At this altitude the human body is dying, whether it is climbing or sleeping, so while plenty of expeditions end up spending a day or two in the high camp due to uncooperative weather or the need to rest up, extra time up high is ill-advised. Willie was even more surprised to see that, at least when he encountered them, Nils and Gustavo were not breathing bottled oxygen during their downtime. He spoke to both climbers and recalls that neither had to take off an oxygen mask to respond to him.

"That is always bad, bad, bad, bad, bad," Willie said. "Nils is extremely strong to be without oxygen going all the way to the South Col."

The day before, Willie had made a point of arriving early at the last camp before the summit so he had plenty of time to prepare for his team's attempt to reach the top. Late in the afternoon he checked on the progress of the other climbers on the mountain, and watched as Gustavo and Nils made their last few steps onto the Col. They were quite late—Willie had noticed they usually arrived late in camp—and he had been troubled then to see that neither of them was breathing supplemental oxygen.

"What are you thinking?" Willie said to Gustavo.

Although the altitude clouds Willie's recollection of the event, Damian, in Salt Lake City, noticed how clearly his brother's outrage came through the satellite phone that evening. For Willie, the most important rule of guiding is making sure to match each day's challenge to his client's abilities, not his own. But the few times he ran into Gustavo and Nils on the mountain, he could see that the guide was driving his elderly client hard and passing up obvious opportunities to lighten their loads and save their strength for the summit push. Gustavo and Nils headed out with huge packs on their backs into the blazing, midday sun when most other climbers on the mountain were burrowing into what little shade they could find to recover from the day's work. It was simple lack of experience. Anyone who had been up Everest before knew to start each day's climb early to avoid the sun. Willie visited their tent to offer his help to Gustavo.

"Come to my camp and any questions you have, just ask me," Willie said.

As much of a bother as it could be, Willie knew that giving some advice low on the mountain was a lot less trouble than getting drawn into a rescue later on. And he knew that if there was a disaster, he was certain to get called on to help. His offers of advice to inexperienced teams were like the crevasse rescue training he offered to anyone in Base Camp who wanted it—an investment in the safety of everyone on the mountain, including himself and his clients. A few weeks later, higher on the mountain, Willie ran into Gustavo and made his offer again.

"Anything you need, just ask me," he said.

Gustavo wasn't interested in his help.

Camp Two, at some 21,200 feet, is the last place on the south side of Everest to really have a rest, and most teams make a point of arriving there early to get as much downtime as possible. Willie had been in camp for a few hours and was hanging out with friends from a team of Basque climbers when they were shocked to see Gustavo dragging slowly into camp sometime between six and seven in the evening. Gustavo had spent more than eight hours making his way from Camp One, climbing through the hottest part of the day and carrying gear that any veteran guide would have handed off to Sherpas. When Willie asked about his client, Gustavo indicated that Nils was at the bottom of the last gully that led to the camp— perhaps 700 or 800 feet behind his guide. It could take him twenty minutes to make it to the camp, or it could take two hours, but Gustavo wasn't looking back to see which.

"I imagine you're taking a rest day off tomorrow?" Willie asked.

He couldn't be certain if it was exhaustion or ego that kept Gustavo from answering or accepting a sip from the water bottle that Willie offered.

After his descent from the summit, around noon on May 17, Willie checked in with the Irish expedition leader Pat Falvey and his *sirdar*, Pemba, both old friends from previous Everest expeditions, who were starting their own summit attempt sometime before midnight. Willie filled them in on the condition of the ropes and the route and did the same with Gustavo and Nils, who, after their day resting in Camp Four, were heading up as well. The next morning, when Willie headed out for Base Camp, Gustavo, Nils, and the Irish team were nearly twelve hours into their own summit pushes.

When he got to Base Camp, Willie learned that Gustavo had already updated his Web site with a recounting of their meeting in Camp Four between their respective climbs to the summit. "In the morning Willie Benegas made the summit and his information about the route of the summit ridge is good although in his fourth time on the summit he was slower than usual," the blog read, in Spanish. Willie was a bit steamed.

"I fixed a lot of the ropes and I am guiding," he said. "You take your time when you're short-roping for your client. You take care of your client. We call it babysitting."

It was obvious to Willie that Gustavo had different ideas about guiding.

A few hours later, when news began to trickle into Base Camp, Willie learned just how different. When he heard that a climber was missing, Willie got on the radio with his friends from the Irish team, still in Camp Four, to try to find out what was happening. Josu Feijoo, the leader of the Basque team that Juan Carlos Gonzalez and Gustavo had climbed with in 2000, was back on the mountain. He recalls Willie coming to his team's dining tent, trying to organize a rescue. Climbers from other teams crowded in to find out what was happening, their jaws dropping as each meager detail was radioed down the mountain. Pat Falvey reported that his Sherpas had found Gustavo Lisi in the middle of the night and dragged him back to their tent. But Gustavo had come down alone, they reported, and said nothing of his abandoned client to his own rescuers. Willie soon realized that with the weather turning, sending a team up to get the missing climber wasn't an option. He called his brother.

"Damian, there's a guy missing on the mountain."

Willie and Damian had both seen news of deaths and injuries in the mountains get posted on expedition Web sites before anyone notified the victims' families.

"We have to do some damage control," Willie said. "Lisi lost his client. Let's . . . make sure that we contact the family before the media gets hold of this and creates another typical Everest thing."

That was going to be challenging, Willie explained. "We don't even know this guy's name."

How can a guide just leave someone behind like that?" Fabiola asked when Damian finished telling her what Willie witnessed of her father's climb with Gustavo.

"I don't know," he said.

Fabiola told Damian that if nobody else was going up the mountain to find her father, she would do it herself. He responded as gently as he could. If none of the hard-core mountaineers in Everest Base Camp could mount a rescue, there was little chance that a woman in London with no climbing experience could put one together.

Nonetheless, by the following morning, Fabiola had put a plan into action. She and her husband, Davide, were going to Nepal on a Sunday morning flight. If they couldn't rescue her father, then they were going to do everything they could to find out what happened to him. In the meantime, her brother, David, flew to D.C. to take care of their mother. Fabiola had already withdrawn $5,000 and Davide was arranging their flights when she called Damian.

"I don't know anybody there," she said. "How am I going to get in touch with all of these people?"

Damian cut her off. "I'll throw what I can in a rucksack and I'm there," he said. "The only problem is, I don't have my passport."

As part of the preparations for the twins' upcoming climb in

Karakorum, Damian had sent his passport to the Pakistani embassy to get his visa. It was Friday, the Islamic holy day, so it seemed unlikely that he could round up anyone at the embassy to send it back for at least a few days.

Damian said he would see what he could do and, in the meantime, Fabiola booked three tickets to Kathmandu. She got a satellite phone number from Gustavo's webmaster, but got no answer, so she called Manuel Lugli, the Italian expedition organizer who had made her father's arrangements, who in turn gave her the number of an Italian couple who were sharing the same Base Camp as Nils and Gustavo. They seemed to be expecting the call. Gustavo, on the other hand, sounded shocked when one of the Italians handed him the phone.

"I didn't leave your father . . . ," Gustavo said between coughs. "You have to understand, I was in terrible condition. I was dead."

"Yeah," Fabiola said. "I understand that Pat Falvey's Sherpas had to bring you down."

"No, no, no," Gustavo protested. "I don't know who told you that, but you are mistaken. No one pulled me off the mountain, I came down myself."

It was Gustavo's first contradiction of what Fabiola already knew through Willie and Damian.

"I can take your dad's things back with me to Argentina and I can send them . . . ," Gustavo said.

"There's no need," Fabiola replied. "Because I'm coming. I'm coming to pick up my father's things."

Gustavo seemed puzzled. Such a long trip for just a few things, he said.

"All of your dad's things are just in that green sack," Gustavo said. "That's all he had."

"My dad footed the whole bill for that expedition," Fabiola recalls thinking to herself. How could everything he bought fit in a little duffel bag?

"When are you getting into Kathmandu?" she asked Gustavo. "Because I'll be waiting for you there."

On Saturday morning, Damian was chasing down a FedEx truck after spending much of the previous afternoon finding someone at the Pakistani embassy who would overnight his documents to Utah. The only flight he could book from Salt Lake City to London departed just after noon. Fabiola called his cell phone every half hour.

"Did you get the passport? Did you get the passport?" she asked.

As the morning grew late, Fabiola called the airline with her unlikely story: Her father was lost on Everest, and the man who could help her find out what had happened to him was chasing down his passport in Salt Lake City. Could they please cut him some slack if he was late for check-in? An hour later someone called her from the airline. The plane was in the air and Damian was on board. He had arrived fifteen minutes before takeoff.

Damian called Fabiola from his layover and she asked him what he looked like—five feet seven, light brown hair, shorts and a rucksack, he said; probably a little scruffy compared with the rest of the passengers on the flight. There was only an hour between his flight's arrival in London and the departure of the one to Kathmandu, and the planes were using different terminals. Damian's cell phone wasn't going to work in London. At the airport, Fabiola rounded up a manager with British Airways and described Damian to him.

"This is the guide that's coming to Nepal with me to search for my dad," she said.

Twenty minutes later, they escorted Fabiola and Davide to the counter where Damian was checking in, and Fabiola realized all the descriptions and searches were probably unnecessary. Among the business suits at the counter, the man in shorts, sandals, and a worn T-shirt stood out from 100 yards away. She didn't know who looked worse, him or her. Neither of them had slept, and they were both frazzled. Fabiola threw her arms around him.

Damian's only piece of baggage was the small knapsack on his back.

"I have two pairs of underwear and an extra T-shirt," he said. "That's all I had time to pack."

When Fabiola had offered to pay him for his help during their first conversations, Damian wouldn't hear of it. She hadn't had time to wire him the money for the flight to London, and last-minute international tickets are not something that fit easily into a mountain guide's budget.

"I don't have any more money, and that's the maximum I can put on my credit card," he said, laughing. "Do you have fifty bucks I can borrow?"

For the first few hours of the flight, Fabiola grilled Damian for everything he knew about her father's climb and what they would do when they landed in Kathmandu. Eventually Davide put his hand on her shoulder.

"He looks really tired," Davide said.

"No, that's OK," Damian said, but he was asleep within minutes and hardly woke during the hours that their flight was in the air.

In Kathmandu, Fabiola, Davide, and Damian checked into the Yak and Yeti, the hotel where her father had stayed six weeks earlier. Nils had initially registered at one of the city's more modern hotels, but Fabiola immediately saw why he had moved. The Yak and Yeti is palatial, but worn and threadbare in places—like a faded photograph of the subcontinent's colonial past. Nils Antezana, educated in one of Bolivia's British boarding schools, had always enjoyed the bittersweet taste he got looking at relics of the fading empire.

In the duffel bag her father had stored with the concierge, Fabiola found a few dollars and a pamphlet from an Italian church he had visited on his way to Nepal, along with a white, long-sleeve shirt that was freshly laundered and pressed—something dapper to slip into as soon as he made it back to the hotel. She also found a stack of correspondence and documents that Nils had exchanged with Gustavo and Manuel Lugli.

When Fabiola and Davide woke the next morning, a little after eight a.m., Damian was already up and working the phones. They went over the logistics at breakfast. Pat Falvey and Clare O'Leary, Irish climbers who were the only ones to see Gustavo and Nils during their summit bid, wouldn't be back for two more days and were flying out of Kathmandu just five hours after they got to the city. There was a very narrow window to sit them down for an interview—at one p.m. on Wednesday. Steven Brault, at the U.S. Embassy, would meet with them at eleven a.m. on Tuesday. Other climbers who had met Nils and Gustavo on the mountain would look up Damian as soon as they were back in town.

Eight

For spectators of the mountaineering arena, the summit of Mount Everest seems the culmination, a final chapter. But many of the climbers who head for the mountaintop look for a new beginning there, for the few minutes they spend standing atop the peak to change their lives. From the summit, some see financial opportunities. Others look for something less tangible. Lhakpa Sherpa knew that, more than any other point on the globe, the summit of Everest had the power to transform its visitors. And she was determined to get there.

It was May 2000, four years before she led my team to Everest, when Lhakpa made her first trip into the death zone above 8,000 meters on the mountain. She was one of only two women remaining from an all-female Sherpa expedition that was trying to get the first Nepali woman to the summit and back down alive. Three others had already retreated and were gathered at the mountain's Nepali Base Camp in a large tent with a radio. But as the remaining climbers made their way to the summit, as Lhakpa told it, they transmitted their encouragement not to her, but to another Sherpani, the youngest member of the team who, like them, was from the Solu Khumbu, the valley below Everest. Lhakpa was the leader of the expedition, but her teammates conversed little with her over the radio. Even before the climb had begun, they had spoken little with the illiterate single mother from outside the Khumbu. She was from the wrong side of the peaks, she told me.

But in a yak herder's house high on the slopes of Makalu, the world's fifth-tallest mountain, Lhakpa had her own fan with a radio. That night her father, alone but for his animals, took the weakening batteries from the transistor radio his daughter had given him and warmed them next to his fire. Then he put them back in the radio so he could learn whether his daughter had climbed Mount Everest—or perhaps died trying. When he heard that only one member of the expedition had made it, he hiked for two days down to his home village with his radio. But when he got there, the batteries in the radio were dead. The villagers had only his word that Lhakpa Sherpa, his daughter, had climbed Everest.

Lhakpa had been looking at the mountain since her birth in the village of Khandbari. By the time she was ten, Lhakpa had realized that Everest was a bright light for the Sherpa people—their best way out of poverty.

"From when I was a girl," Lhakpa told me, "I wanted Everest's summit. It's always my dream."

Each year more than 25,000 trekkers and mountaineers visit the Solu Khumbu valley below Everest, which is inhabited by some 3,000 Sherpa. The hordes of tourists make the Khumbu the wealthiest region in the country, and the economic opportunity they bring to the Sherpa tribe there is unimaginable to those who live below the other great mountains of the region. Makalu's beauty will never make up for the fact that the mountain is just one of Everest's lesser siblings. Lhakpa herself comes from a family of eleven children. Eight were female, and like Makalu compared with Everest, girls would never have the prospects that their brothers had.

Lhakpa and her siblings spent most of their childhood at her father's yak house, in the middle of a national park high up the slopes of the mountain. Her father herded some fifty yaks, occasionally hiring them out to expeditions. The children helped, looking after the animals, milking them, churning butter.

Lhakpa's dream of climbing Mount Everest to make the kind of money Sherpa men did was outrageous, even to her family. Still, at eleven, she persuaded her uncle, an expedition *sirdar*, to hire her on as a "kitchen boy" on a climb up Makalu. She said she broke her leg carrying a heavy load of cooking gear during one of her first trips, but was back at work as soon as it healed.

Four years later, Lhakpa told me, a young man named Lopsang Sherpa came to a teahouse where she was working, on his way to a job on Makalu. In Lopsang, the entire tribe saw how high mountaineering could take one of their own—and how far a Sherpa could fall. Lopsang was a rock star in the Sherpa world. He tied his long hair in a ponytail, wore the latest outdoor fashions, and rode a motorcycle through Kathmandu. Lhakpa moved with him to Kathmandu, she told me, and bore him a son, Nima. Lopsang went off to work on Everest as *sirdar* to veteran American guide Scott Fischer, renowned for his boast of a "Yellow Brick Road" to the summit of Everest. His company was called Mountain Madness, the outfit for which Willie Benegas sometimes worked.

On May 10, 1996, the world watched as a storm descending on Everest wrought one of the worst mountaineering disasters in history. Among the eight climbers who died was Fischer, Lopsang's boss and mentor. Lopsang was accused of contributing to the deadly traffic jam on the mountain by assisting a wealthy client to the summit instead of fixing the ropes for the other climbers. He said he was just following orders, but with his boss dead, there was nobody to back him up. Late that summer, Lhakpa says, Lopsang said good-bye to her and headed back to Everest. The avalanche that took his life, high on Everest's Lhotse Face, was reported in the newspapers before Lhakpa heard about it. She still keeps a newspaper clipping about it, although she has no idea what it says.

In Kathmandu, the only work she could find was serving tea.

However, Lhakpa knew there was one job that could change the future for her and her son: She could climb Everest. To have that chance, she would face what, for her, was an equally difficult challenge: writing a letter.

The correspondence asking the Nepali government to help her put together an Everest expedition took her the better part of a year to write. It was the Kathmandu police chief, she said, who finally completed the task, sitting at the counter in the teahouse where she worked, writing down her words as she spoke, then reading them back to her.

"My people go climbing on mountains. Husbands die in mountains. [Their] children will be poor Sherpa," she told me, paraphrasing. "Many Sherpa die young in the mountains and his wife has no job and no education. Sherpa women stay in the house making food and making children. I no want just that. . . . Women can do everything. Can be doctor, lawyer, engineer. I no have education. I can climb a mountain."

When her letter reached the prime minister, Girija Prasad Koirala, he gave it to his daughter, Sujata, who helped fund and organize the expedition.

In the end, the five Sherpani climbers arranged more than two hundred sponsors, among them influential Nepali mountaineers, political leaders, and businessmen, including Ang Tsering Sherpa, owner of the most successful trekking agency in Nepal. For her persistence, Lhakpa was named leader of the Nepalese Women Millennium Everest Expedition in the spring of 2000, organized "to celebrate the predominant role Nepali women are expected to play in the coming century."

The other team members were from the Solu Khumbu. Although the valleys below Everest and Makalu are barely twelve miles apart, the wealth and privilege that Westerners had brought the people living below Everest often left Lhakpa feeling as if she had as little in common with the Khumbu Sherpa as with the foreign climbers for whom they worked.

"The Khumbu has [Edmund] Hillary schools, Hillary doctors, Hillary hospitals," Lhakpa told me, with both admiration and jealousy. "In Makalu we have nothing. No doctors. No hospitals. No schools."

Lhakpa told me about one of her cousins who had developed complications while pregnant with her third child and perished on the trail while her husband, brother, and friends took turns carrying her on their backs during the five-day walk to the nearest hospital. Lhakpa hoped that, if she successfully climbed Everest, she could bring Makalu some of what Hillary had brought to the Khumbu.

But to the Khumbu Sherpani, Lhakpa said, her leadership of the expedition was demeaning. They had attended school, could read, and owned lodges and teahouses. Some had studied mountaineering in Austria. The other Sherpani climbers complained that Lhakpa walked too fast and talked too slow. *Frontline* producers filming the climb for public television spent little time with Lhakpa, she said, because she was uneducated.

"It's difficult for me to walk slowly," she said in the documentary. "When I hike, I like to be in my own world."

"That's not good for a leader," Mingma Yangzi Sherpa, the deputy leader, said in response to Lhakpa's distance from the team. "She's supposed to oversee things."

The team started strong from Base Camp through the ladders of the Khumbu Icefall, but when the time came to push to the summit, only two women remained. Dawa Yangzi Sherpa was strong, but insisted on stopping for a rest and a drink before the Hillary Step. When she took off her oxygen mask, she vomited from altitude sickness. The young Sherpani descended in tears. Lhakpa continued to the summit with the team's male Sherpas.

Climbers on top of Everest may find a powerful and magical place, but few are truly transformed. Lhakpa Sherpa, however, knew her final steps to the summit were the kind of event that can change a person. Or a family. Or a nation. Snow blowing off the slopes blocked her view of the valley where she had been born. What she could see was her future. She could see her son in school. And from the summit of Mount Everest, Lhakpa could see America, where many Sherpas who succeed in the mountains find new opportunities. For a few minutes, Lhakpa said, she stood not only above the rest of the world but above gender, caste, and ignorance.

Birendra Dahal, an aide to the prime minister whom Lhakpa had recruited as fund-raising coordinator for the expedition, honored a bargain struck before the climb had begun. He took her team first to Lukla, in the Khumbu, and then to Makalu, in a helicopter.

"When we landed in Lukla, I couldn't believe it," Dahal told me. "Four or five thousand people came to respect them. I think there were more than twenty thousand people to receive us in Makalu."

The sprawling Kathmandu restaurant Rum Doodle is named for a fictional mountain in a book, *The Ascent of Rum Doodle* by W. E. Bowman, that parodies everything about expedition climbing. Cardboard yeti footprints decorated by returning trekkers and climbers cover every square inch of the restaurant. Everyone who summits Everest gets a free meal a day for life, as well as his or her name on the wall, which makes Rum Doodle something like the Mount Everest winners' circle.

At a party honoring the Sherpa women's team, Lhakpa moved away from the crowd and into a corner, where she shared her few words of broken English with a lanky Romanian-American climber—George Dijmarescu. He had just completed his second ascent of Mount Everest, this one without supplemental oxygen. Later that year, Lhakpa visited her sister Cheng Kipa Sherpa, who lives in Florida. George came to see her there. They climbed Everest together the following year, in 2001. Like several other famous Sherpa, Lhakpa came to Hartford to work for George's contracting company. Unlike the others, she stayed. They married in a civil ceremony on November 14, 2002.

"I got married in my pajama bottoms," Lhakpa recalled, laughing.

Lhakpa said she hoped to learn to read and get her driver's license. She does her grocery shopping—one of the few outings she makes from her Hartford home—by remembering how the labels look.

Back in Kathmandu, Nima, her son, attends the Ekita International School with his cousin Sonam Sherpa, whose father was killed in an avalanche while working on Dhaulagiri, another of Nepal's 8,000-meter peaks. Lhakpa winced when asked why she doesn't bring her son to the United States to be with her.

"He have good life in Kathmandu," she said. "He's very good writing and very good speaking."

She and her sisters in Florida and Paris pay for the children's schooling. Nima lives with another of Lhakpa's sisters in Kathmandu. Back in the States, the culture is far less tolerant of a mother who would leave her child for months on end to climb the world's highest mountains. When Lhakpa was making her third ascent of Everest in May of 2003 with George, he came to her with an urgent message. His family was outraged that Sunny, at a year old, had not been christened before they left on their climb. They wanted to take the child to a Greek Orthodox church for the ceremony. Sunny was christened as her parents made their way to the high camps.

A few weeks later, Lhakpa stood for the third time atop Mount Everest. Her brother Mingma Gelu and her fifteen-year-old sister, Ming Kipa, known as Doni, joined her there.

"If I climb Everest," Lhakpa recalled her sister saying, "you send me to school."

After the climb, Doni joined Lhakpa's son at the International School.

But Lhakpa said her accomplishments on Everest also made her family the target of Maoist rebels. When Lhakpa's mother begged her not to climb Everest in 2003, Lhakpa was ready to argue that it was her life and mountaineering was her job. She broke down in tears when her mother explained that it wasn't out of fear for her daughter that she wanted her to stay away from the mountains, but out of fear for her family. The rebels had visited the yak house where Lhakpa had grown up to try to coerce assistance from her father. Down in the village, they had burned many of her family's possessions. On top of the pyre they had dropped a gift she had given her mother: a photo of Lhakpa on the summit of Everest. It wouldn't be the last time that Lhakpa seemed a victim of her success.

I had hoped to hear Lhakpa Sherpa's story—how an illiterate girl from the high Himalaya ended up seated beside the king of Nepal—during the frigid trip into the Presidential Range before we left for Everest in 2004. But when her husband and the rest of the team headed into the New Hampshire mountains, Lhakpa had to stay behind in a rented room at the foot of the mountain to take care of Sunny. The shy smile she always seemed to wear when I had first met her cracked—she wanted to climb too, she said. As we headed out the door, she stopped my wife.

"You stay here with me, OK?"

Carolyn wasn't about to drop her backpack and thus we wouldn't get another chance to talk with Lhakpa alone until months later, when we were leaving for Nepal.

When I finally sat down with Lhakpa at her dining-room table in Hartford, she was wearing the same pajama bottoms and orange cotton jersey that she'd worn in New Hampshire. She's bigger than most Sherpani, and I could see, as she hauled her daughter around on her hip, the strength that got her up Everest.

In each corner of the living room, Lhakpa has hung one of George's summit certificates from Everest, but none of her own is on display. She brought me the gold medal she was presented by the king of Nepal, the Order of Gorkha Dakshina Bahu, in its red velvet case, and pulled a picture of her with Sir Edmund Hillary from a cardboard box. Elsewhere she kept a ring that she said Lopsang Sherpa had given to her, which she wore only during her annual trip home to climb Everest and visit her son. She showed me her passport to confirm the spelling of her name—Lhakpa Sherpa—but George, who had spelled his own name G-H-E-O-R-G-H-E until a few years earlier, seemed to have a thing against "h" and convinced Lhakpa to spell her name without that letter too.

"You be quiet," she snapped when he interrupted our interview.

"You're stealing my story," he shouted as he left the room, laughing.

. . .

When they first met, Anne Parmenter, Lhakpa's co-leader of the Connecticut expedition, was taken with Lhakpa's story of the Nepali women's expedition. Gender issues gave Anne her own entrée into Himalayan mountaineering and have defined her career as a collegiate coach. During a climb of Aconcagua, in Argentina, the three men Anne came to the mountain with abandoned the climb. She was left crying in Base Camp—strong enough to make it to the summit, but unable to do it safely by herself. A guide with another team, upon learning that Anne was a coach of women's sports, offered to let her climb with his team, on one condition. He had a desperately altitude-sick climber who was halfway through a sex change. None of the other guides wanted anything to do with the climber they nicknamed "She-He-La." Anne cared for the sick climber, then summited the mountain. Her success on Aconcagua led to other guiding opportunities during her summers, when she wasn't coaching at the college. She made it to the summit of Aconcagua again the next year, then to the top of Denali, and finally to the Himalaya.

Anne was thrilled to learn that the Sherpani who had summited Everest lived just a few miles from her office at Trinity College. After she heard Lhakpa's story, she invited her to tell the story at the college's women's center.

I was also fascinated by Lhakpa's story. But in Kathmandu, I began to find some cracks in it that I couldn't ignore. One of Lhakpa's cousins laughed when I repeated Lhakpa's claim that the village she'd grown up in didn't have a school or a hospital and that she'd hoped to correct that by raising money through her climbing. He went to school in the village, he said. Although the educational opportunities in the Makalu region were certainly more meager when Lhakpa was growing up, there are now six schools that serve the village, and three medical facilities. I couldn't find anyone in Nepal who knew of Lhakpa's relationship with Lopsang Sherpa. Two documentary producers and a radio journalist who covered the women's expedition, as well as Mingma Sherpa, the co-leader of the team, all said Lhakpa had never mentioned a relationship with Lopsang. Lhakpa told the producers of the documentary that Nima's father was alive in 2000, but Lopsang had been dead for nearly four years.

Nobody doubts Lhakpa's climb to the top of Everest with the women's expedition or any of her subsequent summits, but her teammates on the women's expedition and the press who covered it dispute her recollections, pointing out that it was Lhakpa, the leader, who wanted little to do with her teammates, not the other way around. Mingma, the assistant leader, has a teahouse in Tengboche, a popular stop along the way to Everest's Nepal-side Base Camp. When I visited her there, she recalled that Lhakpa had refused to hike, climb, or share tents with the other women on the expedition. Lhakpa instead tented with the *sirdar* of the expedition, who was Mingma's cousin.

Ramyata Limbu, the *Frontline* producer, found that Lhakpa started out friendly, but became increasingly evasive, slinking away from the filmmakers when it came time to interview her. After the expedition, Sapana Sakya, Ramyata's co-producer on *Daughters of Everest*, had hoped to profile Lhakpa, but her subject wouldn't see her. Lhakpa told me that she wouldn't cooperate with the filmmakers unless they gave her money for the schools and hospitals she planned to build.

But Lhakpa's evasion of the press is matched by how aggressively she courts it.

"I want to set records by climbing [Everest] again and again," she told a press conference before the women's expedition set off for the mountain. In subsequent interviews, she predicted she would reach the summit ten times.

In 2005, Lhakpa summoned Stephanie Marsh, a journalist working in Everest Base Camp for the *Times* of London, to a tent where she was having a lunch of sheep brain soup. She announced plans to lead another all-women's ascent of the mountain.

"Lhakpa, who received me on her collapsible chair as if on a throne," Marsh wrote in the *Times*, "had sought me out specifically to write about her next great adventure. She is to lead an all-female expedition to the top of Everest next year. Her unique selling point? This venture is to be bankrolled by Oprah Winfrey. When her team of women reach the top, it will plant a flag representing 'woman power' on the pinnacle. This flag will bear a picture of Winfrey's face."

At a press conference in Kathmandu a few weeks later, Lhakpa said she had placed photos of the king and queen of Nepal, as well as President George W. Bush and First Lady Laura Bush, on the summit of the mountain.

"I will meet U.S. President George Bush soon and talk with him about his help to promote tourism and mountaineering in Nepal," she said.

Six months before the Connecticut team left for Everest, Lhakpa was honored in *Ms.* magazine as one of the world's most notable women.

The expedition from New England that Lhakpa was leading needed a lot of help when we arrived in Kathmandu. Our time in the mystical and filthy capital of the Himalayan kingdom would be critically short, and complicated by the country's escalating political crisis. Nepal's Maoist rebels had called for a strike that would shut down the country just a few days after our arrival. Violent demonstrations against the king drew mobs into the streets every day that left a number of people dead and scores injured. Homemade bombs rattled the windows of the team's $3-a-night Imperial Guesthouse hotel. Cadres of Maoists marched noisily through Thamel, the tourist section of Kathmandu, prompting shopkeepers to slam their doors shut. Shops elsewhere in the city were ransacked, and buses and cabs were burned for operating during the strikes.

To complicate matters more, we had landed in the Himalaya without such vital gear as boots and stoves, which we had to round up before we could get out of town. Our Sherpa celebrity told us not to worry. Her friends and family would take care of the Connecticut team. With their help, she had advised us, it would be easier to find gear in the local shops than it would be to cart it from the United States in our already overweight bags.

"You wanna meet the king?" Lhakpa asked me, not only unfazed by the upheaval in the streets, but confident that she would be granted an audience. She told us that she had planned a party for the team at one of Kathmandu's finest hotels and promised visits from various VIPs from the mountaineering world and the Nepali government.

Amid the chaos, I was troubled that some on the team seemed more interested in partying—hanging out at bars, seeking out belly dancers, or hunting the streets for something to smoke—than preparing for our climb. Still, even I was looking forward to the Sherpa family reunion.

Lhakpa's only consolation at leaving her twenty-month-old daughter in the States was the chance to see her son, Nima, age nine, whom she hadn't seen in ten months. Her family had come from the high Himalaya as well as Florida and France for the celebration, which was held around a backyard campfire.

Nima answered the door and spent most of the night orbiting his mother, cautiously making his way into her arms. The Sherpas who had traveled from Makalu were in traditional Sherpa aprons and coats. Those living in Kathmandu and Florida wore the latest fashions. Lhakpa wore short red soccer shorts and a tight white T-shirt.

At the fire, Lhakpa's family surrounded her to hear tales of her adventures on Everest and in America. Her niece sang her a song about a woman who isn't afraid of mountains. George sat far away in the darkness with the other Western climbers, but he approached Lhakpa's parents late in the evening. Lhakpa's sister Doni had at age fifteen set the youth record on Everest while climbing with George and Lhakpa in 2003. George wanted her on our expedition in 2004, too, but her parents didn't want her climbing Everest again.

Doni stepped away and stared at her shoes as George argued with her family.

"Look at her," he said. "You can tell she wants to climb."

"I no climb now," Doni protested. "I go to school."

• • •

The next morning, I joined Lhakpa at Asian Trekking, the company that handled all of the Connecticut expedition's arrangements. Ang Tsering Sherpa, Asian Trekking's owner, is revered as the most successful Sherpa businessman in history. His company is the best-established tour operator in Nepal, arranging more Everest trips than any other. In his office were dozens of honors from some of the most famous mountaineers, adventurers, and businessmen in the world. But on the wall opposite his desk, one large photograph hung above the rest: Lhakpa Sherpa, sitting in the traditional striped apron of the Sherpa women, hands folded humbly in her lap, head bowed, before King Birendra. She'd had two audiences with the monarch before his son murdered him and most of his immediate family. She'd also met his brother, Gyanendra, the current king, after he took the throne.

Lhakpa's brother Mingma Gelu was the first climbing Sherpa brought onto the team, and he was eager to shop for the gear we still needed. Lhakpa had insisted that "Sherpa prices" were cheaper than what Western climbers could find either stateside or in the Himalaya, but a thermos came with a $65 price tag. Chuck Boyd complained when he learned that his Sherpa's oxygen would cost him $1,200. I brought up the mounting expenses during dinner at a restaurant appropriately named Fire and Ice.

George responded: "I suppose you're going to claim that I didn't tell you that you must pay tips to your Sherpas for the trips they make to higher camps, either." He hadn't.

Asian Trekking charged $3,200 for each climbing Sherpa, but their tips and oxygen would more than double the tab for each climber who summited with a Sherpa—a total bill of about $6,500. Anne told me later that when I stepped away from the table, George complained about my questions regarding money and said the Sherpas know who the cheap climbers are. When I returned, he told of an Austrian climber who had failed to return a tent and a sleeping bag George had left for him in a high camp on Everest. The climber was back this year.

"I'm going to Camp One and cut his tent loose and throw it off the mountain," George said. "And I'm not going to do it when he's acclimatizing. I'm going to wait until he's making his summit push." (None of the Austrians on the mountain in 2004 reported any problems with George or their tents.)

On our last night in Kathmandu, amid frantic packing, Lhakpa indeed threw a party at one of Nepal's finest hotels. She was paying for the event, she said, with money left to her by Lopsang. The team trickled in fashionably late to find a conference room filled with journalists and government officials. Lhakpa sat on a stage with several Nepali dignitaries. Nameplates showed that Anne and I also were expected to speak.

George growled at Anne for her tardiness and glowered at me when I arrived a few minutes later. As we took our turns at the microphone, he paced in front of us, videotaping the announcement that Lhakpa Sherpa, the first Nepali woman to climb Mount Everest, had come from her adopted home in the United States to lead the first Connecticut expedition to Everest, after which she would climb K2.

The press conference was a surprise to the rest of us. So was Lhakpa's insistence that we keep her marriage to George a secret. She asked us repeatedly not to mention her marriage to anyone in Nepal and told Everest historian Elizabeth Hawley that she and George weren't married.

There were other things to hide. For months, George had warned Carolyn and me to conceal our profession because, if the Chinese found out we were journalists, they would prevent us from coming into Tibet or, if we were already there, arrest us. But when my turn came to speak at Lhakpa's press conference, I was introduced as a journalist in front of representatives from the Chinese embassy.

"If he gets busted," Chuck joked, "we're just going to take his gear and split it up."

After the press conference, the party was held on the hotel lawn, complete with Asian delicacies, an open bar, and a healthy dose of stress brought on by our impending departure at four a.m. and the growing tensions on the team. At a table by the gardens, George argued loudly with Dawa Sherpa, the business manager of Asian Trekking, about how many yaks he had arranged to haul the expedition's gear to Advanced Base Camp. Anne stepped in to negotiate a compromise. Bill Driggs reminded George that we still had no fuel for our mountaineering stoves, prompting him to bark a last-minute order to Dawa.

"It will get better when we get to Base Camp," Anne said.

At midnight, as the team packed amid the obstacle course of expedition barrels and duffel bags clogging the hallways of the Imperial Guesthouse, where we were staying, Carolyn returned to our hotel room to find Mingma Gelu, having opened one of our barrels and picking through our gear. He'd removed only a roll of tape, and when Carolyn confronted him, Mingma Gelu told her that George had sent him for it. Other climbers told us, sometimes as warnings, sometimes as jokes, of "Sherpa gangs."

In the few times I met them, I found Lhakpa's parents and sisters to be charming, helpful, and hospitable. But it's not surprising that within a tribe that is among the poorest in Asia, working for some of the wealthiest adventurers in the world, a few are less than honest. I did the math and realized that each of the five bottles of oxygen that I would use for my ascent cost more than twice what the average Nepali earns in a year and nearly four times a Tibetan's per-capita income. And while it's sad to see the actions of a few erode the well-earned reputation of the many, the crimes and betrayals some of them are accused of are small compared to the abuse they endure. Each year, climbing Sherpas die trying to earn, at best, a few thousand dollars by carrying loads and preparing the climbing route for Western mountaineers. Among the porters, who are not equipped or trained to climb, the toll is worse. Hundreds look for work carrying loads up to twice their own weight into the high mountains. The bribes they have to give to the *sirdars* in charge to get hired often offset the small salaries they are paid, so they are dependent on the tips of the tourists whose loads they are carrying for what small income they make. While just the chance that a single English mountaineer was abandoned on Everest makes the news around the world, the West rarely hears of the dozens of porters and Sherpas who die on the trail, or of the Western climbers and trekkers who have simply walked past when the stricken men carrying their loads fall. In one case, when a freak storm dropped several feet of snow in the Khumbu, a helicopter was sent to rescue trapped trekkers, but the leader of the group refused to allow their porters onto the chopper, dooming the workers to horrific frostbite that crippled many of them for life and left them unable to make even the meager living they had.

The tape that Mingma Gelu helped himself to wasn't worth getting upset about, but finding him in our gear worried me.

Nine

While Damian Benegas was tracking down climbers who might have seen Nils and Gustavo high on Everest, people who had befriended them elsewhere during their expedition were just learning of the tragedy. The Swiss climbers Peter Gschwendtner and Kilian Volken were back in Kathmandu after summiting when they heard an American had died on the mountain.

"My—and Kilian's—thoughts went in the same direction: Nils and Gustavo???" Peter wrote on their blog.

Peter went straight to the Yak and Yeti Hotel's reception desk to ask about the two men they had befriended in Base Camp, but they had no information. When the last of the Swiss crew returned from the mountain two days later, however, they confirmed Nils's death.

Meanwhile, Edurne Pasaban, the Basque climber who had been on Everest with Gustavo, Juan Carlos Gonzalez, and Silvio Mondinelli in 2000, was in Spain preparing for a trip to Pakistan. Two months later, she would reach the top of K2, and for two years would hold the honor of being the only woman to conquer the "Savage Mountain" and not have died climbing in the Himalaya. When she heard that Gustavo had abandoned a climber high on Everest, she broke from her preparations to call Fabiola in her room in Kathmandu to express her outrage.

Andres Delgado, leader of the Mexican/Canadian team on Everest, responded to Fabiola's pleas for information with an e-mail from Base Camp. Nils and Gustavo were on the same permit as Andres, but didn't climb with the Mexican's team.

"First of all I want to express my most sincere condolences for your father's unfortunate and unnecessary departure of this material world. I know Guillermo Benegas has information pertinent of how things happened as Gustavo and your father descended from the summit," Andres wrote. "I am very sorry to know that another stupidity from Gustavo ended with the loss of your father's life."

Fabiola and Davide's room overlooked the Yak and Yeti's gardens, but they spent their first night in Kathmandu looking at the floor. They sat on the carpet amid the papers they had found in a binder in the bag Nils had stored at the hotel: invoices, requests for services, itineraries and e-mails that Nils and Gustavo had exchanged with Manuel Lugli, the Italian agent who had organized their expedition. They laid out the pages like pieces of a puzzle that might eventually show how Nils and Gustavo ended up together on Everest. In a couple of spots, Fabiola saw that Gustavo noted he was a guide certified by the International Federation of Mountain Guides Associations—IFMGA—the occupation's gold standard.

"How could someone with such high qualifications let this happen?" she wondered.

When Fabiola first called Manuel Lugli on his cell phone, she found him out to dinner with his family in Italy. He was a bit annoyed at the interruption when she insisted he find the phone numbers and e-mails for climbers she could contact on the mountain. He hadn't heard about the accident. But Manuel had been with Nils and Gustavo during their trek to the mountain six weeks earlier. He had left Everest just as his clients were starting their climb but had come back to Italy worried.

Manuel had met Nils Antezana on the flight from Rome to Kathmandu in early April, but he had been in constant contact with him since October, shortly after Gustavo Lisi had contacted Manuel to say that he had a client for an Everest climb. Gustavo wanted Manuel's company, Il Nodo Infinito (The Infinite Knot), to make all the arrangements for the permits, porters, cooks, Sherpas, and supplies he and Nils would need to climb to the top of the mountain. Nils had called Manuel every month since signing on to discuss the arrangements. Although Gustavo was overseeing the climb, Nils was paying for everything, so Manuel had had no problem with Nils's probing but polite questioning about every detail.

Manuel knew Gustavo because the company he had worked for before starting his own adventuring business had arranged the Basque expedition that Gustavo and Juan Carlos Gonzalez had climbed with in 2000. But news of the stolen photos hadn't made it to Manuel, so he had no problem making arrangements for another of Gustavo's climbs.

Although Manuel had seven Italian climbers on the flight headed for Everest Base Camp, they were all climbing Lhotse, the peak next to Everest. All Manuel's clients would share facilities at the bottom of the two mountains, but Nils and Gustavo were on the Everest permit of a team led by Andres Delgado, the Mexican climber. Spots on the permits cost some $10,000 each, but in the end they are formalities that often mix and match mountaineers who have no plans of climbing together. Nils and Gustavo knew they would be climbing independently of the others, but they would have the support of two Sherpas—Big Dorjee and Mingma Sherpa— whom Manuel arranged for through the Kathmandu expedition organizers Cho Oyu Trekking.

After a few days in Kathmandu, they flew to Lukla, the village from which the climbers began the weeklong trek to Base Camp. Manuel and Nils had a lot in common—Manuel had been a physician before he got into the adventure business, and Nils's son-in-law, Davide, was from Sicily—so they spent a lot of time walking together during that first week. Manuel was eager to see how Nils held up to the rigors of altitude and noted that the doctor was very slow on the trail. But many younger climbers are just as slow, and speed on the trek doesn't necessarily equate with performance on a climb. Manuel was more concerned by Nils's relationship with Gustavo.

Things went well as far as Namche Bazaar, the bustling village that is the heart of the Sherpa culture, where every expedition spends a day or two resting and shopping. But at dinner in the village, Manuel said a local shopkeeper accosted Gustavo and accused him of trying on a pair of pants in his store and then sneaking them out by putting his own pants on over them. Nils defended Gustavo, but the merchant went to Gustavo's room, found the trousers, and threatened to go to the police. Gustavo continued to deny the accusation, but eventually settled up with the shopkeeper, claiming that he was willing to pay money he didn't owe to bring the altercation to an end.

The next day's hike ended with a long, uphill climb to the monastery at Tengboche, which Gustavo reached hours before Nils did. The guide regularly hiked ahead of his client, but this time Nils commented to Manuel about it. Manuel heard Nils and Gustavo arguing that night. By the time they reached Base Camp, the tension between client and guide had reached the point where Manuel felt he had to sit them down to work out their differences or else put an end to their climb. It was a long, strange meeting with Manuel and his business partner, Davide Arrigo, mediating between Gustavo and Nils. Although Spanish was Nils's first language, he insisted on speaking English and having Manuel translate to Gustavo. The tensions between them had become such that they literally didn't speak the same language. During their calls before the climb, and throughout the trek, Gustavo and Nils had been clear about their relationship as guide and client. But Manuel was surprised that they couldn't agree on what that entailed: whether Gustavo was supposed to hike with the man who was paying his way, help him with his gear, or provide advice. By the end of the meeting, Gustavo had promised to climb at his client's pace and wait for him when he fell behind, but, Manuel said, Nils remained suspicious.

"[Nils] wanted to be very clear about the strategy on the mountain, especially related to the Sherpas," Manuel recalled later. "He wanted to have the last word on any decision."

Davide Arrigo speaks Nepali, and gave strict instructions to Big Dorjee and Mingma so there could be no confusion later: Nils was to have priority on the way to the summit and back. The Sherpas were to answer to Nils.

"I think that in the end . . . he had the fear . . . that Gustavo could go ahead and leave him behind," Manuel said. "That Gustavo wanted to summit at any cost."

CHINESE BASE CAMP—APRIL 12, 2004

Most Himalayan expeditions begin with weeks-long walks that acclimatize the climbers to the higher altitudes. But on the north side of Everest, where I staged my assault with the Connecticut team, drivers with the Chinese Tibetan Mountaineering Association (CTMA) truck climbers to Base Camp in a matter of days. Because they haven't acclimatized, the 17,000-foot elevation makes many visitors sick for a few days. My teammate Chuck was vomiting with a stomach bug before we even arrived in Base Camp. I was taking my first round of antibiotics to clear up a bad cough. We all tied scarves over our faces to protect our lungs from the dust, smoke, and cold. The masks made us look like bandits. We fit right in.

The settlement looks more like a mining town than a mountaineering camp. Gray Chinese tents spread like row houses cheek to jowl up to a fetid pond. Yaks were tied in alleyways and wandered on the surrounding hillsides. Large expeditions sprawled out into subdivisions all the way to the rocky snout of the Rongbuck Glacier on the vast moraine beyond a hill topped by the Chinese liaison officer's house. In 2004, there were some fifty tents in a commercial strip Chuck called Shakedown Street and others simply referred to as Tibetantown. Two years later, from the top of the hill, I counted eighty-three tents.

Cardboard signs scrawled with names intended to lure Westerners—Hotel California and the Everest Bed and Breakfast—offered booze and bunks. Stoves burned yak dung and trash for heat, filling the tents with thick, pungent smoke. Stacks of colorful Tibetan blankets and pillows lined the canvas walls for overnight visitors. During my first expedition, boomboxes with feeble batteries played Chinese Muzak versions of American hits, but two years later, most of the tents had portable solar panels and some had full-size stereos with speakers blasting tunes into the street. Cases of beer departed on the backs of porters and yaks for the 21,500-foot Advanced Base Camp. The sharp odor of animal dung and human waste was eased occasionally by the scent of burning hashish.

Expedition doctors were known to treat venereal diseases and brawling injuries as well as altitude sickness. Pony carts hauling tourists back and forth between Base Camp and the Rongbuck Monastery and Everest View Hotel a few miles down the road cruised like shrunken stagecoaches into the camp past Land Cruisers, tour buses, and a yellow metal post office that was well stocked but almost always closed. A woman swung inside one of the carts as it passed into the camp and grabbed the mountain guide there by the arm.

"Sleepy, sleepy with me?" she ordered more than asked.

On the dusty main drag, a man standing in front of a tent grinned at me, then gestured to his crotch and his mouth and pointed to the women inside the tent. Tibetan and Chinese women approached tourists in the streets and snuggled, unsolicited, beside them in the teahouses.

"All I know is a woman grabbed my arm and was trying to pull me into a place that I was definitely not going into," Chuck said. "You're in the Wild West. Or the Wild East."

Those working the mountain use ice axes rather than pick-axes, but most are there to scratch a living from the Earth's hide. They surround the goddess mountain with satellites, tie her down with ropes, and tame her with computer-analyzed weather reports. And for every person who reaches Everest's summit, many more arrive in Base Camp just looking for a piece of the action.

Aside from the guides and Sherpas, nearly every climber on Everest is paying, or at least is supposed to pay, his or her way to the top. Tens of thousands of dollars change hands here with no legal oversight. And in this wilderness, money is like blood: It's sure to draw predators.

The permit to climb the Chinese side of Everest works out to cost less than a third of what it does on the Nepal side, where Nils Antezana and Gustavo Lisi had also just arrived in Base Camp, but you definitely get what you pay for, at least as far as the mountain goes. Climbers in the Nepal side Base Camp are surrounded by high, dramatic peaks—Pumori, Nuptse, Lhotse, Ama Dablam, Cholatse. The trek in leads hikers through wooded valleys; past scores of Buddhist shrines, monuments, and temples; through a dozen villages nestled below massive, snowy pyramids and gaping passes. Every step offers adventurers something new to climb, visit, or explore. Some climbers take numerous side trips, perhaps even climbing a lesser peak to acclimatize on their way into the city of nylon at the base of the mountain. Base Camp itself is a short walk from the start of the Khumbu Icefall, which, while perilous, is an ever-changing kaleidoscope of snow and ice. The festive camp is known as the highest party in the world. During the 2006 season, one millionaire brought a chef and thirty-some coolers of gourmet food, a Polish Playboy bunny was ogled all the way to the top of the mountain, and a Sherpa outraged the country by violating the sacred summit with his claim that he posed nude there (a mountain guide with him at the time told me he had really only stripped to the waist). Some wealthy mountaineers commuted by helicopter between Base Camp and the Kathmandu Hyatt.

Everest's Chinese Base Camp is the opposite side of the mountain in more ways than one. On the five-day Land Cruiser ride from Nepal to the mountain, all climbers are required to stay in the same lodges in the same three settlements—Zang Mu, the truck-clogged border town known as Little Bangkok for its abundant prostitution; a small city called Nylam; and the decrepit Tibetan village of Tingri, where we watched children stone a puppy to death, then wondered if that's what we were served for dinner. Aside from acclimatization hikes on the hills over Nylam and Tingri, the only side trips allowed are bathroom breaks on the daylong truck rides. The hills and peaks surrounding this Base Camp are piles of crumbling stone, only occasionally clothed with ragged scraps of snow. The real climbing starts above Advanced Base Camp, still thirteen miles of rocky trudge away, a trip we would make repeatedly as we acclimatized.

Some fifteen miles from Base Camp and 12,000 feet higher, the summit of Everest fills the sky. A teammate stared at it and whispered, "My precious." I traced the route up the mountain's Northeast Ridge to the peak with my finger. Then I crawled into my tent in the low camp and tried not to vomit.

Our electronics also suffered. George's laptop had died before we reached Base Camp, his generator proved unreliable, and his satellite phone was out of order for days on end. In the States, George had delayed buying the phone for months until finally Anne ordered it for him a few days before we departed. In Kathmandu, he couldn't get it to work, so Bill Driggs figured out how to set it up. Now, in Base Camp, the team quickly exhausted all the satellite time George had paid for. In the meantime, Carolyn and I were filing stories, posting to a blog, and transmitting photos and video almost daily. When our workload left little free time or bandwidth on the *Courant*'s equipment for teammates to use, their resentment mounted fast.

Snowfall delayed the Connecticut team's first trip to Advanced Base Camp, and the inevitable snowball fight turned ugly. Three of our teammates pelted Bill as he tried to read. The game devolved into a wrestling match in the stony slush. Carolyn tried to make a video of the fracas, but Guillermo Blaizac threw a snowball into the lens of her camera. When the snow melted, they threw rocks. Carolyn asked them to move their target practice away from the tent where we kept all of the media equipment, and Guillermo again responded, this time by pegging her with a rock to the laughter and cheers of the other competitors. At six feet tall, slender, and blond, Carolyn was already a lightning rod for the team's brewing storm.

"It will get better when we get to ABC," Anne told us at dinner that night.

Ten

Two days after Fabiola and Davide checked into the Yak and Yeti, a woman left a note for them at the front desk. They found Rhonda Martin and José Luis Abreu waiting for them in the hotel restaurant. Rhonda had befriended Nils when he spent a few days during his trek to Base Camp in Pheriche, where she was working as a nurse. When she got wind of the accident, she e-mailed friends on the mountain, including José, the Base Camp manager for the Mexican/Canadian climbers whose permit Nils had shared, to find out what had happened. When José told Rhonda that Nils's daughter had come to Kathmandu, they tracked her down at the hotel.

"I just wanted to tell you what a wonderful man your dad was and that he was so excited to climb Everest," Rhonda told Fabiola. "And . . . to let you know that there was trouble brewing weeks ago."

José mentioned that another Everest veteran, Hector Ponce de Leon, also witnessed some things that Fabiola should know about. Fabiola and Davide rejoined Rhonda, José, and Hector at the Kathmandu Hyatt a few days later.

• • •

For more than a decade, Rhonda Martin had pursued backcountry medical skills the way climbers train for the peaks. She studied with the Wilderness Medical Society in Bozeman, Montana, and at the University of Glasgow, and joined the venerable Explorers Club in New York. After visiting the Annapurna region of Nepal in 1997, she found herself between jobs and, in 1998, took a temporary position in a Kathmandu clinic and then trekked to Everest Base Camp.

Rhonda specialized in emergency room and intensive care nursing, but was always looking out for ways to use extended leaves from her job at Brigham and Women's Hospital in Boston to practice her craft in places where it would really make a difference— doing research in remote locations or assisting with international disaster relief. She befriended Dr. Buddha Basnyat, medical director of the Himalayan Rescue Association, and Dr. Luanne Freer, the resident physician at the Everest Base Camp Medical Clinic. On Pike's Peak, she studied whether the herb ginkgo biloba can prevent altitude sickness. When Basnyat and Freer organized a similar study along the trail to Everest, they asked Rhonda to help out. The results have been promising.

Pheriche is one of the last villages along the trail through the Khumbu to Everest's Nepali Base Camp. And while the hamlets closer to the mountain are frigid outposts, Pheriche is comfortable enough and close enough to Base Camp that many climbers will descend to it for rest days during their climb.

Constructed of plywood, the Pheriche Hospital seemed primitive, but in the six years since Rhonda had first seen it, the clinic had made strides. It had a second Gamow bag—a coffin-shaped tent that inflates to mimic the air pressure of lower altitudes to save the most desperately altitude-sick patients. The doctors and nurses who took seasonal positions at the clinic often left behind medical equipment, so each season the hospital was slightly better stocked. Rhonda liked the idea of doing her research near the clinic, where she could put her downtime from the study to use, so she set up shop next door at the Himalayan Lodge.

Between Lukla, where an airstrip nestled at 9,000 feet was the welcome mat for the thousands of visitors to the Solu Khumbu, and Everest Base Camp, twenty-odd miles up the valley, volunteers for the study tracked the wellness of two hundred trekkers and climbers. But by the time they reached Pheriche, at just over 14,000 feet, most of the guinea pigs had dropped out due to illnesses, changes of plans, or a failure to stick with the scheduled dosage of the pills they were given in Lukla.

"[The study] would take an hour or two of my day, and the rest of the day I was free and tended to hang out at the clinic," Rhonda said. "I was able to treat a lot of the locals and help out with a lot of the evacuations."

Each afternoon of the trekking season, the staff of the clinic gives a presentation on altitude sickness. Rhonda often took the lead role in the daily performance, perhaps because she so often found herself treating people who couldn't keep their eyes off the mountains around them long enough to learn how to survive them. Climbing teams from around the world would approach Rhonda to ask advice. If they weren't sick yet, they knew that few Everest climbers avoid illness altogether and they wanted to be prepared.

"My first job is research," she said. "My second job is staffing the clinic, and my third job is social butterfly."

She had watched dozens of mountaineers heading off, but a pair of them stood out.

Rhonda met the guide before his client, and remembers the Argentinean strutting through the lodge and flirting with the women. He was Hollywood handsome, and he made his way through the lodge with the confidence to match, eager to let everyone know that he was a guide on Everest. Gustavo asked Rhonda for tape so he could stick his business cards next to those of other guides and Sherpas on the most prominent spots of the lodge's walls.

She didn't meet Nils until her next shift at the clinic.

"Can I help you?" she asked when Nils walked in. "Are you feeling well?"

"Oh, I'm just fine," Nils replied. "I'm just over here exploring what's going on."

For the first time since he had headed into the Himalaya, Nils was in a place where he felt at home.

"He was fascinated by the clinic," Rhonda recalled of the doctor who smiled as he looked around the room at what surely was one of the crudest medical facilities he had ever visited. Business, for the moment, was slow, so Nils pulled up a chair and sat down.

"Wow," he said. "Had I known that opportunities like this existed when I was younger, I would have been over here."

For a moment he seemed to find mountain medicine more adventurous than mountain climbing. Rhonda could hardly answer his questions fast enough.

"Who runs this? What's the [Himalayan Rescue Association]? How did you get your job? How did you end up with this research?"

They compared notes about Boston and Washington, D.C., recreating each step of the different paths that had led them from very different places to one of the highest hospitals in the world.

"The conversation was going a million miles an hour," Rhonda recalls. "I asked how he had come to climbing, and he told me about his practice in D.C. and how he started flying airplanes and that he had come to climbing late."

When he told her that he was sixty-nine, Rhonda didn't believe him.

"Fifty-nine or sixty, tops," she responded.

He said climbing Everest was a lifetime goal of his. When Rhonda asked how he had come to be part of the Italian team, he said Gustavo had arranged it. Nils explained that he was originally from Bolivia and he still considered that country his home. He had done most of his mountaineering there, and he met Gustavo during one of his climbs.

"The first time they climbed together, Gustavo was a client, not a guide," Rhonda recalls Nils telling her. The next time they climbed together, Gustavo worked as the doctor's guide. During that trip, Nils told Gustavo of his dream to climb Everest.

"Gustavo told him he had climbed Everest already, from the

north side, and summited," Rhonda remembers Nils saying. "And he would be willing to take him back and be his guide."

Nils was quite clear. The fact that Gustavo had already reached the summit of Everest was the primary qualification that convinced Nils to hire him to lead him up the mountain.

After Nils left the clinic, he and Gustavo took an acclimatization hike into the mountains around Pheriche. When they returned, Rhonda noticed that Nils was knackered. A little while later, she ran into Gustavo, and although Rhonda's Spanish was no better than Gustavo's English, they managed to converse. He told her how his father had taken him into the Andes when he was seven. Ever since, he had wanted only to be a mountain guide. He'd led clients through the mountains of Italy, Bolivia, Argentina, and Chile. Gustavo told her that he had reached the summit of Everest a few years earlier, climbing from the north, and was looking forward to climbing the south side of the mountain. And this year, he said, he was taking a client up there with him.

That evening Nils joined Rhonda and an intern at dinner. As they dined, Nils talked of his children, and the intern piped up. He had crossed paths with David Antezana when he was in medical school. Small world, they laughed. But as the threesome talked their way around the planet, Rhonda was troubled.

"I noticed that Gustavo didn't come over to eat with us," she said. "Aside from the hike they took together, they seemed like they were not very close."

Rhonda almost always spoke to climbers in teams. A question to one of them often brought answers from the entire group. She had seen dozens of expeditions pass through the lodge, and even the ones that weren't getting along well took their meals together. Looking at the daunting task before them, climbers worked hard to get to know the teammates whose lives and livelihoods would be roped to their own just a week or two later. Yet Gustavo and Nils spent most of their time apart, and even when Gustavo and Nils sat side-by-side, they hardly spoke to each other.

Rhonda had a bad feeling about Gustavo, and her concerns grew during the two days that he was in Pheriche.

"He tended to be mooching things off people constantly," she said.

The morning of his acclimatization hike with Nils, Gustavo approached Rhonda at the clinic. She was used to guides coming to her for first-aid supplies. He asked Rhonda to get him some toothpaste and sunscreen—things she would have to provide from her personal supply. His stock of the items, he said, had been carried ahead to Base Camp. Rhonda was bothered more by the fact that a mountain guide wouldn't have such basic necessities than by the sense of entitlement that would motivate him to send a complete stranger to fetch them. At this altitude, pink blisters of sunburn rise right beside the black ones brought on by frostbite. Surely a guide who had already climbed Everest knew how sharp the sun is in a place with so little atmosphere to blunt it.

"Guides usually pride themselves on being organized and prepared," she thought as she watched Gustavo approach another team of climbers to ask for other supplies that he didn't have.

"He was very demanding, very aloof," she said, noting that he rarely spoke with other expeditions unless he needed something. "The people he did talk to were all females. A little bit of a predatory personality."

"I would not want this guy as my guide," she thought as she watched him prepare for his hike. "There's something off here."

On their third morning in Pheriche, the day that Nils and Gustavo would continue their trek to Base Camp, Nils stopped at Rhonda's table during breakfast. He looked drawn and tired and sick.

"I don't feel too well," he said. "I have a really bad sore throat. Will you look at it?"

Rhonda looked at his throat outside the clinic, took his temperature, and asked how he had slept.

"Not a wink," he said.

Sleep disorders are very common at high altitude, and although they usually pass, they can also spiral into more serious illnesses.

"If he can't sleep here, how's he ever going to sleep on the mountain?" she thought.

She started to express her concerns to the doctor, but he cut her off.

"There's actually more to it than that," Nils told her. "I'm having problems with my guide, Gustavo. We're only starting out, and already we're at odds with each other."

On their hike up to Pheriche, Gustavo had ignored his client and routinely left Nils behind. Out of sight of his guide, Nils took a wrong turn and had nearly reached the village of Dingboche, in a parallel valley to the east of Pheriche, before other trekkers sent him back down to the trail junction and up to Pheriche. It was dark when Nils trudged into the village. He was freezing, exhausted, angry, and more than a little spooked. When he stepped inside the lodge, he found his guide sitting by a fireplace, drinking tea.

"Why did you leave me?" Nils asked Gustavo. "I don't expect you to stand right next to me like a mother and child, but you need to be watching out where I am."

Gustavo, Nils told Rhonda, lashed out at him.

"The problem is that you are so slow," Gustavo had snapped. "It's that you're too hot. I'm your guide and I was telling you, 'You need to take off more clothes and drink more water.' You're staying too far behind."

"He was rude and brazen. I paid him a lot of money. I paid his air ticket from Argentina. To be treated like this is just so disrespectful," Nils vented to Rhonda. "I know when I'm hot. I know enough to know how to dress in the mountains. . . . I know when I'm hydrated. He was absolutely wrong in his assessment of that. I'm a seasoned climber. This little thirty-three-year-old guide is ordering me around like I'm the kid and he's the dad."

Rhonda wondered why Nils didn't just sign on with one of the better-known guiding outfits working on Everest. She wouldn't be surprised, she thought, if Nils and Gustavo split up by the time they got to Base Camp. When she asked how they had left it, Nils said Gustavo had promised to stay within his sight for the rest of the climb.

"Give him a little while, but if it doesn't go well after Base Camp . . . ," Rhonda said, but she didn't finish her sentence. Who was she to be giving a mountaineer advice?

As Gustavo and Nils prepared to hike out of Pheriche later that morning, Rhonda approached them and gave them each a small bundle of brightly colored fabric—strings of prayer flags.

"Would you put this on top of Everest for me if you make it?" she asked Nils.

"I would be thrilled," he replied.

Rhonda posed for photos with the client and his guide, gave hugs all around, and promised to visit them when she made her own trip up to Base Camp. She had sent off dozens of climbers from Pheriche, but in the weeks to come, she couldn't get Nils and Gustavo off her mind.

"I have a bad feeling about this," she thought to herself as she watched them head into the mountains. "I have a really bad, bad feeling."

Rhonda looked forward to visiting Nils during her own trip to Base Camp a few weeks later, but when she arrived, she learned that he and Gustavo were acclimatizing higher on the mountain, so she never got a chance to check up on Nils once he was on the climb.

On May 16, Rhonda arrived in Kathmandu, her work for the study completed. She checked MountEverest.net every day to follow the progress of her friends on the mountain. On May 18, the top headline was CLIMBER MISSING. Rhonda sent e-mails to several Base Camp managers to find out who it was.

"I didn't hear and I didn't hear," she recalled later.

"You can't be 'missing' high on the mountain," she thought after another day of reports of a climber unaccounted for. "You're dead. . . . You don't stay up there two days in the death zone. You've either fallen off or something dreadful has happened."

It was three days before the missing climber was identified. Rhonda wasn't completely surprised that the climber who had worried her most was almost certainly dead, but the trickle of news from the mountain posed more questions than it answered.

"How can he be missing," she thought. "Where were the Sherpas? Where was Gustavo? How come there is no information? Is Gustavo missing too?"

She sent another flurry of e-mails and rifled through her bags to find the card that Gustavo had given her, then logged onto his Web site. "Summit," it said, and told how Nils had achieved his dream. But otherwise it didn't mention the doctor. Rhonda recalls the site telling how Gustavo had planted the Argentinean flag on the summit along with the flag from Salta, his hometown.

"It was a whole paragraph of nothing but accolades about himself," Rhonda said. "Nothing about Nils being lost."

"How can this be?" she thought.

It wasn't until the first teams were returning to Kathmandu that José Luis Abreu filled Rhonda in. José's friend Hector Ponce de Leon had been climbing the mountain as part of the Discovery Channel expedition and had run into Nils and Gustavo several times on the mountain.

"What a surprise," Rhonda thought as Hector told his story to Fabiola. "This is what I saw about Gustavo. He never had anything on him that was necessary. Gustavo was always expecting the Sherpas or somebody else to supply it for him. Everybody else was doing the wrong thing. He blames the victims. . . . This guy's a sociopath."

Eleven

Climbing teams on the world's highest mountains move like yo-yos—climbing up the mountain to set a new high point, spending a night or two there, then descending to recover from the effort and adjust to the thinner air. To acclimatize on the north side of Everest, most climbers will make one or two trips from Base Camp to Advanced Base Camp and back, before moving in at the higher camp. When they feel comfortable there, they make a round trip or two up to Camp One, the first of the three high camps that lead to the summit.

For their summit push, climbers plan to spend a night or two in each of the high camps on their route. On their summit day, they start climbing before midnight in hopes of reaching the climb's most difficult section—the aluminum ladder scaling a bluff called the Second Step—around first light. By midmorning, they should be standing on the summit in order to have enough time to descend to a lower camp by early afternoon.

The first hike to ABC and back is vital, both for the human

body's acclimatization to the altitude and for the team's adjustment to working together. For most, Interim Camp is essential to that trip—a rugged way station that breaks the thirteen-mile climb from the 17,000-foot Base Camp to the 21,500-foot Advanced Base Camp into two arduous but manageable parts.

But on the morning of the Connecticut team's first hike up the mountain, we stood amid bedlam. Dozens of yaks arrived in small herds. Their drivers weighed our loads and haggled angrily through the morning as team members packed and repacked the barrels and duffel bags that would ride atop the beasts to ABC. Anne had resolved George's dispute with Dawa Sherpa over the number and cost of the yaks Asian Trekking was providing us, a deal that George resented. "Anne has stabbed us in the back," he said when the subject came up. Now as the yaks moved out, George and Lhakpa, our Everest veterans, stayed in the cook tent while those of us who had never been there before struggled to make sense of the mess.

Carolyn and I, with coughs and stomach illnesses to recover from and dispatches to send back to the States, decided to ascend a day after our teammates. It was imperative that we have a tent in Interim Camp. We had hardly spoken with Lhakpa, our "leader on the mountain," since our arrival in Base Camp, but we stopped her twice before she headed up, and she assured us that we would have a shelter. Later, the rest of the climbers reported that the chaos only worsened in the intermediate camp. They waited for hours in the cold before the yaks with their tents and sleeping bags arrived, and few of them could find their gear before the sun set. Dinner—some salty water soup—wasn't ready until after dark. In the morning they could barely stomach their breakfast and had no water for the six-mile hike to ABC, 2,000 feet higher in the atmosphere.

As the team started out on that day's climb, Anne, our other leader, reminded the Sherpas who were breaking camp that they needed to leave a tent for Carolyn and me. She was told that our Tibetan porters would know where to take us: a small mess tent nestled in the hills. All the mountaineering tents were broken down and packed onto the yaks. But back in Base Camp, we were only just hiring the porters, so there was no way they would know where we were intended to camp.

By the time Carolyn and I completed the hike to Interim Camp late that day, snow was lashing sideways and darkness was falling. Our fingers were numb, our feet soaked, and our lungs sucked desperately at the thin air. We stumbled over the rocky hills that separate the 19,000-foot-high camp into clusters of tents in between the seracs—pinnacles pushed up by the moving glacier—that circle the moraine like fifty-foot sharks' fins made of ice, but we couldn't find our shelter. The two teenage Tibetan porters who helped us carry our gear spoke no English and looked both puzzled and frightened as we hunted for the dome of nylon that our teammates were supposed to have left for us. Without it, we were looking at a night out in a storm on Mount Everest.

The large military mess tent was our last hope.

"I don't know where your camp is," said a man in sneakers and jeans slouching in the corner. "But at least come in for a cup of tea. It's really miserable out there."

We dined in that tent with commercial expedition leader Dan Mazur and many of his thirty-eight clients. After dinner, we slept there with Arnold Coster, a Dutch climber, and four Tibetan mountaineering porters who complained that they had never had to share a tent with white people before. The next night, with our phantom tent still eluding us, Coster invited us to crowd into the mountaineering tent he had set up. We slept, with overwhelming gratitude for the strangers who had taken us in and angry frustration with our own climbing partners who had left us without one of the basic needs for surviving in the mountains. When we left, Mazur told us he usually charges $200 a day for trekkers and climbers who drop in on the expeditions of his company, Summit-Climb. This might seem an outrageous price for a couple of meals and space in a tent, until you consider the cost of getting food and gear up high on Everest. However, five minutes after taking our money, Dan came back and returned it to us.

"Let's just keep this on the favor basis," he said. "You'd take in a couple of my climbers in a storm, right? It's a shame, what's happening to your team. Everest makes people grow horns."

When I continued up to Advanced Base Camp that day, I ran into my teammates Chuck, Dave, and Dan Lochner, who were descending. Chuck had vomited regularly since our arrival in Tibet. He could hide his illness lower on the mountain, but in Advanced Base Camp his swollen, listless face was impossible to miss. Dave and Dan were also sick and were making the torturously slow descent with him. By noon it started to snow, and wind blasted the mountain. They reached Interim Camp at three p.m. and Dave decided to stay there.

"I could have slept anywhere," he said, noting that he had a sleeping pad and a down suit with him. "I didn't feel like I wanted to walk anymore, and I didn't need to."

Dan decided to stay with him, but had nothing to keep him warm overnight. Members of a Greek expedition gave Dan a blanket, fed the two of them, and put them up with their Sherpas for the night. Chuck, however, wanted to continue down, so he found a doctor, told him about the condition of his friends, and headed out.

"By the time I got down to Base Camp, I was pretty much hallucinating," he said later. "I was shot."

After he staggered into Base Camp, Carolyn, who had also returned to the low camp that day, expressed shock that Chuck had left his friends behind. She also complained about the missing Interim Camp tent.

"This is a hard-core mountaineering expedition," Chuck responded. "If you can't hack it, you shouldn't be here."

The next morning, the Greeks fed Dave porridge with nuts that caused an allergic reaction and made him vomit. The team's doctor gave him medication that left him holding his knees on the ground. He, like Carolyn and me, sought help in Mazur's Interim Camp mess tent.

Staying healthy is often a greater challenge than the climbing. Some mountain maladies are killers: Pulmonary edema drowns climbers in their own blood; cerebral edema fills the skull with fluid. The body, desperate to increase the density of oxygen-carrying red blood cells in a climber's veins, will pull fluid out of the blood and store it elsewhere. Skin gets puffy, limbs occasionally swell, but these edemas are generally harmless. If the fluid builds up in the lungs or the brain, however, the condition will quickly turn fatal. The only cure is getting to a lower elevation, fast.

Other illnesses are just uncomfortable and inconvenient. Acute mountain sickness brings nausea and headaches to many climbers. Cheyne-Stokes respiration, while generally harmless, causes climbers to hold their breath when they sleep so they awaken gasping and terrified. Third World sanitation gives others water- and food-borne illnesses such as giardia and dysentery. And in this oxygen-poor environment, even common colds and sore throats are guaranteed to get worse without a trip down, a round of antibiotics, or both.

After everyone was back in Base Camp three days later, we gathered in our dining tent for a debriefing.

"If we make these kinds of mistakes up high," George said, "I guarantee you it could be fatal. . . . To this point, we've had other expeditions help us a lot, and that's going to get embarrassing."

We wouldn't have had to rely on other expeditions during our trip to ABC, Anne pointed out, if we had played like a team. "It was two days of every man for himself," she said.

Back in Base Camp, it was not the persistent illnesses and relentless cold but boredom that caused the most discomfort. Books, stereos, and countless trips to Hotel California for beer and cards passed the time as the climbers acclimatized. Computers provided e-mail during the day and action films on DVD at night: *Kill Bill* at the Himalayan Experience camp; *Gladiator* at ours. Nobody brings romantic comedies to Everest. Beer flowed every afternoon. Vodka and whiskey marked special occasions.

During an evening of drinking, George gave Chuck a blow-by-blow account of the tension and infighting that had plagued the Romanian national expedition he had climbed with in 2003. But it was talk of raiding other teams' caches of oxygen that troubled Chuck.

"This is the Connecticut Everest Expedition. This is my name and my reputation. We're not stealing oxygen," Chuck told Anne afterward.

But a few days later, Anne and Carolyn were surprised to hear Chuck say that there was plenty of excess oxygen and abandoned equipment in the higher camps, and that he would take whatever he needed.

"They've told me how to do it," he said, explaining that with found bottles of oxygen, you could just open up the valves inside a sealed tent, which then inflates with oxygen, thereby avoiding the inconvenience of wearing the oxygen mask while sleeping.

Although in dire circumstances climbers will take advantage of whatever resources they must to survive, most try to compensate the people whose supplies they use. However, the value of the tanks of oxygen—around $450—has made them a constant target for theft, and dozens of tanks are reported stolen every year. Veteran guide Wally Berg recounted to me how an entire shipment of his oxygen tanks vanished one year. One of his Sherpas tipped him off that a Russian team that claimed to be climbing without using supplemental oxygen had stolen his gas. Wally visited their camp and found a strangely shaped table in their mess tent. He pulled the tablecloth off, and there was his crate of oxygen tanks.

I couldn't believe Chuck would appropriate anything vital to the survival of other climbers. He had enough oxygen to get to the summit without helping himself to anybody else's. And for all I know, he got there using only the gas he had purchased.

To some mountaineers, rows of tents stocked with equipment are a buffet. With only a thin sheet of nylon and a zipper in between them and whatever resources they need to get to the top of the mountain, survive a desperate situation, or increase their earnings when they get back down, many just help themselves. But even petty thefts at this altitude can be deadly.

Marcin Miotk, a Polish climber, arrived at Everest's Chinese Base Camp in May 2005, after making an unsuccessful attempt to climb Annapurna, the deadliest of the 8,000-meter peaks. He planned to ascend Everest solo, without Sherpas, and using no supplemental oxygen—the first Polish mountaineer to climb Everest without it. On

May 29, Marcin started toward the summit, stocking tents at Camp One and Camp Two with gear, but retreated to ABC due to high winds that made a summit attempt without bottled oxygen too dangerous. Austrian friends who continued up left a sleeping bag for him in Camp Three, the highest camp on the mountain.

Two days later, an unprecedented late weather window opened and Marcin headed for the summit, climbing fast enough to make it to Camp One at midday, which proved to be fortuitous. When he opened his tent flap, he found that it had been raided. The Gore-Tex clothes he had left there for extra warmth had been stolen. He was irritated, but could get by without the clothes, and had planned to climb all the way to Camp Two that day anyway. But when he arrived at Camp Two hours later, he discovered his tent there had also been pillaged, this time burglarized of equipment crucial to his survival—his sleeping bag, gloves, windstopper pants and jacket, socks, and headlamp. With night coming on, the situation was desperate, so Marcin borrowed an unused sleeping bag from a nearby tent, which he returned in the morning before heading up again. With no supplemental oxygen or extra layers of clothing, Marcin was vulnerable to the cold, but the loss of his headlamp was the real problem in continuing his ascent. Without it, he wouldn't be able to start the climb from Camp Three to the summit in the middle of the night as almost every other climber does, forcing him to make his summit bid dangerously late in the day and leaving him little time to make it back to his tent before dark. Since he was climbing without bottled gas, he already had very little margin for error. During his climb to Camp Three, Marcin passed nearly fifty climbers heading down the mountain and asked many of them to borrow a light. Nobody would lend him one. He moved in at Camp Three, set up his gear for the night, and started for the summit at five thirty the next morning, climbing without a backpack so as to move more quickly. All the other climbers he saw were on their way down, having already summited or turned back. Marcin reached the top at two thirty that afternoon, the last summit of the season. He was back at his tent between seven and seven thirty; the setting sun was just touching the horizon. Exhausted, he wanted only to crawl into his sleeping bag and start his stove. But his tent had been looted again. Marcin picked through the mess that was left and tried to find his equipment, but it was all gone. His sleeping bag, stove, extra clothes, even his medications had been stolen. And with the sun going down, he had only a few minutes to find replacements before he froze to death.

"Everything that seemed of any value was gone," Marcin wrote in an open letter to various mountaineering Web sites. "At 8300 meters, during summit push! . . . No shame, no ethics—only money counts."

Marcin crawled out of his tent screaming, although the wind was strong enough that nobody else in the camp heard him. Earlier in the season, Camp Three had been crowded by dozens of tents and climbers, but now there were only six or eight tents left. Everyone in camp would have known that the person they were stealing from was in the midst of his summit bid and would be desperate for the gear on his return.

"The robbery I experienced at Camp 3 was simply a robbery on my life," he wrote. "Had I been just a bit more tired, I would probably have entered the tent and my body would have been found there the next season."

Five hours earlier Marcin had summited Everest in the best of styles—alone, and without bottled oxygen. Now, after all three of his high camps had been burglarized, he faced the very real possibility of dying for lack of a stove and a sleeping bag. He summoned the last of his strength and staggered from tent to tent in the growing darkness to beg from the Sherpas still in camp for enough equipment to survive the night.

"Probably the same guys who stole my gear in the day," he wrote.

"The Sherpas have lost their honor in the past years. You can't even imagine how cunning they have become. Daring even—who will steal more, who will grab the most valuables—this is what the Sherpas are talking about when they are playing cards in Base Camp.

"In 98% of the population, Sherpas are great guys. But [they make] me think of them all in very dark colors . . . Because they tolerate the bad 2%."

It's a cold irony, Marcin points out, that often the best climbers, who are in small, independent groups or alone, are the easiest prey for thieves up high.

In an effort to preserve mountaineering's wholesome image, many expedition leaders and guides dismiss thefts as rare; but as weather windows opened up on other popular Himalayan peaks in 2005, it became clear that high-altitude burglaries were not isolated incidents. On Ama Dablam, an Italian climber who had remained in Base Camp while his teammates were climbing high on the mountain awoke in the night to a knife cutting through the back of his tent and a hand reaching in to grab his equipment. When he got out of his tent, he found the team's two other tents had already been slashed and emptied. Meanwhile, at Camp Two on the mountain's southwest ridge, guide Luis Benitez arrived to find climbers in his sleeping bags and helping themselves to his food and fuel. In late June, not a month after all three of Marcin's high camps were robbed, Czech climbers arriving in Camp Two on Nanga Parbat, the second-highest mountain in Pakistan, found that someone had used up or stolen all of their stove fuel. Three weeks later, a team of Kazak climbers on K2 in Pakistan returned to their Advanced Base Camp after resting lower on the mountain.

"At their arrival in ABC, the guys found out that someone has stolen all of their equipment, including crampons," the Web site Russiaclimb reported. "The final summit push is not happening."

The thefts ended the Kazaks' climb, but it could have been far worse, as an incident reported a day later from the mountain next door showed.

Don Bowie was already disgusted when he headed up Broad Peak, a mountain neighboring K2, for his second summit bid. During his first climb up high, Don had been in Camp Two when a renowned Polish climber, Artur Hajzer, who was at 7,850 meters on his way to the summit, fell and broke his ankle. At that altitude, many climbers consider a busted leg synonymous with death, but immediately after the accident, ten climbers from various countries formed a rescue team that would spend three days bringing Artur down. Don, who works with a Sierra Nevada sheriff's department search and rescue, headed up from Camp Two toward Camp Three to join in the effort. Though the mountain was packed with up to fifty climbers, they had about half as many people as they needed for the operation. Yet during the three days that Don pleaded over radios with climbers in every other camp, nobody else joined in the rescue. From Camp Two, he could look down on a large commercial team throwing a party in Base Camp. But when he called down for help, only one other climber pitched in. Some said they needed to save their strength for their summit bids. One commercial leader didn't even pass the request for help on to his team. And the climbers descending from Camp Three just passed by the rescuers. When the exhausted team got to the bottom of the peak, the other expeditions sent cooks and kitchen boys with no mountaineering equipment to help carry Artur to Base Camp.

Don was happy that the mountain was deserted when he went back a week later for his second attempt on the peak. There wouldn't be anybody around to rescue him if he got into trouble, but after his experience with Artur, he knew there were few people he could count on for a rescue anyway. Nonetheless, Don let everyone know that he was heading back up onto Broad Peak alone.

Don made it to Camp Two in a couple days, where he waited out a storm, passing the time with food, fuel, and a coffee-table book salvaged from the trash left by other expeditions. When the weather cleared, he climbed on to a point just below Camp Three, at 7,000 meters—23,000 feet. But he recognized that the fresh snow had created serious avalanche conditions. Climbers on K2 he spoke to over his radio reported that storms were about to slam the weather window shut. And the rescue a week earlier had weakened him far more than he had realized. Don gave up on reaching the summit and headed back down the mountain fast. Fresh snow and avalanches had buried the fixed ropes, and digging them out further drained the already exhausted climber. He was rappelling down the rope below the last camp on the mountain when he happened to look over his left shoulder.

"I caught something in my eye and immediately stopped," Don said.

The rope had been cut. He was within three feet of sliding off the end of his line and falling down the mountain.

"What the hell is going on?" he thought.

Maybe an avalanche or rockfall cut the line, he hoped, optimistically. Don got out his ice ax and downclimbed to a rock tower where he remembered that the next set of ropes was anchored. When he got on top of the pinnacle, he peeked over the edge. The rope and all the anchors that kept it in place were gone. In all, some 1,600 feet of rope had been taken from one of the most dangerous parts of the route. And like Marcin, Don was certain that the thieves knew they were likely killing the climber still high on the mountain above them.

Below, a thin layer of ice covered the steep gullies and vertical faces. If he didn't die in a fall when some piece of the mountain gave way, the rocks coming loose and tumbling down the vertical bowling alley would probably take him out. But it was the only way down. Don scrambled into the gully with no safety line.

The first rock to hit him, the size of a baseball, put a hole in his pack, smashed some gear, and nearly knocked him off the mountain. Even with his helmet on, it probably would have killed him had it struck his head.

"The very first one I took was a death blow," he said. "I thought my chances of falling or getting knocked off by rocks was pretty high. I was really surprised when I got down to lower sections of rock and mixed rock and ice that I had not been hit at that point any worse than I had."

It took two and a half hours for Don to downclimb a section that would take about fifteen minutes to rappel. He staggered away from the mountain, so exhausted that he was falling over, and having to sit and rest after each hundred meters he walked. He tried to remain vigilant; he didn't want to die on horizontal ground after making it through a downclimb that by all rights he shouldn't have survived. When he got to the alcove where he had stashed his food and equipment, he found what he expected: All of his supplies were gone.

The following month, the Alpine Club of Pakistan issued a press release.

*The Alpine Club of Pakistan has taken a serious note of theft
incidents which occurred on K-2 and Broad Peak recently,
and has decided to set up an Inquiry Committee under the
Chairmanship of renowned Pakistani mountaineer Col Sher
Khan to investigate into the allegations, identify the culprits,
and recommend suitable remedial measures for the avoidance
of such like incidents in the future.*

On September 7, at the Ministry of Tourism in Pakistan, an Inquiry Committee from the Alpine Club of Pakistan searched and
questioned a porter who had been working on K2 when the series
of thefts occurred on that mountain and Broad Peak next door, but
found none of any team's missing gear. No further investigation of
the thefts that plagued the 2005 climbing season has been reported.

Don Bowie learned for himself how effective law enforcement
was in the high peaks when, two years after his desperate retreat
from Broad Peak, he reached the summit of K2 during his second
trip to the Karakorum mountains. He and two teammates rescued
a collapsed climber as they climbed down from the top. But when
Don went to continue his descent the morning after he reached the
summit, he discovered that someone had taken his crampons—
theft would again threaten his life. With no way for his boots to find
purchase on the steep ice as he descended from the high camp, Don
eventually fell and would have slid off the mountain if he hadn't
crashed into a snow bank, tearing several ligaments in his leg.
Fearing he had broken his ankle, Don crawled down the mountain,
pleading for assistance from more than a dozen climbers who literally stepped over him rather than help. He eventually threatened to
impale passing climbers with his ice axe if they didn't drop a rope
for him to continue his descent.

Twelve

At 21,500 feet, Advanced Base Camp on the Chinese side of Everest is higher than the summit of North America's loftiest peak. Bodies waste away during the weeks climbers wait for their bones to squeeze out enough red blood cells to make a few minutes of survival at the summit possible. Nothing heals. Many mountaineers use pulse oximeters to test how saturated their blood is with oxygen, but even then, it's a guess as to when a body is prepared to climb to the summit. Until we felt we were ready, exhaustion and cold isolated us in the sprawling, nylon city.

Carolyn and I spent most of our time buried in sleeping bags so big they seemed like down caskets. We scratched notes into pads and tapped on keyboards until our fingers went numb, then shoved our wooden hands deep into the bags to bring them back to life. During storms, winds coming off the summit sounded like trains, rumbling in the distance, then blasting through the camp. The snow and subzero temperatures were inconveniences. But the wind was a killer, turning snowflakes into needles and driving the cold deep into our bones. After the windstorms, climbers staggered through their sites to gather their shredded tents. Some camps looked like the debris fields from a tornado, full of snapped poles and tattered fabric, but with tables full of food left untouched. Our tents survived the mountain weather, but the closer we moved to the summit, the more Everest seemed to tear at the fabric of the team.

We drew names from a hat to determine which Sherpa would work for which climber, but Chuck interrupted the ceremony.

"I want to talk about e-mail," he said.

George had hounded Carolyn and me to provide e-mail and satellite phone service to him and the rest of the team. He bristled when we responded that we didn't have enough resources for everyone. Now Chuck, who had initially complained that we were bringing any communication equipment at all, chimed in with a new tune.

"I've got a business to run," he said.

Later, Bill called another meeting. "We've got to drop all this fighting," he said tersely, trying to end the bickering. "It's hurting the team."

Although George had told us he preferred to spend his time in the cook tent, most of us were surprised at how rarely he came into the dining tent where his teammates gathered, and that he shared none of our meals. But during the Buddhist ceremonies, known as *pujas*, held to bless the team, George took center stage, kneeling beside the monk for the duration of the event, while the other climbers gathered at a more respectful distance. Sherpas won't climb without holding a *puja* to ask the gods' permission to climb. But Lhakpa, a Sherpa who grew up Buddhist, attended none of the hours-long ceremonies, and her absence made us uneasy. As we moved up the mountain, our co-leader was even more remote. She refused to wear sunglasses in the withering glare of sun on snow, and was laid up snowblind when we moved in at Advanced Base Camp.

I heard her arguing with George.

"I want to go down," she said.

"It's like *Survivor*," Anne said. "With all the alliances."

"Or *Lord of the Flies*," Carolyn responded.

Walking past the cook tent, Bill overheard George showing off his new camera to Dan Lochner. He could afford it, Bill recalled George saying, because he didn't need to hire a Sherpa. He knew members of the Connecticut team weren't going to make it. He would use their Sherpas.

"It will get better when we start climbing," Anne said.

"Yeah," I responded sarcastically. "Sure. It will get better when we get to the 'death zone.'"

Dan Lochner and Dan Meggitt nicknamed their parlor-size tent the Pleasure Dome for its music, Christmas lights, and beer. Although women allegedly led the Connecticut team, a stack of pornographic magazines discouraged them from visiting what quickly became the expedition's most popular common area. So when the Dans invited not only me, but also Carolyn, into their Pleasure Dome, something was up. When George's generator had broken down a few days earlier, we had asked the Dans if we could use theirs. Now they had decided against helping us.

"I can't see where you two have done anything for the Connecticut Everest Expedition," Dan Meggitt declared, a surprising statement considering neither of the Dans were a part of the expedition or had had anything to do with putting it together.

Until then, Carolyn and I had managed to file blogs or stories almost daily, even when one of our computers died and the other's battery failed. Now we were doomed to spend days hiking tent-to-tent to panhandle 21,000 feet above sea level for the power to do our work. George was the only other member of the Connecticut expedition in the tent when we were cut off from the generator. He sat with Guillermo on a cot and looked away when we glanced at him.

A few minutes later, when we told Anne and Bill about our

MICHAEL KODAS

predicament, Guillermo stuck his head into the dining tent to ask for Bill's credit card to pay for George's satellite phone fees.

"That's not the way a team's supposed to work," I heard Bill snap when he left the tent to speak with George.

"This expedition is a fraud," he said when he returned. "I feel extremely betrayed by George. All those e-mails I got before we left [the United States] to get me to do things, saying, 'You can't say no to me this time.' You never even see him unless he needs something from you.

"I kept thinking that when I got up on the mountain, I would get more excited about climbing and get past the troubles. It hasn't worked that way. I just can't get past the B.S. It has changed this mountain for me. I just don't have the patience for it anymore.

"I know I can climb this mountain," Bill said. After watching him claw his way up the steep snow and ice to the North Col, none of us doubted it. The grin beaming from his face when he got back showed how much he wanted it.

"But I can't sleep at night worrying about the things that are going on with the team," he said. "I am up every night thinking about it. I can tell you how many squares of ripstop [fabric] are in the roof of my tent."

The following night, after dinner, Bill broke out a bottle of Canadian whiskey and broke the news. This was no longer a team he wanted to be a part of.

"I am probably going down tomorrow, and I am not coming back up for a lot of reasons that some people know about and some people do not," Bill told the startled group. "There is a lot of stuff I'm going to leave, so let me know if you're going to need anything. I am going to leave a lot of food. I'm leaving a sleeping bag for Dawa [his Sherpa].

"Dave," he said to teammate Dave Watson, "if you want a Sherpa, I've paid for him and already given him a pretty good tip."

He left us his oxygen, too—four bottles worth more than $400 each. Altogether his gifts to his teammates were worth nearly $6,000.

George and Lhakpa, dining in the cook tent during Bill's announcement, didn't find out he was leaving until he was putting on

164

his pack early the next day. George pulled him aside to try to patch things up, but Bill was fed up. He was going home.

Fabiola waited a long time for Hector Ponce de Leon to come down from his room at the Kathmandu Hyatt. Short, with a goatee and glasses, Hector normally looks a bit bookish. When Fabiola first saw him, he seemed small and remote. She worried that his remorse about her father was making it difficult for him to speak with her. He was hoarse from his climb, his voice little more than a whisper as he told her how sorry he was. But as Rhonda Martin and Fabiola told their stories, she could see anger brewing in Hector. His voice was no longer soft or slow when it was his turn to speak.

Hector had been suspicious of Gustavo Lisi the first time he met him, which was in Base Camp on Cho Oyu. It was 1995.

"We were just absolutely shocked about how can anyone like him with such poor judgment, such incompetence and such a character could even think about climbing a mountain like Cho Oyu," Hector, who was leading the expedition, said. "Quite young, inexperienced, not a strong climber, not a skillful climber. I didn't like him from that very first moment."

Many climbers get in a bit over their heads on their first 8,000-meter peak.

"He'll learn," Hector had tried to convince himself.

But as the weeks on Cho Oyu rolled by, he worried that Gustavo didn't take the dangers and difficulties of high-altitude climbing seriously.

"He was always hiding something," Hector says. "He was not straight about what he was going to do or how he felt. And if there was any kind of obstacle or setback, his reaction was not at all, from my point of view, good."

When carrying gear to upper camps, Gustavo returned to Base Camp with his pack still loaded with equipment critical to the climb up high. The blunder brought on chuckles from other climbers, but Hector noted how the Argentinean just shrugged off his responsibility, along with his backpack of gear.

"Even back then, I thought 'There's something wrong with this guy.'"

Neither climber had made it to the top of Cho Oyu on that trip, but in the years since, Hector had put together an impressive résumé in the Himalaya. He had climbed Pakistan's 8,000-meter giants Broad Peak and Gasherbrum II. He was on the north side of Everest during the killer storm of 1996, on K2 in 2002, and had guided Everest for Mountain Madness during the 2003 anniversary season. For the 2004 season, he had come back to Everest as a cameraman and character in the Discovery Channel's *Ultimate Survival: Everest.*

When Hector got to Base Camp, he checked in with some of his friends on the other Spanish and Latin American teams. Despite the coverage in *Desnivel,* the Spanish climbing magazine, the story of Gustavo's theft of Juan Carlos Gonzalez's summit photos and his false claim of reaching the summit in 2000 was still unknown among most mountaineers. But among many of the Spanish-speaking climbers Hector visited, there was a palpable sense of outrage that Gustavo not only was back on the mountain but had someone paying him to lead him to the top.

"How in the world did this poor man happen to fall into Gustavo's hands?" Hector thought to himself. "Does he have a clue who this person is?"

Annabelle Bond, a subject in the documentary that Hector was filming, wondered if Gustavo's client knew about his guide's past and whether they should say something.

For Annabelle, the Khumbu Icefall proved the most terrifying part of her trip up Everest, and perhaps of the entire year she spent climbing the Seven Summits, which she did faster than any woman had before her. But as dizzyingly out of place as she felt on the catwalks across the icefall's crevasses, the Hollywood-polished blonde would have looked right at home on a fashion-show runway. The daughter of Sir John Bond, chairman of HSBC Bank, Annabelle had been born in Singapore, grown up in Indonesia and Hong Kong, and attended boarding school in England and finishing school in Switzerland before moving to New York when she was seventeen. She had ridden a horse across Ecuador, run the Inca Trail, and learned polo in Argentina and mountaineering in New Zealand and South America. Her climb on Everest had been born when Lady Bond—probably the only woman in history to arrange for her daughter to climb Mount Everest—met Chilean banker Andronico Luksic at a party in London. Andronico was putting together one of the most elaborately provisioned Everest climbs of the 2004 season.

"My daughter's a climber," Lady Bond had said, as if she had just found the perfect summer camp for her child.

The ladders of the icefall, often several of them lashed together to cross the widest of the huge slots in the ice, are clichés in the mountaineering world. That doesn't inspire any extra confidence in climbers who are making their first steps on the sagging, springing, swaying spans. Annabelle first crossed them on her hands and knees. Seracs towered over the climbers like the buildings Annabelle had worked among in Hong Kong. Blocks of ice the size of houses had fallen from some of the pinnacles.

Annabelle and the rest of the Chilean expedition had made a few forays into the icefall before they dared to climb all the way through it, heading to the first of the ladders to practice crossing them so that when the time came to make their way through the maze of ice, they could get out of the danger zones fast. On their first trip as a team into the icefall, they had stopped at a wide crevasse that was crossed by two ladders tied together. Another climber was already clipped into the rope, taking a lesson in crossing the crevasse from a Sherpa. The climber awkwardly moved his spiked feet from rung to rung until he made it back onto solid snow, then looked up from his feet to see the Chileans. He smiled back at Annabelle when she said hello, then introduced himself to Rodrigo Jordan, the leader of the Chilean team. He said his name was Gustavo, and explained that he was a guide. He was leading someone up the mountain.

"A guide training with a Sherpa?" Annabelle thought. "And

where's his client? Why isn't that person getting this lesson? Does he know that his guide doesn't know how to cross the ladders in the icefall?"

Even with her limited experience at high-altitude mountaineering, Annabelle saw that it was a strange situation, and it worried her. Although the Sherpas are the best performers at altitude, few of them have the communication and logistical skills to guide, teach, or lead. It was like an airline pilot getting flying lessons from a flight attendant.

"I'm glad he's not my guide," she thought to herself.

Rodrigo, a professor of management at a Chilean university and one of a handful of climbers to scale Everest's Kangshung Face, ran his expedition with businesslike precision. When Annabelle gathered with him and the rest of her team, she found that they were chatting about the strange situation while they waited their turns on the ladder. Kiko Guzman, a guide with Annabelle's team, noticed that Gustavo seemed awkward and uncomfortable on the ladders. In the weeks to come, Kiko crossed paths twice with both Gustavo and Nils as they made their way up and down the mountain. But he never saw them together, which, considering that Gustavo had only one client to look after, struck him as strange and reckless.

Annabelle and her teammates didn't think too much more about Gustavo until they sat down with Hector Ponce de Leon in Base Camp.

"I wouldn't go anywhere with Gustavo," Hector said. "I can say that much."

But in the end, none of the climbers in Base Camp who knew of Gustavo's past warned his client. When Hector finally met Nils, he ended up having to lead him out of harm's way himself, and that alone, he hoped, would be enough to show Nils how dangerous his guide was.

On May 7, Hector had a big day ahead of him. He started from Base Camp before dawn and made it to Camp Two at about seven a.m. About an hour later, as he continued up, Hector noticed three people climbing ahead of him on the Lhotse Face, and was immediately worried. The rising sun bakes the face, and as the snow softens and ice begins to fall with the rising temperature, the climbing becomes difficult, dangerous, and slow. Almost every other climber between Camps Two and Three had set out by five in the morning to finish their climbs before the sun reflecting off of the Lhotse Face made them feel like they were walking on lava rather than snow. Hector was late himself that day because he was climbing all the way from Base Camp to Camp Three—effectively cramming three days' climbing into one. It was after one p.m. when he reached Nils, Gustavo, and one of their Sherpas.

"How can anyone move so slow?" he thought.

He didn't exchange words with any of them, but he remembers Gustavo's cough. The frigid, dry, often gritty air of high altitude had Gustavo heaving over and hacking between each step.

Hector headed for his tent, which he had set up well away from the rest of Camp Three, only to learn that the climbers he had just passed were camped right in front of him. That was when he recognized Gustavo and said hi to him, but not much more. At least he speaks Spanish, Hector thought after chatting briefly with Nils, so he might already know about Gustavo's previous trip to Everest. Big Dorjee and Mingma arrived, and they argued about a problem with the team's food, although Hector couldn't tell what. As it turned out, neither Gustavo nor the Sherpas had brought food for their stay up high, leaving them only crackers and a few snacks to fuel their efforts. Hector dropped by their tent to give them some coffee when he learned they had nothing to brew into a hot drink.

The next morning, Hector and two Sherpas fixed ropes and shot video above Camp Three. They started back down for Base Camp by noon, again noticing that there were only two dots on the glacier below the Lhotse Face, on their way down to Camp Two.

"Wow, they're really moving slow, even going down," Hector thought.

When Hector looked down at Gustavo and Nils again, he was shocked. One of the climbers had moved well ahead of the other and was making his way into camp. The other was at least an hour away from the tents, struggling to find his way alone through the crevasses between the face and the camp. Although there are ropes to cross the worst of the slots, a few required jumps where a stumble could lead to an injury or worse.

"That's terrible," Hector thought, "Gustavo's left him behind."

For Hector, there is no exception to the rule that a guide is "roped up" with his client in crevasse terrain. It was absolutely incomprehensible that a leader would leave a paying customer behind on an unfamiliar glacier.

Hector was reminded throughout his expedition of what it felt like to be left behind. Andres Delgado, his former climbing partner and a man he had himself rescued, abandoned Hector when he had fallen in a crevasse a few years earlier. With Andres back on Everest, the tension between the climbers became a subplot in the Discovery Channel documentary.

Hector made his way down the Lhotse Face as fast he could, jumping across the large crevasse at the bottom so that he could reach the abandoned client before something terrible happened. When he caught up with Nils, the doctor was trashed—badly dehydrated, disoriented, and delirious. He was past the worst of the crevasses and on an obvious path that had been beaten into the snow by hundreds of boots, but Nils told Hector he couldn't see the way to go.

"Just stay right behind me," Hector said. "And in twenty or twenty-five minutes we'll be in Camp Two."

Once Hector had Nils away from the slots and within 100 meters of the camp, he raced ahead and found Gustavo lying on his back, taking in the sun outside his tent.

"What the fuck are you doing?" he cursed at the guide. "Your client is back there. Go back and get him."

Gustavo walked out to lead his client into camp. Hector thought about warning Nils about his guide, but continued to Base Camp without saying anything.

"I still regret [not saying anything]," Hector told Fabiola. "I want to think it would not have made any difference. I thought then, 'This man really, really doesn't have the strength to climb Everest—the physical stamina or strength. He just moves too slowly.' So I thought if Gustavo still has some honesty, decency, whatever you want to call it, he should turn him around."

Gustavo Lisi had made plenty of serious mistakes during the climb, Hector points out. But lies were not mistakes. They were intentional frauds against his client. Had Nils known that Gustavo hadn't really been to the top of Everest before, not only would he never have hired him to guide him there, but the lie, and the theft of Juan Carlos's photos that he committed to support it, would have prevented the doctor from climbing with him at all.

"He really, really had to summit," Hector told me of Gustavo. "Of course, Dr. Nils could at any point also make that decision for himself, like, 'This is as far as I'm going.' But that's why you hire a guide. The guide is there to tell you no matter how badly you want to summit, 'OK, I am sending you down.' That's for me the main responsibility that you have as a guide on an 8,000-meter mountain."

While Nils Antezana was making life-and-death decisions based on a lie, in Gustavo, Hector believes, the hidden truth turned into a cancerous summit fever that could only be cured by reaching the top of the mountain.

"I think Dr. Nils's fate was sealed the moment he hired Gustavo as a guide. [Gustavo] had a personal agenda . . . there is no way he was going to turn Dr. Nils around."

Thirteen

On most mornings, climbers on the steep headwalls atop the Rongbuk Glacier look like fence posts in the snow. Their movements are almost imperceptible as they march a serpentine route through snowy slopes and ice cliffs to the North Col, a saddle-shaped dip in the North Ridge of Everest. At Camp One, atop the Col, more than fifty red and yellow mountaineering tents were spread in rows atop the glacier like jewels on satin.

Anne Parmenter and I took nearly seven hours to complete our first trip to Camp One. We were desperately out of breath throughout the frigid, strenuous, wind-blasted slog. It was the most fun we'd had since leaving the United States. "We're finally climbing," Anne said, grinning between gasps.

My own smile faded when I saw my wife upon my return to Advanced Base Camp, where she had waited while Anne and I climbed. It struck me that she was emaciated. Altitude sickness had had her throwing up most of her meals during the previous weeks, leaving her weak with hunger. Eventually, my already slender wife

Dan Meggitt asked to videotape our current argument while it was raging, but an uneasy truce developed before he got his camera set up. George agreed to let us use his repaired generator. I asked George about the conversation Bill had overheard about taking other climbers' Sherpas. He replied that climbers who turned back surely would let their resources go to the good of the team, wouldn't they?

Outside, Carolyn and Anne sat with Lhakpa, with whom they had not conversed in weeks. When they asked if George had forbidden her to talk to us, her eyes filled with tears. She changed the subject.

Carolyn and I descended to Base Camp the following morning. Anne, hoping to clear a bad cough, came down a day later. While Carolyn and I were on our way down, my editors at the *Courant* received an e-mail from George Martin, the proprietor of EverestNews .com. Attached was George Dijmarescu's four-and-a-half-page rebuttal to my stories, Carolyn's blogs, and the "serious accusations" they contained. He requested that the *Courant*, as well as Martin's Web site, print his version of events:

Let me [start] by saying that the idea of this expedition belongs to me and I did pull all the members into it.

. . . I would [inform] you that the friction was started when those employees of Hartford Courant *changed the rules during the game . . . The friction was and is constant because these people want to drive this truck where their corporate bosses wanted to.*

After his initial complaints that the *Courant* and I weren't providing him and the rest of the team with e-mail and satellite phone service, he accused Bill Driggs, ironically the team's only admitted George W. Bush supporter, of promoting a "socialist-liberal philosophy" with his desire for teamwork.

[Bill's] socialist agenda wasn't going to work here and he eventually find himself on a collision course with my philosophy of climbing . . . I lived in communist Romania [where] I

would lose twenty-five pounds. Her hair fell out in clumps and her teeth ached from the lost enamel.

While I was at Camp One, Carolyn had spent her time alone in the dining tent in ABC. At lunch the cook brought her a plate with some coleslaw and two pieces of bread, meager rations compared with what the climbers were served. When she went to the cook tent to get more food, she was shocked to find Mingma Gelu, Lhakpa's brother, serving himself a plateful of stew. She described the event in her blog.

"I want what everyone else is eating. Chicken, I don't care," Carolyn said.

Lhakpa followed her back to the dining tent. "You want chicken, you must pay!" she insisted.

The cook returned to the dining tent with a smile and a steaming serving of yak meat, rice, and soup for Carolyn.

The broth went down OK, but Carolyn vomited the stew on top of the rest of her meal. For a few moments she considered forcing the whole mess back down her throat. "Dogs do it all the time, don't they?"

Instead, she dumped her plate into what she thought was a trash bag, but was actually a sack of food. Our cook was understandably angry.

George responded to Carolyn's blog posts complaining about the rations in his own blog, filed days later, in which he told of a party celebrating Dan Lochner's twenty-second birthday, held while Carolyn, Anne, and I were away. The event was complete with "Jell-O shots" provided by Chuck and Dave and a cake too big for the climbers to finish. His report appeared on EverestNews .com, where George has filed extensive reports during his Everest climbs.

"Carolyn is a reporter with trekking permit, we cannot let our kitchen resources go to a person who has no ambition or right to climb this mountain," he wrote after Carolyn complained that she couldn't find the cook and get a meal in Base Camp. "How unfair for her to claim that some how Asian Trekking should send a cook down and [leave] us climbers exposed with only one cook."

George didn't mention that, even after one of our kitchen boys took sick, we still had two cooks and, according to Dawa Sherpa at Asian Trekking, Carolyn's $3,800 permit paid for the food and services of the cook that George claimed she had no right to.

Anne and I had other problems with food.

Our Sherpas, Dawa Nuru and Mingma Gelu, surprised us the morning we left for the North Col by demanding $200 each to buy "Sherpa food"—the food they would eat in the high camps. It was the first we had heard of the special meals our Sherpas expected us to provide at high camps, and the price they quoted was more than twice what we had already spent on high-altitude food. Although we had brought more than enough to feed them too, our provisions didn't suit their tastes. We asked them to wait a day for the money so we could complete our climb to Camp One, but when we returned from our overnight on the North Col, they announced they were quitting. To stay on, they demanded that we not only pay for their high-altitude food—we gave them $100 each—but also fork over more than $1,600 each for work they had yet to complete, tips they normally wouldn't receive until the end of the expedition. Anne asked Chuck and Dave if they had paid their Sherpas the same fees.

"Yeah, we've worked it out," Chuck said.

"You guys just need to develop a personal relationship with your Sherpa," said Dave, who had never before climbed with a Sherpa but was now using the one that Bill had paid for.

I thought it unlikely that the Sherpas we paid more than $6,000 to hire and equip would abandon us because we weren't pals. But the morning after Anne and I agreed to our Sherpas' demands, Lhakpa, angered by some of Anne's comments on Carolyn's blog, ordered her brother to dump Anne's gear out of his pack.

"You no help Anne," Lhakpa shouted.

Mingma Gelu pulled the gear from his pack, but in the end carried it up for her anyway.

In the days before our climb to the North Col, Anne had watched as Lhakpa, who rarely carried a pack herself, checked the bags carried by friends and family working for other expeditions. Lhakpa coaxed those whose packs seemed light to carry some of her own

gear. When Anne ended up carrying some of the equipment that Mingma Gelu was supposed to haul to Camp One, she wondered aloud whose gear the Sherpa she was paying had in his pack.

"Anne, you a big mouth," Lhakpa shouted when she heard of Anne's comments. "You no want Everest. Go home!"

My relationship with our Everest veterans was even worse.

I'm going to sue you, or I am going to whack you!" George screamed when I stuck my head into the Pleasure Dome.

"Are you threatening my life?" I asked.

"Yes, motherfucker," he screamed. "I am threatening you!"

George had been unable to read my stories and Carolyn's blogs when his computer broke down. But since reconnecting to the Internet with Dan Lochner's computer the day before, he had been raging about our reports about the disintegrating team. Carolyn and I had planned to hike down from ABC to Base Camp in hopes that the richer air would help Carolyn get over her nausea and heal my sore throat. As we prepared to descend, we heard George boasting of the ways he could "make an accident" happen to me, such as tampering with oxygen equipment.

"I'm going to burn their tent down!" he shouted.

Before we headed down, I stopped at the Pleasure Dome, both to offer George the chance to air his grievances in my next story, and to find out if it would be safe for me to rejoin the climbing team when I returned to Advanced Base Camp.

The squabble lasted nearly four hours. George bragged that he had most of the residents of our camp working against me. Chuck's and Dave's change of heart about technology and demands for e-mail, he said, came from him. When I loaned George our satellite phone for an emergency call to Kathmandu, Guillermo had dialed through the device's menus to check the numbers we had called, the Mexican climber told us. George claimed that he sent D Lochner to eavesdrop on the phone calls Carolyn and I had m from our tent, and that the Dans had secretly videotaped us they told us they were cutting us off from power.

was told when and what to speak. If some members of this ex-
pedition long for such a [socialist] life style, they are free to
[live] in such society, I found Capitalist America and I love it.

George denied that the snowball- and rock-throwing caused any tension, and took offense that we somehow implied that Lhakpa had participated, although we never wrote anything about Lhakpa throwing rocks. He admitted to cutting us off from power with "a video camera rolling which secretly recorded all the conversation, so dear *Hartford Courant* don't run garbage journalism cause I have it on tape . . . Yes I cut Michael and Carolyn from the generator but nobody else."

George claimed our descriptions of the problems with food were also inaccurate. "Carolyn got the same rations as everybody else," he said. Dawa Nuru and Mingma Gelu quit working for Anne and me because, although we had offered them all of the same food that we had, he claimed that the "sherpa were left with no food."

He said my reporting was hurting his family and his business:

I spoke with my family this morning and they informed me
that lots of my customers and neighbors came with the paper
in hand asking for some sort of explanations . . . my mother
started crying and it ripped my heart.

He finished his screed with barbs for the flagship of the *Courant* and a long-distance embrace of his daughter.

Chicago Tribune gets [sic] this trash out of Advance Base
Camp of Everest, there are already enough polluters here.
  Best wishes to all and especially: Sunny my dearest daugh-
ter, I can't wait to see you, you give me the joy and strength to
do this again, and I will do it for you . . . This misleading jour-
nalism should not effect [sic] you, your father is a decent man
and a man of honor.
  . . . I want only peace and good will to all the members . . .
Connecticut I am not the villain.

. . .

Carolyn, Anne, and I didn't need to stay at Interim Camp during our climb down to Base Camp, but we knew we would have to on our return trip up to ABC. During our descent, we each checked on the tent we had left at the midway camp, which the entire team had agreed to leave set up to make sure sick climbers had a place to stay in an emergency. The tent was missing again.

I saw George's note when I arrived in Base Camp. And there were other unexpected messages. Russell Brice wanted to talk to me. Brice, an Everest legend from New Zealand, has been climbing in the Himalaya for thirty years, ten of them running commercial expeditions to Everest. In 2003, on his thirteenth Everest expedition, all his clients reached the summit. In 2004, more than 100 people lived in his tents, which spread out in long rows like a suburban subdivision. By 2006, Russell's company, Himalayan Experience— or HimEx—had put 270 people atop 8,000-meter peaks. He'd lost only one client, a friend of his who died while trying to snowboard from Everest's summit.

In the frontier town that is Everest Base Camp, Russell is something akin to Wyatt Earp. Not everyone agrees with the rules he and the rest of the mountain's most experienced guides try to impose, but while they are certainly most beneficial to the guides who impose them, they're the only order high on the mountain. On a hilltop overlooking his sprawling camp is a collection of memorials to legendary climbers who perished on Everest, such as Peter Boardman and Joe Tasker, who vanished in 1982 trying to climb the Pinnacles on Everest's Northeast Ridge—a route that Russell himself eventually made the first ascent of. As we sat amid the shrines talking, it was clear that Russell saw me and the rest of my team as badly out of place.

Everest guides are a moody bunch. With hundreds of thousands of dollars invested in an endeavor that is, by definition, uncertain; an army's worth of equipment, logistics, and staff to manage; and the very real possibility that the service they are selling will kill some of their customers, it's not surprising. Russell is as gruff as they come, known to simply walk away in the middle of conversations without so much as an "excuse me." But after the years he's worked on Everest, he has good cause. He had problems with our expedition, and George in particular.

"He's cheating you guys," Russell said. "He organizes an expedition and doesn't take responsibility."

He was getting cheated too, Russell said. We proudly told climbers outside our team that, although we had two Everest veterans on our expedition, we were climbing without guides. But Russell said we were really just parasites feeding off the work and resources of better-provisioned expeditions. Each year, Russell hosts a meeting in Advanced Base Camp to determine what each expedition will contribute toward installing the ropes that are critical to the safety of all the climbers on the mountain. George had us descend from ABC the day before this year's conference. The rest of the team didn't hear about the meeting for nearly a week, but Russell said he had notified George about it. A sponsor had provided ropes for us to contribute to the effort. When we picked up the ropes from our outfitter in Connecticut, I watched Chuck swap the spools of narrow cord most appropriate for fixing on high mountains for thick ropes best suited for the kind of rock and ice climbing he guides in New England. Chuck kept the team's ropes in his expedition barrels. Now Russell told me he had never received them, and he wasn't interested in getting them anymore. Months later, when we returned to the States, Chuck announced that he had kept the ropes to put to use in his guiding business.

The expeditions that did pitch in to the effort to make the climbing route safe managed to fix ropes only up to Camp Three, the last camp before the summit. Russell had enough cordage to equip the rest of the route to the summit, but wouldn't put it up until his clients were climbing. Those who went for the summit earlier would hang on old and dangerously tattered lines.

Stringing more than 10,000 feet of cord from ABC to the summit of Everest is not a negligible expense. In 2006, when Russell's Sherpas fixed the ropes up the entire route and set a record early summit in the process, his records showed he spent $32,160 on the ropes and anchors, and the salaries and bonuses of the Sherpas who put them up. Although most teams on the mountain promised to help out with manpower, ropes, or cash, Russell's spreadsheet showed that he got $14,800 back—less than half his outlay.

The human toll, however, was far higher. Tuk Bahadur Thapa, a new employee of Himalayan Experience, developed pulmonary edema during the early effort to fix the ropes. His co-workers carried him off the mountain, but barely a mile from Base Camp, he died. Days later, on the south side of the mountain, a tower of ice collapsed in the Khumbu Icefall, killing Ang Phinjo Sherpa, Lhakpa Tseri Sherpa, and Dawa Temba Sherpa, all of whom were preparing the route for the coming onslaught of climbers on the Nepal side. More than a third of the death toll for the season—the second highest on record—would be Sherpas who were putting in the equipment to keep Western climbers safe. Russell wept when he gathered his team in a dining tent to tell them of his employee's death. The insurance Russell provided, along with the salary, bonuses, and tips Tuk Bahadur had earned before his death, would help provide for the dead Sherpa's family. Russell promised to raise money to send his employee's children to school. Nonetheless, a family in the poorest nation in south Asia had just lost their breadwinner, and most Sherpas and porters working Everest are not as well taken care of as Russell Brice's. So it's understandable that the boasts of "solo" climbers, who claim that they made it to the summit without Sherpa support but in reality clipped into the highway of ropes that Russell's Sherpas risked their lives to put in place, ring dissonantly in the guide's ears.

On the other hand, it's not surprising that many mountaineers bristle when they arrive at a peak to find a toll road to the summit. Some suspect those who collect the fee of running a money-making scheme rather than trying to make the mountain safe. But to me, $100 each to have fresh ropes well anchored to the route seemed a bargain. Other climbers, including several on my own team, didn't agree. In the end, more than half the climbers on the north side of Everest in 2004, including the Connecticut team, clipped into the ropes without making any financial or physical contribution to putting them there. Anne and I offered to pay our share when we learned that our teammates hadn't contributed the ropes we had brought for the effort, but Russell, disgusted by the whole affair, declined our offer.

He said our expedition was causing problems lower on the mountain too. One of our three cooks was sent down alone to Base Camp when he became altitude sick. Sherpas from another expedition found him in our cook tent three days later and were convinced he was dying. They took him first to a nearby Russian expedition that medicated him, then to an Indian expedition where he was put in a Gamow bag. When Russell heard about the sick cook, he brought him to his camp and put him on oxygen. Despite his tough exterior, many climbers recall Russell having provided them oxygen, food, medications, and shelter when they were in trouble. When I first met him, he told me that HimEx climbers had been involved in fifteen rescues on Everest. But he also pointed out that two of his own climbers refused orders to turn back in 2001, got stuck out overnight, and were rescued by guides from International Mountain Guides— a point he shared to highlight how some commercial operations help one another out. Expeditions like ours, which can't even take care of their own, now show up on the mountain, whether they admit it or not, in the position of having to piggyback on well-resourced operations for more than just rope.

"The kitchen boy was sent down with no support and no medicine," Russell charged. "I used two bottles of oxygen to care for [him]. Am I ever going to get that back from George?"

Experience made him confident he could forecast our future. "You're going to run out of food," he said, predicting as well that the shortage of provisions would end some climbers' chances for the summit.

"He probably didn't tell you about the tip structure for the Sherpas' trips to high camps," Russell added. We told him that George had each climber who wanted help from a Sherpa hire one individually.

"That's not how you do it," Russell said incredulously. "You hire your Sherpas as a team."

Russell said that when he had first come to Everest, climbers had banded together and helped one another out. Today, he said, many hide to avoid responsibility or lurk in the shadows to exploit other teams.

"These people are in my tents, in my sleeping bags, using my gas, and eating my food," he said.

Russell Brice has had oxygen bottles stolen and tents thrown from the mountain, filled with crucial equipment. In 2005, a cache of ropes his Sherpas had stashed high on the mountain—ropes intended to keep every climber headed to the summit safe—was stolen before they could be put in place. In 2006, thieves unbolted and carted away the huge battery that powered the production studio set up by the Discovery Channel.

"I drop oxygen at Camp Three, and [someone comes] and takes it, and it's not there for my client," Russell said. "That's manslaughter."

His tents were once open to any climber desperate for a port in a storm. These days, there are often locks on the doors.

Back at our dining tent, our cook laughed when we told him our own tent was stolen from Interim Camp. He took us into the team's tent of kitchen supplies and opened a large white bag. The missing tent was hidden inside. Lhakpa, he said, had the tent sent down with porters after we had left the camp.

Mount Everest as seen from the summit of Ama Dablam in the Solu Khumbu valley of Nepal. (Photo by Michael Kodas)

Nils Antezana climbing early in the morning on May 16, 2004, the day he reached the summit of Everest and was later abandoned on the mountain by his guide and Sherpas. (Photo courtesy the Antezana family)

Big Dorjee Sherpa, *below*, had reached the summit of Everest ten times by 2004, the year he climbed with Nils Antezana and left his client to die on the mountain.
(Photo by Michael Kodas)

Gustavo Lisi, *right*, guided Nils Antezana on an ascent of a mountain in Bolivia before the two climbers headed to Everest together.
(Photo courtesy the Antezana family)

Lhakpa Sherpa climbs up the East Rongbuk Glacier on her way to Camp One on Mount Everest. (Photo by Michael Kodas/*The Hartford Courant*)

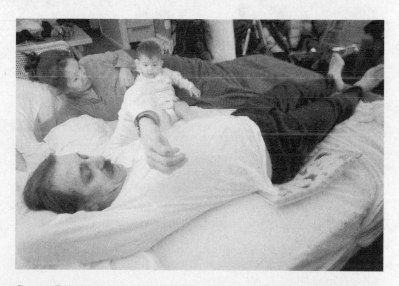

George Dijmarescu, *bottom*, Lhakpa Sherpa, *top*, with their daughter, Sunny, before George headed out for a climb in New Hampshire's Presidential Range. (Photo by Michael Kodas/*The Hartford Courant*)

A porter carries a huge load across the hanging bridge below Namche Bazaar, in the Solu Khumbu valley of Nepal leading to Mount Everest. (Photo by Michael Kodas)

Bill Driggs heads out for a climb from ABC to Camp One on the North Col of Mount Everest in Tibet. (Photo by Michael Kodas/*The Hartford Courant*)

Hartford Courant journalist Carolyn Moreau rests in Base Camp during the meltdown of the Connecticut Everest Expedition.
(Photo by Michael Kodas/ *The Hartford Courant*)

Tibetan women in Chinese Base Camp on Mount Everest peddle goods and services to arriving Western mountaineers. (Photo by Michael Kodas)

Camp One on the Tibetan side of Everest during the 2004 Everest climbing season. (Photo by Michael Kodas/*The Hartford Courant*)

In Camp One, Mingma Gelu Sherpa, *left*, and Dawa Nuru Sherpa prepare to leave behind Michael Kodas and Anne Parmenter, the climbers who paid nearly $10,000 to hire them.
(Photo by Michael Kodas/*The Hartford Courant*)

Everest, *left*, and Nuptse catch the last rays of the setting sun.
(Photo by Michael Kodas)

Climbers on the North Ridge of Mount Everest approach Camp Two
during the 2004 spring climbing season.
(Photo by Michael Kodas/*The Hartford Courant*)

Fourteen

Our days back in Base Camp should have been relaxing. However, our rest was overshadowed not only by the mountain but by the knowledge that we would have to go back up onto it. I looked at the sunny pyramid a dozen miles away, knowing that ragged ropes provided little security for my team's attempt on the summit and that the weather window was closing in around it as well. The Italian team initially planned to summit during the same predicted stretch of sunny, calm days that we did, but had changed their minds. Their forecast now showed the break in the storms closing almost as soon as it opened. Russell Brice wouldn't say when his $10,000 weather report told him to send his climbers up, but he made it clear that it wasn't now. And not only would we race the jet stream on bad roads, but Anne and I would pay for our rest in Base Camp with exhaustion during our summit bid if we stuck to the schedule that George and Dawa Nuru insisted on for a May 20 summit. While the rest of the team had been resting in ABC for weeks, we would have to hike thirteen miles and climb nearly 4,000 feet in the two days before starting the climb in earnest.

Nonetheless, I knew the team would insist on heading for the summit as soon as we trudged back to Advanced Base Camp. The only real shock was that Anne and I went along with it. Two days later, when Anne and I staggered into the Connecticut expedition's dining tent in ABC, we didn't have a chance to sit down before Chuck rushed into the tent to give us our marching orders.

"Get your packs ready," he said. "We're leaving for the summit in the morning."

That night Carolyn and I lay side-by-side in the frigid darkness, unable to sleep, but without much to say. I worried quietly about the mountain I was about to climb, and the man who had bragged that he could ensure my failure. Carolyn could think of little to say to encourage me, but seemed confident that, whatever happened, I'd make it back down. She said she knew I wouldn't give my life for either a climb or a story.

The next morning, after breakfast, George came into the dining tent and sat at the head of the table. Lhakpa stood behind him. It was the only team meeting he organized during the entire expedition.

The meeting had hardly started when the Dans, who had begun their summit bid the day before, called George from Camp One. They both had connected their first bottles of oxygen to their masks incorrectly, blowing out the seals on their regulators and leaving their systems with dangerous leaks. It was a mistake we had all been warned about. Every few minutes the radio crackled as the Dans called their dining-tent "help desk" and my team's conversation veered to their crisis—two rubber rings I could fit on my thumb that were the difference between standing on top of Everest or retreating before they even tried to get there. Chuck suggested they could replace the O-rings with dental floss. I wondered how many climbers, known for cutting toothbrushes in half to save weight, carried that kind of hygiene up Everest.

"You would trust your life to a piece of dental floss?" George snapped at Chuck, who dropped his head without responding.

Although the Connecticut expedition had never climbed as a

team, George insisted we would go to the summit as one. Anne and I suggested that she and I take a rest day, but George was adamant that we all start together. It wasn't fair to the team to split up the Sherpas, he insisted. If someone needed a rescue, we needed all four Sherpas working together to bring the victim down. Dave Watson chimed in with only one question about the summit plan.

"I just want to know, if someone turns back, whether they will allow their Sherpa to work for the team?" Dave asked.

It was a strange question coming from Dave, who had never been able to afford his own Sherpa but eagerly accepted the services of the one Bill had paid for before he abandoned his climb. Of course we would let our Sherpas work for the team, and we'd said it before—when George had asked.

As soon as I answered Dave's question, I knew Russell had been right: For all the talk about having a good relationship with your "personal Sherpa," the Sherpas were a team and they worked for George, who had not paid for their services or any of their tips. Nonetheless, Anne and I tried to salvage our relationships with Mingma Gelu and Dawa Nuru, who allegedly worked for us but remained on strike until we paid them for work they hadn't done yet. Chuck and Dave told us that they had already taken care of their Sherpas, so Anne and I took the money we had kept hidden in camp and ponied up more than $3,200 to get our Sherpas working again.

George's halftime hype proved weak glue for the fractured team, which quickly broke back into the same fragments as it had before. Chuck and Dave headed out, then George, Lhakpa, and Mingma Gelu. Anne left by herself, and I took off last. When I had made it halfway up the climb to Camp One, I saw Anne. She had reached the shade provided by the final headwall of the North Col and was desperate for a drink and a snack. But Hristo Hristov, a twenty-six-year-old Bulgarian who joined her there, wouldn't hear of it.

"No, no. I give you tea," Hristov said as Anne dug out a water bottle.

When she got out some power gel energy food, Hristov had her put it away and handed her a fistful of finger-sized plastic envelopes of his own golden goo.

"No, no. Try this—Bulgarian honey," he said.

As I approached the spot where Anne and Hristo had rested and snacked, the spot of shade they had coveted was turning into long, tooth-shaped shadows. I felt as if I were swimming alone at night into an unknown ocean. I was in over my head, and it was just a matter of time before I couldn't tread water anymore.

The tent Anne and I shared was one of more than sixty that filled Camp One. The stove we had left in the tent during our last visit, which we had purchased in Kathmandu to use on the climb, had vanished. In its place we had been left a feeble hanging stove that took all night to heat our dinner and melt snow for our water bottles.

Even in the daylight, we hardly glimpsed George and Lhakpa above ABC; never shared a single word with either of them during our attempt to reach the top of the mountain. In fact, we spent no time at all with any of our teammates during our summit bid. We were, by any real measure, no longer members of the team, which was both terrifying and reassuring. I worried that there was nobody outside the tent I was sleeping in who would come to my rescue if things went bad; but on the other hand, there was nobody else on my team I would trust to save me even if they tried.

"Anne, do you really think we can make it up this thing on our own?" I asked. "I feel like I barely made it here."

As Anne and I lay down for the night, on the other side of Everest, Nils Antezana, Gustavo Lisi, Big Dorjee, and Mingma Sherpa were climbing from their tents to begin their final day's climb to the top.

KATHMANDU, NEPAL—MAY 26, 2004

Other than Nils's teammates, the Irish climbers Pat Falvey and Clare O'Leary, along with their Sherpas, were the only people who saw Fabiola's father during his final day's climb to the top of Everest. Fabiola, Davide, and Damian caught up with the Irish 2004 Expedition a couple of hours after they returned from the mountain. Pat and Clare were waiting with their teammates and luggage at the Hotel Thamel for their ride to the airport and the flight home to Ireland. They were short on time, but before Pat would pass on anything to Fabiola about what he had witnessed, he had something else to give her that would prove just as valuable. He dug into his luggage and pulled out a minidisc recorder. If she really wanted the truth about what had happened to her father, he told her, get everything on tape.

As a teen, Pat had worked as a bricklayer and a construction foreman. In his early twenties, he made his first million as a developer and businessman, and by his late twenties, he had lost it all. He took to hiking to relieve the stress of rebuilding his business and, on a walk up Ireland's highest mountain, announced he was going to climb Mount Everest. Six years later, he did it, and by the time he was forty, having rebuilt his fortunes, he had left the corporate world to work as a professional adventurer, team trainer, and motivational speaker. With his climb to the summit of Everest in 2004, Pat became one of the few mountaineers to reach the top both from Tibet and Nepal. Clare O'Leary, a doctor, had just become the first Irish woman to summit Everest and, within eighteen months, would hold the same title on the Seven Summits.

At forty-four, Pat's once-thick brown hair was thinning and turning gray. He was still grizzled and lean from his weeks on the mountain, but his cherubic face and soft brogue made him seem warm and kind despite his businesslike approach to the conversation.

In the days before his own summit bid, Pat had spoken with Willie Benegas and David Breashears about the weather. The weather was grand at that moment, but they warned him that conditions looked as if they would change sometime after one in the afternoon on May 18. There was enough time to summit that morning and get back to camp, but the forecast prodded Pat and Clare to start early. Willie had passed on the same advice to Gustavo. The Irish team left the South Col to start their climb to the summit sometime around nine thirty on the night of May 17. Within about half an hour, around ten p.m., Clare heard the distinctive and repeated grating of an ax being twisted into hard ice. She looked up to see a hunched climber leaning hard on his ax and sluggishly moving his feet forward. Clare had heard that someone was attempting the peak with prosthetic limbs, and the climber in front of her was so slow, stiff, and awkward that she wondered if this was the disabled mountaineer. When she realized he wasn't, she thought that perhaps he was climbing without using supplemental oxygen and had become badly hypoxic. But she looked at him as she passed and, although she couldn't see the face of the stooped climber, she saw the telltale hose and regulator that confirmed that he was using bottled gas. Up ahead, Big Dorjee and Mingma were sitting on the snow waiting for their struggling employer.

"What is this guy doing up here?" Clare thought to herself.

"His pace was so slow . . . He just wasn't moving well at all," she recalled. "I really thought that he was going to be turning back very, very soon."

When Pat reached Gustavo, just beyond the Sherpas, he gave the Argentine a thumbs-up to ask how they were. Gustavo returned the gesture. The Sherpas didn't seem worried, so Clare and Pat moved on.

The Irish climbers reached the summit at about six forty-five the next morning and stayed there for twenty minutes before starting their descent. The weather was fine when they arrived, but horsetail clouds in the sky above them portended an incoming storm and, by the time they started down, Pat noticed that the wind seemed to be spinning snow up the mountain.

"It seemed like we were stuck in a vortex," he said later. "We were escaping a lot of it by being on the right side of the blow."

Clare passed Nils and his teammates again just as they were arriving at the South Summit, sometime between eight and nine a.m. She was so convinced that the climbers she saw the night before would have turned back that she didn't realize that it was the same team until later. Pat, on the other hand, immediately recognized the same struggling climber making his way toward the summit and worried that the traverse from the South Summit to the actual summit, which was normally covered with snow but in 2004 was largely bare rock, would prove unexpectedly challenging for Nils. He was having difficulty placing the spikes of his boots on soft snow. It would be that much harder on jagged rocks.

Pat was concerned that a leader still had an obviously weak climber moving up the mountain. With only their two small groups climbing above Camp Four, there wouldn't be many options for rescues. The weather was obviously getting ready to turn, and it didn't seem to Pat that the four men in front of him were showing much teamwork. But it wasn't his place to argue with another leader. He had his own team to think about, and, in seconds, had passed the other climbers.

By eleven thirty a.m., the Irish team had made it back to Camp Four, where Pat and Clare crawled into their tent and fell asleep. When they awoke now and again, Pat would look out of the tent at the Triangle Face above the South Col.

"I wonder if the others are down," Pat said as he watched the weather building on the mountain before falling back asleep early that afternoon.

Far up the mountain, Nils Antezana and his Sherpas had not yet arrived on the Balcony. Pat wouldn't have the answer to his question until five the next morning, when one of the Irish team's Sherpas came to his tent and told him of the shouts that drew them out into the night while the rest of the team slept.

When Pat described the climb to Fabiola, he was focused in much the same way that he was when he was making it. But as he told of the disastrous mess he learned about in Camp Four the morning after he reached the summit, he became increasingly agitated.

As soon as Pat heard that someone might need help, he crawled from his tent. Pemba, Pat's *sirdar*, was already stripping the camp. The team would need to descend soon, Pemba said, because they were running low on bottled oxygen. They had given some away the night before. Two Sherpas—Big Dorjee and Mingma—had straggled into camp, one of them so weak that he couldn't walk without assistance. Three of the Irish team's Sherpas had helped the others into a tent and heard their story of the "crazy men" who went to the summit when they should have turned around. Later they had heard shouts from outside of camp and went out and found an Argentinean climber who had fallen nearby. He was lying on the snow, his down pants were torn, and they could see his headlamp shining a few hundred meters up the mountain where he had lost it. The Irish team's Sherpas helped Gustavo back to their camp, gave him two bottles of oxygen, and sent him to his own tent.

Pat, concerned that he needed to get the climbers whom his Sherpas had rescued farther down the mountain before the weather stranded them all in the high camp, headed to Gustavo's tent. He found the Argentine talking on a satellite phone.

"I went to his tent, and he was on the phone just constantly chatting, making two or three phone calls," Pat said. "Pemba and Jangbu tried to assist the climber, but he took a while to get out of the tent, as he had been on the phone. I asked Pemba who he had been on the phone to, and he said, 'His mother.' "

Gustavo had still not let anybody know that he had left Fabiola's father on the mountain. But by the time he climbed from his tent to speak with Pat, Gustavo's webmaster was updating his site with other news—SUMMIT!!!! GUSTAVO LISI HAS CONQUERED EVEREST!!!!—making no mention that a man was missing. Pat, however, had seen four climbers heading up, and only three were accounted for. More than half a day had passed between the time Gustavo abandoned Nils on Everest and when he told Pat about it. Rescue was already a breath away from hopeless, but Pat turned and looked at the mountain anyway.

"The weather conditions had descended on the mountain, and there were severe gusts and winds high up," he said. "We could see about, maybe 750 feet of the Triangle Face."

The Balcony was painfully close—500 vertical meters away. But with the weather coming in, saving someone there would be like running into a burning building, except far slower. Pat looked in on Big Dorjee and Mingma, but found them so wasted they could barely get themselves down the mountain, much less climb back up to help their client. Then he went to Victor Saunders—the guide who had encountered Nils's descending teammates during the summit bid his own team had aborted just six hours earlier. Victor was shocked to learn that there was still a climber high on the mountain whom he might have been able to help when he was up there.

"Knowing Victor, if he would have been aware, I'm sure that they would have gone to the assistance of the weakening climbers coming down," Pat told Fabiola.

But now Victor and his Sherpas were so exhausted from their climb the night before that they couldn't safely go back up. Pat got on the radio to get the latest forecast. It wasn't good. Rather than head up the mountain, Pat told Victor, they should all head down in anticipation of deteriorating weather. In the end, it would be five days before Victor made another attempt to reach the summit. He and other climbers on their way to the top stopped at the Balcony to look for the dead man that Big Dorjee and Mingma said they had left there. The empty platform of snow they would find was even more disturbing than staring at a frozen corpse would have been.

Pat had Gustavo pack up his gear and sent him down with Pemba and another Sherpa, but by the time he arrived at Camp Two that afternoon, his Sherpas were so angered by the Argentinean's behavior that they refused to help him anymore.

"Pemba got upset because it looked like the Argentinean climber was stronger than he pretended to be," Pat said. "After he got over the Geneva Spur, he continued at a strong rate with Jangbu, eventually getting to Camp Three and insisting that our Sherpas would make him tea and coffee."

Pat's Sherpas complained that Gustavo didn't behave like a man whose life they had just saved, but instead began giving them orders as if they were working for him. He never thanked them or Pat for rescuing him or assisting his descent to the lower camps. But Gustavo's rudeness wasn't nearly so upsetting as what they were learning about his climb to the summit.

"This is what was said by [their] Sherpas to our Sherpas," Pat said to Fabiola. "That they were very, very mad at Gustavo. That they were crazy men; that they were going up too slow; that they had said to them that they were going too slow; that they put [Nils] in an alcove at the top of the Balcony which would have been where the oxygen bottles were."

Pat paused for a moment. Fabiola stared but didn't speak. She could hear her heart pounding.

"What I'm about to say may be disturbing, but it is the facts of what I have heard: that as they went away the Bolivian climber had caught the leg of somebody and that he had asked [him] to stay and [he] had pulled away."

Fifteen

It took me six hours to climb the snow slope from Camp One, at 23,500 feet, to the lowest reaches of Camp Two, about 2,000 feet higher. Anne was fifteen minutes behind me. More than thirty climbers marched single file between the two camps on Everest's North Ridge, holding on to fixed ropes like they were banister rails along a staircase of boot prints in the hardened snow. Ice axes were little more than canes. The ropes prevented anyone from having to stop a fall with his ax, or pull his partner from a crevasse. Success here was a triumph of physiology rather than mountaineering skill.

And in this one-foot-in-front-of-the-other world, George and Lhakpa's strength was obvious. They stayed so far in front of the pack that I wasn't sure which figures on the landscape were theirs. Chuck was about twenty minutes ahead of Anne and me throughout the climb. He would sit on the snow and look back at us between the grueling, tedious slogs up the slope. Dave climbed with Chuck early, but moved well in front of him at the top of the slope.

Sometimes I could rally twenty steps in a row, but usually only three or four before my body simply refused to move and I had to lean on my ax, panting. I felt a burning sensation deep in the pit of my stomach, and it spread to my fingertips and legs. Our pace seemed strong in the morning, but by noon, the previous three days' climbs were taking their toll. Most of the other climbers passed us. Hristo Hristov, the Bulgarian mountaineer who had fed Anne tea and honey during a rest stop on the previous day's climb, could only nod to us as he passed. Shoko Ota, a sixty-three-year-old Japanese woman already breathing bottled oxygen, was close behind him in line.

For the rest of us, bottles of oxygen were like the weapons that video game players win to allow them to fight at the next level of a fantasy world: If we got to Camp Two, we got gas for dinner and right through the night. And we might make it to Camp Three.

"I can't believe a sixty-three-year-old woman passed me," Anne grumbled as she kicked her spiked feet with sluggish resentment into the next steps on the slope.

Six months earlier, Anne had showed up uncharacteristically late for her field hockey team's bus ride to a game in Maine wearing a medal around her neck. When her players asked about it, she told them that she had just finished running the Hartford Marathon— her eighth of the twenty-six-mile runs. She joked that knowing she had a bus to catch improved her time. But the woman coming up the slope behind me now seemed little like the coach who could run twenty-six miles, hop on a bus for six hours, and then lead women half her age in a muddy battle with sticks and cleats.

"It was like we've run four marathons in a row," she said as she stumbled over the lip of the snow slope and staggered grimacing into the gusting wind.

We arrived at a cluster of tents at the top of the ramp of snow just before two p.m., knowing it was going to be a brutal struggle to climb the remaining 1,300 feet over steep, rocky ground to our own campsite. In good conditions, that last scramble takes two hours. This snowy shoulder held only five tents, which some guided expeditions used as an additional intermediate camp to break up the trip to Camp Two over separate days. I sat on my pack amid them and had a cup of tea while waiting for Anne to arrive, then helped her into a tent with a friend in the camp.

"Why the hell don't we have a tent here?" Anne snapped, looking at the storm-lashed ridge above us. "Why did they put our tents all the way up there?"

We had known for weeks that the Sherpas were putting the Connecticut Camp Two as high on the ridge as they could, and nobody had protested. When I had learned that some guides used an intermediate camp, I had called it "Camp Two Minus" and never thought that I might be one of the laggards who would want to use it. Now I was desperate for a port in the storm.

Without sleeping bags or fuel, the tents before us were empty promises. We would certainly survive the night inside one, but without down bags to warm us enough to sleep and a stove to melt snow and heat food, we would be no better off in the morning. I stepped up toward two of the tents to see what might be inside. I could see how summit fever could turn a climber into a thief. The idea of cashing in our chance to reach the top for want of a bit of food or a warm place to sleep was unbearable. Maybe we could radio down to Russell and offer to pay for what we used, I suggested, peeking through a cracked tent door. But there was nothing to buy. They were empty.

We had been at the tents for twenty minutes when Dawa Nuru and Mingma Gelu arrived. It was the first we had seen of them since we'd left Advanced Base Camp.

"You must go up," they said. "Or go down."

In the end, the math was simple.

This definitely wasn't how I wanted to climb any mountain. Barely holding myself together enough to crawl into camp at dark, skittishly awaiting the next crisis on my team, and peering desperately into the doors of other teams' tents, wondering if it was OK for me to take just what I needed to make up for everything that had been taken from me. Maybe we were strong enough to climb to the top of Everest and back. But I wasn't convinced that we could battle through a storm or recover from an accident. And I didn't know who we could count on to help us.

We retreated in silence, lone figures stumbling down the now-empty ridgeline. Anne seemed on the verge of tears as we fell into our tent at Camp One. I felt twenty years older than when I'd arrived in Nepal. The next morning, Mingma Gelu and Dawa Nuru brought us cups of tea before they climbed back up the mountain to rejoin the team.

"Enjoy it," I told Anne. "It's the most expensive cup of tea you'll ever drink."

Two days later, on May 20, George, Lhakpa, Chuck, and Dave reached the top of the world along with the expedition's four Sherpas. They were the first to reach the summit among some fifty climbers who made the attempt that day. Whiteout conditions blocked their view of the curved Earth below, but not of the ragged ropes that threatened to drop them into the void—or the dead and dying climbers along the route.

My story ran the next day on the *Courant*'s front page, under the headline EXPEDITION TRIUMPHS.

"In many ways, it was the best climb of my life," Chuck said when he got down. "For eight people to move together that fast was amazing."

The entire Connecticut team was back in ABC within twelve hours of reaching the top. Dave Watson stumbled into our mess tent like a character from a mountain monster movie at two fifteen in the afternoon, just seven hours after he had left the summit. The battered climber still had the oxygen mask over his face and the crampons attached to the boots he had strapped on at eleven p.m. the night before.

The horror show that had begun unfolding the day before was only just becoming apparent. The Connecticut team had survived what proved to be the deadliest storm on Everest since the 1996 disaster that had killed eight climbers. By the time our brutal summit window had shut tight, seven mountaineers, including Nils Antezana, had perished.

On his return, George cited the worst conditions, both of the weather and the route, that he had encountered in his six trips to the top of Everest. My teammates, who had contributed no resources or manpower to equipping the climbing route, complained bitterly about its condition. Russell Brice should have completed fixing the ropes, George said. Many Sherpas who did fix ropes did it poorly.

"The rope is old and trashed, with the core showing through half of it," Dave said. "We did almost the whole [climb to the summit] in the dark. It wasn't bad at night 'cause you can't see the abyss and what would happen to you if you blew one of these moves and the rope broke. You'll probably kill everybody around you 'cause you're all just five feet apart and you think, 'Holy shit, I wish it was dark again so I don't have to look at that.'"

Our campmates Dan Lochner and Dan Meggitt had replaced their damaged oxygen regulators and reached the summit a day before the Connecticut expedition. On his way up, Lochner said, he passed a Korean climber who had collapsed and was hanging from a fixed rope at the base of the summit pyramid. The man asked for hot water, but Dan, at his wits' end, pushed to the limit physically, and driven hard by his Sherpa, continued on past the dying climber. Wednesday night, after Lochner had descended to Camp Three, word spread among climbers at Advanced Base Camp that two Sherpas were trying to deliver oxygen, a sleeping bag, food, and hot water to the Korean, who was reported to be stricken with snow-blindness and frostbite on his hands and feet.

"There's nothing our entire team put together could have done for that guy," George said.

Lower down the route, another member of the Korean team fell below the ladder that climbs the Second Step, and broke his leg. A South African climber, Andre Bredenkamp, came upon the Korean just after the accident.

"He was lying in the snow with people around him, and he was begging them not to leave him," Bredenkamp, High Commissioner with the South Africa Scout Association, told *The Witness* newspaper. "We looked at him and we had to leave him and walk on. We simply did not have the capacity to carry him or drag him. We could hardly keep upright ourselves. Some people took out their spare jackets and covered him and we told him to relax.... They were really urging him to go to sleep and die peacefully."

"We covered him up with snow and he just went to sleep," Bredenkamp told the *Cape Times* upon his return to South Africa.

A third member of the Korean team turned around and headed back up the mountain to assist his friends after descending from the summit.

The next morning, all three of the Koreans were dead. When the Connecticut team reached the spot where Dan Lochner had passed the Korean, the body was on its back on the slope but still attached to the rope. His hands were bare and pressed together in front of him as if he were praying. Snow covered his face in a ghastly, open-eyed death mask.

"Above the third step, on the snow pyramid, you're traversing this hand line on totally sketchy loose rock," Dave recalled. "There's a Korean guy with no gloves on. . . . He's hanging on a tether so you can't use the hand line, so you're traversing above him hoping you don't fall on [him]."

Shoko Ota, the Japanese woman who had passed Anne and me near Camp Two, topped out the same day as the Connecticut team—the oldest woman to ever reach the summit. But descending the Second Step, she fell. She died there dangling from a rope as her teammates tried to help her. Hristo Hristov, exhausted from his climb to the summit without oxygen and separated from his teammates, sat down above the step a few hours later, went to sleep, and never woke up.

"Everest to me just seems like bragging rights," Dave said, when asked whether it was worth it. "But it means something to me—walking past all these dead bodies of people whose dreams died there."

Two days later, when members of the Bulgarian team came looking for information about Hristo, George told them that he had seen him near the summit, exhausted and pounding his head against a rock in frustration—comments that, along with my story including these statements, angered many climbers in Bulgaria. George would eventually claim that he was referring to a different member of that team. The grim expressions of Hristo's teammates were a counterpoint to the sunny smile another Bulgarian climber, Mariana Maslarova, had brought to our camp a few weeks earlier.

A furry red cap made forty-two-year-old Maslarova one of the most recognized fixtures in Advanced Base Camp. Maslarova's uncle, also named Hristo—Hristo Prodanov—had died while descending Everest twenty years earlier. The Bulgarian expedition was commemorating the trip made by Hristo. His niece wasn't climbing with them, however, but with an international expedition. She had her own commemoration planned.

Mariana's climb, which she had planned to make without supplemental oxygen just as her uncle had, was not going well, she told us when she visited. Her Sherpa wouldn't go high on the mountain, complaining of headaches, she said.

But other Sherpas in ABC said Mariana, wife of the head of the Bulgarian Federation of Alpine Clubs, was suicidal in her bid to become the first Bulgarian woman to climb Everest. Mariana's Sherpa was doing everything he could, including feigning illness, to keep her from going high. On her first climb to Camp One, which she made at the same time as my teammates and I, Mariana moved far too slowly to consider reaching the summit without oxygen.

Nonetheless, on May 18, Mariana headed back to the North Col, passing the other way as Anne and I retreated from our own summit attempt. She had neither her Sherpa nor her backpack with her. There was no honey or tea during this encounter. She shared just the single word and gesture that had become Mariana's trademark answer to those asking how she was.

"Summit!" she sang out as she pointed to the sky before resuming the slow slog up the glacier toward Camp One.

At Camp Three she had to search for a tent to stay in for the night. The next day it took her thirteen hours to reach the Second Step, and other expedition leaders could be heard voicing concern, and curses, over their radios as she created a dangerous bottleneck at the ladder that led up the step.

"Get her out of there!" one screamed over the radio.

At least twenty people tried to convince Mariana to turn back, but she continued up into a night that she was almost certain not to survive. She was last seen at 28,500 feet—the same place where her countryman Hristo Hristov had died just days earlier.

Suicide by Everest struck me as rare until a year later, when Duncan Chessell, an Australian guide, posted a desperate note on his Web site and in other media titled KAMIKAZE—INDIAN WOMAN SUKHI VOWS "SUMMIT OR DEATH."

Duncan labeled his client "*the worst climber on the mountain.*"

After two attempts Sukhi had failed to climb more than 150 feet above Camp Two. Guides insisted she descend, but before she would, she called her family to ask permission. Instead of giving it, Duncan said, they contacted the team's trekking agent, offering to pay more money, insisting that Sukhi summiting was very important to the family's prestige. When guides tried to bring the girl down after the call, Duncan said, she threatened to jump off the mountain.

"Sukhi is in such a mentally controlled state by your family that she cannot reason any longer," he wrote. "You do not care about her, only about your family name, which is going to be put into the newspapers of India as to how you killed your daughter any day now."

Sukhi descended after the letter appeared, but said later that her family had not pressured her to climb. Nonetheless, she had soon announced plans to return to Everest. The following year, a different Indian climber, this one on the south side of Everest, threatened to jump into a crevasse when she failed on her third attempt to reach the summit.

CAMP TWO, MOUNT EVEREST, NEPAL—MAY 19, 2004

Dave Morton, a guide for Alpine Ascents International, had just ascended to Camp Two with the group of clients he was taking to the summit when he learned from Pat Falvey, who was on his way down, that Gustavo Lisi's client was missing and presumed dead.

"It's just a fucking mess up there," Pat said.

A few weeks earlier, Gustavo, whom Dave knew from working in the Andes, had dropped by the Alpine Ascents tents in Base Camp for a cup of tea. Dave was surprised to learn that the Argentine guide had a client on Everest. He was even more surprised that he would bring the man to the Alpine Ascents camp, considering the only other time the two guides had spent any time together in the mountains, Dave had ended up firing Gustavo.

It was in the year 2000 and Dave had brought two clients to the Andes to climb several Bolivian peaks, but he needed another guide. Bernardo Guarachi, the first Bolivian to reach the top of Everest, had made the arrangements for Alpine Ascents in Bolivia. He recommended Gustavo, who had been working for Bernardo's company for a few months.

Dave, Gustavo, and the two clients headed up Huayna Potosi, a mountain overlooking La Paz. At high camp, one of the clients faltered and Dave turned around with her. Gustavo and the other client, a man who had already climbed Everest with Alpine Ascents and had taken nearly every other trip the company offered, headed for the summit. But before they went up, Dave pulled them both aside.

"It's our policy to rope up on this mountain," he said.

Plenty of climbers head up Huayna Potosi unroped, but Dave was firm—anyone guiding the mountain for him was expected to tie themselves to their client and keep the rope on until they made it back down.

"It seemed to go well," Dave told me. "I met them back at Base Camp, and that night we were all going out to dinner."

But the clients announced that they wouldn't be joining the guides for dinner, and Dave got an inkling that although Gustavo and his client had successfully reached the summit, things hadn't gone as well as it had appeared.

"The next day, this guy Paul said it was a nightmare. 'I don't want to see that guy again.'"

Gustavo had never tied in with his client. What's worse, once they reached the summit, there simply wasn't a rope long enough for both of them to wear. Gustavo had raced down the mountain without his client, leaving the climber to find his way down alone, unroped and frightened. When Dave confronted Gustavo about not tying in with the man whose life he was responsible for and abandoning his client, the guide brushed off the complaint.

"I stayed with him most of the time," he said. "But he was really slow."

Before heading to Illimani, the next mountain on the schedule, Dave spoke with Bernardo.

"We don't want to have Gustavo work for us again," Dave said. "Period."

The next time Dave saw Gustavo guiding was on Everest, where, on two different days, he passed the Argentinean leading Nils up the icefall as his own team members made their way down. Both times Gustavo and his client were the last on the route, but Dave didn't think too much about it.

"Oh, so slow," Gustavo commented as he waited some twenty feet in front of his client.

To Dave, it was quite clear that Gustavo was guiding Nils and, in fact, he was happy to see the man he had fired for leaving a climber behind sticking tight to the one he was leading up Everest. Perhaps he had learned his lesson.

It wasn't until Camp Two that Dave got to know Nils, and he couldn't help but feel a bit of envy at the classy client Gustavo was leading in the mountains. While climbers nearby boisterously recounted tales from the mountains and told off-color jokes, Nils and Dave sat outside taking in the sun of a perfect, windless day and talking quietly, sometimes in English, sometimes in Spanish, about world affairs, medicine, Nils's family, and the one place that they both loved—Bolivia. Dave likes talking about climbing as much as the next guide, but he thought Nils would be a dream of a client—somebody with enough going on outside the mountains to provide a couple months' worth of conversation. How did someone like Gustavo get a guy like that to come to Everest with him?

Dave ran into Gustavo a few more times on the mountain, but he never saw Nils again.

When he arrived in Camp Two on his own team's summit bid, Dave learned that Gustavo had again abandoned a client, and that this one was almost certainly dead. He wasn't sure he wanted to take the time from his own climb or walk through such a dark cloud at a time when he needed to be as positive as he could for his own climbers. But he spoke Spanish and he knew that Gustavo, unable to speak English, would be isolated with his grief. He walked over to Gustavo's tent.

"I'm sorry," Dave said. "What are you going to do? What are you going to tell the family?"

Gustavo's voice was ground down to a ragged whisper. "I don't know what happened," he said. "I don't know what I'm going to do."

Then he changed the subject.

"It was so beautiful," Gustavo said. "It was a perfect day, such a gorgeous day, you wouldn't believe it . . . Let me show you the photos."

As Gustavo took out his digital camera and started scrolling through the photos, Dave just stared blankly at the screen.

"You've gotta be fucking kidding me," he thought to himself.

The man had just gotten his client killed on Everest and all he wanted to do was show his photos, talk about how pretty it was.

"It was as if he had had this profound spiritual experience," Dave said.

Dave spent fifteen minutes in the tent; however, all but the first five were blurred by his shock. If Gustavo seemed to have had some sort of enlightenment while the man he was guiding was dying, Dave was now having his own, albeit much darker, epiphany.

"Jesus Christ, what the hell happened up there?" he thought as he walked back to his camp.

Four days later, while waiting for his teammates to catch up with him at the Balcony during the Alpine Ascents summit day, Dave searched for signs of the man he had so enjoyed chatting with in Camp Two. Victor Saunders, the guide who had seen Gustavo, Big Dorjee, and Mingma during their descent, made his second summit attempt with his own clients during the same weather window as Dave, and he also looked for the abandoned climber. Neither guide could find any sign of Nils Antezana—no body, no footprints, no jacket or oxygen bottles. Perhaps Nils had managed to get back on his feet and tried to get himself down the mountain and ended up falling, getting lost, or collapsing someplace where he couldn't be found. But both Dave and Victor were puzzled that there was no sign of his having been there.

When he descended from the summit, Dave sought out some Sherpas who could tell him what Nils and Gustavo's Sherpas had told them. Big Dorjee had told them about how Nils had grabbed at Mingma's legs as they left him, about how he had begged them to stay with him, but Mingma interrupted Dorjee as he spoke with the other Sherpas and told him to stop telling that story.

"Don't tell them that he was still alive when we left him."

Sixteen

While the rest of the climbers in our camp were down from the summit by the night of the 20th, for thirty-six hours, there was no sign of Guillermo. The Mexican camped with the Connecticut team but climbed without supplemental oxygen and summited hours later. Nobody expected him to make it back to Advanced Base Camp the same day he reached the summit.

The next day, though, he was one of several climbers from various expeditions who were unaccounted for in the deteriorating weather.

"If he doesn't come down tomorrow, he's dead," George said.

"Maybe we see him next year," Mingma Gelu added darkly.

Most of the Sherpas returned to Camp One to begin breaking down the team's gear. Anne visited other expeditions to see what they knew of Guillermo. Later George asked her to take him to Russell Brice's camp.

"I normally wouldn't help you," Anne recalled Russell telling George. "But this is a human life."

That night, while we worried about Guillermo, Chuck broke out the scotch he had brought to the mountain to celebrate reaching the summit. When Bill had served up whiskey with his announcement that he was leaving the expedition, it had helped calm Carolyn. But Chuck's booze, served up in a tent full of tense teammates, had the opposite effect. Carolyn fell into our tent cursing me for bringing her along on my misadventure.

"Fuck you," she snapped at me when I asked what was wrong. "What the hell are we doing here? Guillermo's probably dead, and for what?"

For half an hour she crawled back and forth across our tent, zipping herself into her sleeping bag to weep, and then fighting her way out of the bag to stick her head out of the tent and vomit into the subzero night. Carolyn had come to detest Guillermo, who had pelted her with snow and a rock and spread porn through the camp. But she didn't want him dead and was guilt-ridden for her animosity.

The next morning, Russell Brice made a rare appearance at the Connecticut site. One of his Sherpas had found Guillermo in a tent at Camp Three, making tea. He had a bit of frostbite, but Russell was convinced he could make it down on his own.

Dave Pritt, a British guide, also visited us. He was in the Pleasure Dome early in the afternoon when George radioed our Sherpas in Camp One and ordered them to climb up to assist Guillermo. They hadn't brought warm enough clothes, they responded, and the weather was bad. They stopped answering the radio.

"Guillermo no need a rescue," Lhakpa said angrily. "Guillermo a lazy boy. My people can die up there too."

George asked Dave Pritt to send his Sherpas to help.

"You know, George, I've only just met you today, but I've heard the stories, many stories about you being unwilling to help others," Pritt said. "Now you come with a guy in your group that needs help and people say, 'Why should we help George?'"

Pritt's climbers, still in high camps, needed his Sherpas, but he loaned Anne a pair of radios. The ones my teammates brought didn't work, so we borrowed others from whomever we could.

George began radioing offers of money to our Sherpas. A promise of $5,000 prompted two Sherpas—Ang Mingma and Dawa Nuru—to help Guillermo. They found him late that afternoon, still resting in the tent at Camp Three where Russell's Sherpas had seen him.

Ang Mingma cursed Guillermo loudly for causing their storm-bound trek through the "death zone" while he napped. Guillermo begged their forgiveness. The Sherpas strapped an oxygen mask onto Guillermo, Ang Mingma said, and the Mexican walked down unassisted while the Sherpas stripped gear from the mountain.

It was well after dark—nearly twelve hours after Russell's Sherpas found the Mexican—when George decided to join the rescue. He radioed Ang Mingma with orders to continue descending through the night rather than stopping at Camp One, where Guillermo and the Sherpas could have safely waited until morning to continue their descent. He was coming to lead them down in the darkness. Before departing, he marched through camp, shouting out orders for down coats, headlamps, batteries, and thermoses and cursing those who couldn't provide what he wanted.

"Do you want him to die?" George shouted.

At seven thirty p.m., George, Dave, and Dan Lochner headed out.

Three hours later, the summit-weary climbers were halfway back up the North Col. Dave, a ski patroller, mountain guide, and the only person there with search-and-rescue training, watched as Dan Lochner, one of the least experienced climbers on the mountain, crawled up the snow-loaded slope on his hands and knees. He could hear avalanches letting loose on the slopes nearby.

Chuck, who teaches avalanche safety, refused to go.

"[George] put three people in danger at night on an avalanche-prone slope when Guillermo wasn't really in danger and could have stayed another night at the North Col," he said.

Dave, Dan, and George never made it to Camp One; they waited on the ropes halfway up to the camp for the Sherpas to escort Guillermo down. The next morning the weather began to clear, as Russell Brice's weather report had predicted. We had ten days left on our climbing permit, and George had assured us that everyone would get a second chance to summit. But the last hope Anne and I had of standing atop Everest died the next morning as another of Russell's predictions came true.

"There is no more food," George announced.

In reality, I knew there was little chance that I would take another shot at the summit. I'd had trouble breathing since my first attempt. Even the hike to Base Camp was agonizing.

BASE CAMP, MOUNT EVEREST, NEPAL—MAY 21, 2004

As Guillermo's "rescue" was unfolding, Willie Benegas, on the other side of the mountain, was departing Base Camp for Kathmandu. He, along with the rest of the Mountain Madness team he was leading, left Everest on May 21, the same day that filmmaker and mountaineer David Breashears and American climbing legend Ed Viesturs headed out. David and Ed were climbing the mountain in 2004 to make footage for a feature-film project about the 1996 disaster, a tragedy they both witnessed while climbing the mountain together to make another movie—the IMAX film that David co-directed, in which Ed was a featured climber.

Most climbers leave the mountain by retracing the thirty-mile walk to the Lukla airstrip, but Ed and David said their good-byes to Willie in Base Camp and hopped in a helicopter. While Willie and most of the other climbers would spend three or four days making their way back to Kathmandu, Ed and David would arrive there that afternoon.

But no sooner had the Everest celebrities arrived at the Yak and Yeti Hotel than they ran into the man they thought had just started walking back from the mountain, already washed up and in a fresh change of clothes. Their jaws dropped. Willie Benegas had just outrun a helicopter through the high Himalaya. At least, that's what they thought.

Damian Benegas jokes that his own nickname is "Willie" because of how often he and his twin are confused for each other. Although he would have loved to hobnob with two of America's most famous climbers, he wasn't about to puncture the myth blowing up around his brother, even if it would only last for a day or two, even if it involved a trick they hadn't played on anyone since boarding school.

"How did you get here?" Ed and David asked the man they thought they had said good-bye to on Everest a few hours earlier.

"Oh, I'm very fast," Damian replied. He flashed a sly grin and then sauntered away before they could catch on.

When Willie did arrive at the Yak and Yeti a few days later, it was like he was walking toward a mirror in the middle of the corridor. His reaction to seeing his twin was just as incredulous as David's and Ed's had been, but it was fired with irritation rather than amazement. The brothers hadn't spoken over the sat phone since before Damian had agreed to come to Kathmandu with Fabiola and Davide. He was supposed to be preparing for the twins' attempt to put up a new route on Latok I, a Pakistani mountain with the potential to be the most dangerous and difficult climb of their career. Damian recognized the anger in his brother's eyes. How could he blow off such important work to party? How could he squander what meager funds the guides had managed to put away for their own dreams on an expensive flight to Kathmandu when he wasn't even climbing?

"What are you doing here?" Willie demanded.

Damian told his brother about Fabiola, her desperate pleas, her family's hopes that, if they couldn't save Nils's life, if they couldn't find his body, they could at least dig up the truth about what had happened to him.

"I'm sorry, Willie," Damian told his brother. "I had to help these people."

That night, Willie joined his twin at dinner with Fabiola and Davide. They sat on the balcony at Rum Doodle, where Nils Antezana, like almost every climber who reaches the summit of Everest, would have celebrated. Willie handed Fabiola three colorfully woven bags wrapped in the white scarves Sherpas bless climbers with. The bags contained rocks from the top of the mountain—one each for her, her mother, and her brother. Willie had intended to give them to some other friends, but they were the only way he could think of to connect Fabiola with Nils.

"Your father would have wanted you to have some of these," he told her.

"I didn't think there were guys like you in the world anymore," Fabiola said.

Whether they were on another mountain right beside it or on the other side of the planet, the twins couldn't seem to keep from getting dragged into Everest's dramas. Willie knew the events that had made his brother into the kind of person who would fly halfway around the world to help a stranger. Many of the memories that inspired the Benegas brothers to help Fabiola had occurred in the previous twelve months, in the year that began with the twins' last trip to Nepal together, and Everest's Golden Jubilee.

By 2003, Willie Benegas had stood on the summit of Everest three times, each of them with clients, placing him among the most sought-after guides for the trip to the top of the mountain. So he was expecting the call that January, offering a spot guiding during the coming fiftieth anniversary of the mountain's first ascent.

"I knew this year could be the biggest nightmare in the mountain's history," Willie wrote in the 2004 *American Alpine Journal*. "There were going to be too many expeditions, too much press and too many ego-trippers . . . From my experience, a mix of poorly run private expeditions meeting in Base Camp is a formula for disaster."

The night after he descended from Everest's summit in 2002, Willie learned that a Hungarian mountaineer was unaccounted for.

"It seems his 'friends' had decided that in some mystical way he would manage to return safely to camp, even though he had collapsed at 8,200 meters," Willie said in his report. He went out alone and found the climber lying at the base of the Triangle Face, gave his oxygen to the stricken man, and dragged him to camp, certain that without the warmth provided by the bottled gas, he would lose some of his own digits to frostbite. Memories like that make climbers' fingers ache, particularly when they're holding a telephone offering the chance to do it all over again. Willie turned down the job guiding Everest during the anniversary season. If he was going to suffer like that in 2003, he would do it with his brother rather than clients he would probably never see again. He wanted to get as far from the Everest circus as he could, which proved to be barely two miles away.

He called it "Fatai Sarpa Nuptse"—the Crystal Snake of Nuptse.

Of the triumvirate of peaks that makes up the Everest massif, Nuptse seems the poor sister, most famous for how often its summit is mistaken for the top of the world in photographs. Willie first saw the Crystal Snake during his maiden voyage on Everest in 1999, when the clouds parted briefly to reveal a line of ice and snow that weaved toward Nuptse's 7,855-meter summit. Ice like glass made up the most spectacular line he had ever seen.

Climbing Nuptse is far more challenging than any of the standard routes on the "Big E." By 2003, there were more than a dozen routes up the tallest mountain, but only two to the top of Nuptse. Nearly 2,000 people had climbed Everest. Only a handful had made it to Nuptse's main summit.

Willie and Damian used the same Base Camp as the climbers who were celebrating Everest's anniversary, so they lived in relative luxury along with nearly a thousand other people. There were shops selling T-shirts and yak meat, and a tent housing an Internet café with four computers and a satellite connection available for a dollar a minute. A Frenchman of questionable repute wandered the camps offering massages. A British team planned to carry an ironing board to the summit. But in the first week of May, when virtually every other climber there headed up the Lhotse Face toward the South Col of Everest, Willie and Damian veered right, to Nuptse. And then, within a few miles of the most crowded peak in the Himalaya, they were about as alone as they had ever been in their lives.

They spent their first night on the route hanging in their harnesses. Their stove broke at two a.m., leaving them screaming with the frustration of having no way to heat food or melt drinking water from snow. The route, far steeper than they had anticipated, was covered with ice so hard, it crushed their ice screws like beer cans. Damian had broken a rib coughing and stepped through snow that hid a crevasse. They headed back to Everest to round up another stove and some heftier screws, and were back on the Crystal Snake on May 18 with enough food to last four days.

Their bivouacs rarely had enough space for two people to sleep, so the twins nestled as close as they had in the womb. Spindrift fell upon them through the night, filling their sleeping bags with snow, pushing them from their tiny perches, and encasing them in ice.

After four days, Willie led them up the last steep pitch of ice to the head of the Snake and was marching up a slope of deep snow when he realized the slope was about to avalanche. He took a knife and cut the rope from his harness. If the slope cut loose, at least there was a chance they both wouldn't fall off the mountain if he and Damian weren't tied together. They made their way to a small rock that was poking up through the snow and held on "like castaway sailors not wanting to let go of a tiny island."

For two more days the twins ascended crumbling rock and hair-triggered slopes of snow until they reached the top of Nuptse at one p.m. on May 23. Willie spread his arms out in front of Everest and Lhotse for his brother's photos as if he were welcoming people to a party. Then they began their descent to Camp Two on Everest, where they arrived at ten that night and celebrated in the tents of the Alpine Ascents International expedition. But the worst part of their climb was yet to come.

The following morning, Willie and Damian woke feeling more exhausted than they ever had in their lives.

"We weren't sleeping. We were eating nothing. We lost so much weight. Damian had a cracked rib. It was pretty horrendous," Willie said. "We were destroyed."

After breakfast, they lay in the sun with Luis Benitez, a guide for Alpine Ascents, and Willi Prittie, that expedition's leader, who were enjoying the ribbing that Damian was giving Willie for all the gear he had dropped during their climb. They had all seen plenty of sick climbers on Everest, so at first glance, the Sherpa coming down on the arm of another didn't strike them as unusual. As the stricken climber neared, however, they noticed he was groaning and fighting for his breath. When he sat down just below their camp and wouldn't get back up, Willie, Luis, and Willi Prittie went to check on him.

The sick climber, Karma Gylzen Sherpa, was twenty-eight and working for the massive and well-sponsored Team Everest '03, organized by the Coalition of Texans with Disabilities. Days later, the expedition's leader would be the first one-armed climber to summit Everest. A dozen other disabled athletes made a "challenge trek" to Base Camp. Among the hordes crowding the trail to Everest during the anniversary season, the wheelchair-bound trekkers showed the greatest chutzpah as they wrestled their chairs over the increasingly rugged terrain. They had planned to wheel all the way to Base Camp, but no wheelchair can ride over the most difficult trails to Everest. In the end, a huge team of Sherpas and porters did much of the legwork. Disabled trekkers often rode in baskets worn by the natives like backpacks, or with their wheelchairs lashed to the backs of porters. But when the team's Sherpa, Karma, was sent down from Camp Four, the one other Sherpa who accompanied him was nowhere near the amount of manpower needed to get Karma to safety. The climbers Karma was working for, wrapped up in their own summit bids and sicknesses, were unaware of how ill their employee was, or that he needed more help.

Luis Benitez was more than familiar with climbs to raise awareness of disabilities. He had made his first trip to the top of Everest two years earlier as part of the expedition that put blind climber Erik Weihenmayer on top of the mountain.

"So this is how we treat the people who help us reach our dreams," Luis thought as he checked on the sick Sherpa. Trained as a Wilderness Emergency Medical Technician, he found Karma's oxygen saturation and pulse were good, but his stomach was giving him horrible pain.

"No eat, drink, shit, or piss for three days," the stricken man's friend told Luis. The other climbers worked the radio to recruit a rescue team, but despite the heaviest traffic on the mountain ever, they found no takers. The Base Camp manager for Karma's expedition begged other teams for help but was "flat-out refused."

The Alpine Ascents guides, caught between wanting to help and their responsibilities to their clients, assigned some Sherpas to help get Karma down. But Willie and Damian were the only people available who knew how to conduct a rescue, and the effort would require ten or more climbers. The twins wrapped Karma in a sleeping bag and put him on oxygen. Then they ripped loose a ladder that was spanning a crevasse, tied the Sherpa onto it, and dragged the makeshift stretcher down the mountain like oxen pulling a plow.

"Twelve hours or twenty-four hours or eighteen hours—I can't remember how long it was," Willie said. "It was forever."

Willie also lost count of the number of people he asked for help who had passed by the Sherpa fighting for his life without breaking their stride.

"We had French passing through, we had Americans passing through—no regard. Everybody wanted to get off the mountain fast, or they wanted to go on for the summit."

A French climber passed them by on his way down the mountain with two Sherpas carrying his gear, but he refused to allow his employees to put the equipment down and help out.

"He was more interested in his gear than in trying to save the life of [a] Sherpa," Willie said.

Luis stayed in close contact with Willie and Damian. He was already talking about going down to assist when Damian called in from near Camp One. Karma was unconscious, vomiting, and in convulsions. They needed dexamethasone to revive him, and their own syringe of the drug was broken. Luis looked at his boss, Willi Prittie, the leader of the Alpine Ascents team.

"With his eyes, he told me, 'Go, and do the best you can,' " Luis wrote in his report about the incident. "All I remember is running. Running at almost 22,000 feet to try and help a man I had never known before this day."

Luis made it to Camp One in twenty-seven minutes and injected Karma with dex. Karma's eyes were rolled back in his head, his abdomen was as hard as a plank, and he had vomited bile into his oxygen mask. It took the entire team to roll him over and clear his throat. Luis radioed the Sherpa's condition to Luanne Freer, the Base Camp doctor. Then they lifted Karma and headed into the Khumbu Icefall.

They continued to call Base Camp for help, but the only assistance came from above. Manuel Lugli, the Italian expedition organizer who would, a year later, put together the Everest climb for Nils Antezana and Gustavo Lisi, had just attempted a speed climb on Everest with another climber. Despite their exhaustion, the two Italians joined in the effort.

The team moved through the jumbled maze at a crawl that slowed even more when night descended. They pulled Karma across the worst of the icefall's crevasses on ropes stretched across the chasms. When friction made it impossible to pull the litter across one gorge in the ice that was more than 100 feet wide and nearly as deep, Damian climbed out onto the cord and over the litter, then hung in front of it to pull Karma across the chasm hand-over-hand.

Long after nightfall, Karma passed out again. He had no pulse, no breath, and no response in his eyes. Damian kneeled over the Sherpa to administer mouth-to-mouth, spitting out the bile from Karma's throat in between breaths. Luis could feel Karma's ribs cracking as he frantically pumped his hands on the Sherpa's chest. Louder cracks from the icefall reminded the rest of the climbers huddled around them that, even if they couldn't see it in the blackness, crumbling towers of ice made administering emergency medicine here like doing triage on a battlefield.

Damian and Luis refused to give up until long after the other climbers knew it was over. Willie put his hand on Luis's shoulder. It was no longer a rescue, he explained, but a body recovery. Karma was dead. Luis looked up and saw the headlamp beams piercing the steam that came off the bodies that were still alive, and wept. They secured the stretcher with Karma's body for the night and made their way as fast as they could toward the city of tents glowing in the distance. As they exited the icefall, climbers and Sherpas from teams that had refused to help now came to them with tea and cookies, but the rescuers just shoved past and made their way into camp. Luis listened to laughter and cheers coming from the tents of the French team that had passed them without helping. He cleansed himself of his contact with the dead according to Sherpa tradition— juniper smoke, water, and three handfuls of rice thrown into the air. Then he fell to his knees and vomited onto the moraine.

After learning of Karma's death, members of the Coalition of Texans with Disabilities expedition announced that in addition to the funds they were soliciting for their own organization, they would also raise money for the Karma G. Sherpa Memorial Hospital. Four years later a prayer wheel had been constructed in Karma's village in the Solu Khumbu, and members of his family had flown to Texas to attend the wedding of Gary Guller, the leader of the expedition and the first one-armed climber to summit Everest. Construction of the hospital, however, had yet to begin.

Three days after Karma died, Willie and Damian heard a helicopter coming into Base Camp. So did Ellie Henke.

It was Ellie's third year working as the Base Camp manager for Alpine Ascents. She and her partner, the guide Willi Prittie, had complained about the inordinate amount of helicopter traffic coming to Base Camp during the Golden Jubilee season. Many teams were using helicopters to resupply, and others were hitching rides between the Kathmandu parties and the mountain, which struck Ellie and Willi as badly confused priorities. Choppers that carry out injured climbers can save lives, but the ones bringing in supplies and tourists who could get there just as well on foot add a dangerous level of chaos in an exceptionally hazardous place to land. Ellie and Willi had once listened, aghast, as an expedition leader told a chopper pilot coming to evacuate a team member with a back injury to wait until the team could order up some supplies to load onto the flight into camp. The weather turned before the shopping was done, and the injured climber waited for days in increasing agony for the storm to clear so the flight could get through.

During the anniversary season, the bored crowds in Base Camp gathered around landing choppers as if they were greeting rock stars. Himalayan veterans, on the other hand, ran the other way.

They know how little air there is for a helicopter rotor to hang on to at 17,000 feet, and that the platform of stones that the chopper must land on is invariably less stable than it appears, simply because hidden below it is a moving glacier.

The morning of May 28, Ellie heard a chopper that sounded lower and louder than the others. She poked her head out of a tent to watch as it came in and then started wobbling a few feet above the ground.

It was five days after the Benegas brothers had reached the summit of Nuptse, and the day before the fiftieth-anniversary celebrations of Hillary and Norgay's first ascent of Everest. The Russian-built helicopter carried five passengers and a four-person crew to Base Camp, where it was scheduled to pick up climbers, including a Sherpa who had just set the speed record on the mountain, and take them to Kathmandu for the parties. As it descended to land a little after ten that morning, one of its wheels clipped the top of a pile of stones, and the chopper tripped off the landing pad, rolled over a trekker on the trail into camp, and crashed into a shallow, frozen stream. The rotors hurled debris onto the camp, and several people were injured by the rain of rocks and helicopter parts that fell up to half a mile from the site of the crash. Two Nepalis on board the chopper died in the crash, and several other passengers were critically injured.

Willie and Damian were among the first to get to the scene. The blades were still spinning and drove most of the rescuers back, but Willie managed to get past them, along with a military officer who was familiar enough with the aircraft to stop the engine. Another pair of choppers landed, and the twins helped load the injured for evacuation to Kathmandu. Then Willie walked back into camp, rounded up his passport, and loaded his backpack. He wanted nothing more than to get as far away from Everest as he could.

Between the chopper crash and her own team's summit bid, Ellie was swamped with work, but she put down her radio to give Willie a hug. She had watched like a stargazer as Willie and Damian had made their way up the Crystal Snake during the previous weeks, marveling each night at how much higher the lights of their headlamps had moved up the mountain and cheering when she heard that the twins had pulled off their dream climb. But now Willie looked nothing like a champion. His jacket was splattered with blood, and she could see that he had been crying. Despite their accomplishment, there would be no party, no reliving their victory with their friends.

Ellie released her embrace and pushed Willie out the door of the tent.

"Get out of here, Willie," she said. "Just walk out of here and don't look back."

Damian was still recovering, and his girlfriend was on the mountain, so he stayed in Base Camp. But Willie hiked straight through the night to the airstrip in Lukla, more than twenty miles from Everest. He stopped in Kathmandu just long enough to visit the victims of the helicopter crash and give some blood to help with their treatment. But months later, his year still seemed to be going downhill.

Many climbers consider Alpamayo, in Peru, the most beautiful mountain in the world—a supermodel that is one of the most popular peaks on the mountaineering runway. Even Alpamayo's standard route sounds like an accessory for a tall and glamorous star: the Ferrari. The climb races straight up a runnel, a vertical groove in Alpamayo's steep flank. Willie arrived in Peru two months after he left Everest's anniversary party to lead clients up this aloof beauty.

But like many striking celebrities, Alpamayo has a problem you don't see until you get close—a giant serac that drops deadly blocks of ice down the climb. Once he had his clients in camp, Willie took a walk to check out the route. The block of ice hanging off the summit was as big as he had ever seen it, looming over the climb like the beak of a mountain-size bird. He told his clients they would be climbing a different peak. Then he headed to the nearby guide's hut to let the climbers there know what he had seen.

Nearly a week later, on Monday, July 21, a climber came running into camp. The serac had fallen onto climbers on the Ferrari. Willie headed up the trail at a run.

About an hour later, he came upon two climbers who had an Israeli woman tied onto a stretcher. Ofira Zucker, age twenty-two, had promised her family that she would be the first Israeli woman to reach the 19,500-foot summit of Alpamayo. A few weeks earlier, she had e-mailed her father, Menahem, a photo of herself atop another mountain with the caption, "A hug to dad from the summit of the world."

Menahem had tried to talk her out of her climb.

Guy Ben-Ze'ev's parents had made the same pleas to him. Guy, Ofira's climbing partner, had spent a tour with the Israeli Defense Forces clearing explosives.

"When Guy was released from the army, we said to ourselves that he's finished with danger," his father told the Israeli newspaper *Yediot Aharonot*.

Ofira was the lowest of the ten climbers spread out over several hundred meters in the groove that ran up the mountain like a gutter. Above were Germans, a Dutchman, an Argentine, and two Peruvian guides—one of whom had already reached the top. Around nine a.m., the cornice at the top broke loose. Either of the Peruvian guides could have triggered the avalanche, or it might have happened whether they were there or not. Neither of them, however, fell with the block of ice that came down the runnel like a train onto eight mountaineers tied to its tracks with their own ropes.

Afterward Ofira was screaming for help in the crevasse at the bottom of the Ferrari. The others were silent. The climbers who extricated Ofira put her on a donkey for what would be a nine-hour evacuation. When Willie saw Ofira, her face was blue. He tried to resuscitate her with CPR, but couldn't revive her.

To Willie, the site of the accident looked like news photos he had seen of car bombings, with snow and ice and bodies jumbled at the bottom of the route like the debris of a collapsed building. Guy, the man who had served his country by disarming explosives, lay at the bottom of the rubble. Police worked for days to get to his body as other mountaineers stepped past the bloody wreckage to start their own ascents. Damian was leading a trek in another part of Peru's Cordillera Blanca mountain range when he heard that an Argentine guide had died in an accident on Alpamayo. He hiked through the night to get to the mountain, certain that his brother was dead.

Initial investigations pointed to the inexperience of the guides on the mountain during the accident and their lack of familiarity with the climbing route. Some wondered why, of the ten people on the route, the two local guides survived, but eight foreign climbers perished. Why would they crowd such a perilous climb, where any one of them could have brought down a killer avalanche onto the others? But Willie knew that climbers move up mountains the same way avalanches snowball down them. It had taken only one climber to head up the route for the rest to follow like sheep.

Barely a week later, Willie was leading a group up Huascaron, the highest peak in Peru, when he passed a tent in Camp Two with its front door open. When he came back, a local porter told him that someone was in there, and Willie knew what he was going to find inside. The mountaineer in the tent had been just about to light his stove when a heart attack had hit him. Willie rifled through the man's gear to find some identification, then called the police. They asked him to stay on the scene until the next day.

"No way," he said.

In 2003, with their summit of Nuptse, Willie and Damian Benegas made what was among the most acclaimed climbing accomplishments of the year—the mountaineering equivalent of a gold medal in the Olympics. Willie's ten-page story about climbing the Crystal Snake was the first entry in the 500-page *American Alpine Journal* of 2004, touting "The World's Most Significant Climbs." But when the twins look back, they see the clouds before they see the peak—the dozen lives they couldn't save.

"Two thousand three was a really bad year for me and Damian," Willie says.

Willie and Damian didn't tell any of this to Fabiola as she sat at Rum Doodle turning the rocks from the summit of Everest in her hands while successful climbers, fresh back from the top of the world, cheered and toasted at the crowded tables around them.

"I wish my dad would have climbed with you guys," Fabiola said. "He might not have made it to the summit, but he would still be alive."

Willie smiled at the compliment, but Damian, the straight man in the twins' routine, looked at Fabiola somberly.

"We don't know that," he said.

To Damian, Nils's death was yet another one they couldn't prevent. But perhaps this one wouldn't be in vain.

Seventeen

Two days after George's announcement that our team didn't have enough food to support further climbs to the top, I woke up in Base Camp to gaze at a perfect summit day. Russell Brice's Sherpas fixed ropes a few feet in front of the first of his nineteen clients who reached the top. Four Italians, climbing without oxygen, spent two hours conducting experiments atop the peak.

But while it was clear and calm on Everest, a furor was erupting in Base Camp.

Anne, Carolyn, and I were at the Italian camp when we heard Lhakpa's screams late that afternoon. George, Guillermo, and Dan Lochner had just sat down in the dining tent after descending from Advanced Base Camp. Lhakpa had followed them into the tent. When we got there, Maila, our cook, was pulling her from the tent. Lhakpa was shrieking and held a softball-size rock in her hand.

We led Lhakpa to the cook tent and tried to calm her down. "But I must fight," she argued, eyes brimming with tears. "I want to fight. I kill this man."

She said she wanted a divorce. Dave offered a haven with his family in Connecticut. After an hour, Lhakpa said she wanted to visit the bathroom. But we soon heard her in the dining tent again.

"I want a divorce," she screamed. "She's my daughter too."

George shouted vulgarities and insults back at her. "Get out of here, you jungle girl," he yelled.

Anne stepped inside the door. But before she could persuade Lhakpa, who held no rock this time, to leave, she saw George hook a blow with his right hand into the side of his wife's head. The rest of the Connecticut team saw Lhakpa crumple onto the rocky ground just inside the door. She cried hysterically as George grabbed the scruff of her coat. I took a photograph and George dropped Lhakpa to come at me.

"You trigger happy?" he shouted. "I'll smash that camera on your head!"

"She's crazy," Guillermo said, throwing his arms in the air when Anne asked for help.

Dan Lochner sat at the table with his hat pulled down over his eyes and his head in his hands.

"I'll show you how to get this piece of garbage out of here," George shouted, grabbing his wife and throwing her onto the rocks outside, where she fell unconscious.

Carolyn, Anne, and Chuck carried Lhakpa to the cook tent. We could hear George's bellowed curses while we tried to revive Lhakpa, who was in convulsions. Carolyn ran for help, and within a few minutes Italian mountaineers and doctors filled the tent. Maila moved Lhakpa to his own tent when she revived. Anne, Carolyn, and I ate in the cook tent. Carolyn put her open pocketknife on the table.

"Just in case I have to cut my way out of this tent," she said. "If it catches on fire or anything."

George, Dan Lochner, and Guillermo went to a teahouse for the night. When the rest of us finally retired, I regretted leaving my ice axes in Advanced Base Camp. Anne took ski poles into her tent. Carolyn slept with her knife in her hand.

"I'm afraid that he'll just come back in the middle of the night, pick up a boulder, and throw it on one of our tents," Anne said.

In the middle of the sleepless night I heard Carolyn whispering. "I'm so scared . . ."

In the morning, Chuck's eyes were bloodshot and swollen. He said he had confronted domestic abuse during his childhood. "I won't tolerate that. It's unacceptable to me."

At breakfast, he and Dave passed a pipe among themselves, filled from a fist-size chunk of hashish that they had brought with them from Nepal.

When George returned to camp at midmorning, Chuck and Dave followed him into the dining tent. George emerged every so often with his cap pulled down to the top of his sunglasses and his scarf pulled up to his nose. He stalked outside the tents, glaring at Anne, Carolyn, and me, occasionally training his video camera on us or lowering his face mask to puff on cigarettes. We had never seen him smoke before. When the women stared back, he grabbed his crotch or flipped them off.

"Darth Vader in Adidas," Anne said.

Neither woman would go to the bathroom unaccompanied. After a few hours the Chinese liaison officer arrived in a Jeep, and George followed him into the cook tent to confront us.

"Who are the journalists?" the officer demanded.

"Those two," George said, pointing as Carolyn and I raised our hands. "They are the journalists."

Chuck and Dave gathered outside the cook tent to watch. The officer said he had heard we were writing about the political situation in Tibet and reporting unconfirmed deaths on the mountain, although he declined to say from whom he had heard this. Anne stepped in to say she was the leader and vouched that I was a climber with the expedition and only wrote of our own experiences. The officer was satisfied, but showed on his paperwork that George, who had nominated Anne and Lhakpa as the expedition's leaders, was actually listed as the leader with the Chinese government. The Jeeps to Nepal showed up an hour after the liaison officer had left and we frantically packed up our gear. The four-hour ride to Tingri was punishing, and the village seemed more disgusting than during our first visit, but it didn't wear George down.

"She's a fucking journalist!" he shouted, pointing out Carolyn and her video camera to bewildered Chinese workers in the town where we stopped for the night. "You want to take a picture of me with my pants down?"

The next day, at the Chinese border, a waiter led us to the table where the last team meal was served. None of the Connecticut expedition sat with George, Guillermo, and Dan Lochner at their table. When I came to fill my bowl, George bounced a pair of chopsticks off my chest.

"Ask permission, you animal!" he hissed.

The venom in his voice was frightening, and I was thankful he was armed only with chopsticks. He didn't speak to me again for five months.

At the border, Carolyn and I were again questioned by authorities who had heard that we were journalists. After we crossed Friendship Bridge into Nepal, George and Lhakpa hired separate cars and raced down the rough-hewn mountain roads to Kathmandu.

"I thought they were going to start ramming each other," said Chuck, who was riding with Lhakpa.

"Last year as well," Dawa Sherpa at Asian Trekking said when Anne told him our story the next morning. "It has happened before."

Eighteen

When Gustavo finally arrived at the Yak and Yeti with Big Dorjee and Mingma, Fabiola was waiting, standing just inside the door to the lobby with Davide and Damian behind her. The guide and Sherpas looked like hell—ground down and dirty in dingy T-shirts. Gustavo stepped back when Fabiola introduced herself, then hugged her and kissed her on both cheeks. She asked Gustavo for the photos from the climb. He had them on his laptop, he said, and would bring her a CD of photos after he checked into his room and cleaned up. When she asked about her father's gear, Gustavo told her bad weather over the Lukla airstrip had prevented flights from carrying the expedition gear out. It would be coming in a day or two.

When Gustavo stepped away, Big Dorjee realized who Fabiola was and stepped forward. Fabiola was struck by how enormous he was—fully a head taller than Gustavo and Mingma.

"I'm sorry, I'm sorry, I'm sorry," he said, his hand pressed to his chest.

Fabiola saw why her father had trusted the Sherpas. Although they live on the opposite side of the planet, they look much like the Indians in Nils's beloved Bolivia.

"Like two tears on different cheeks," she thought to herself.

That afternoon the Sherpas sat with Fabiola, Davide, and Damian in the rotunda beside the Yak and Yeti's entrance. Nima Noru, the owner of Cho Oyu Trekking, the agency that had assigned the Sherpas to Gustavo and Nils's expedition, translated. They did everything they could to save her father, they said, but he was dead when they left him.

"It was really hard to help your father down, because your father was a big man," Dorjee said. "Your father was a very big man."

"Are you kidding me?" Fabiola responded, shocked. "He was half your size."

At his heaviest, her father had weighed 160 pounds and he must have lost at least ten or twenty pounds during the expedition.

After the Sherpas left, Gustavo came downstairs with a CD of photos. Elizabeth Hawley, the eighty-one-year-old journalist and historian who has documented every Everest expedition since 1961, had just arrived at the hotel, true to her knack for tracking down climbers as soon as they got back to Kathmandu. Damian volunteered to translate for her interview with Gustavo while Fabiola and Davide looked at the photos from the expedition on a computer in the hotel's business center.

Gustavo's story changed, even as he was telling it.

"I must have been a hundred meters further down, more or less," he said of his distance from the Sherpas when they left his client.

But a minute later he told Damian, "No! . . . I never distanced myself so much, never more than thirty or forty meters. In other words, I never became separated more than a stretch of the fixed cord."

Damian asked Gustavo what the Sherpas had said when they caught up with him.

" 'Let's go down because Nils cannot anymore,' " he said the Sherpas told him after they left Nils on the Balcony. " 'He is dead.' "

Seconds later Gustavo admitted the Sherpas had told him Nils was still alive.

"I asked them what was happening with Nils. [The Sherpas] told me he was unconscious, that he was not speaking, was not responding. That they had put on [Nils] the down jacket and left him up there."

When Damian finished quizzing Gustavo on Elizabeth Hawley's behalf, he had more questions than he started with. Fabiola and Davide were equally puzzled. Like those of Juan Carlos Gonzalez, some of Fabiola's questions came down to photographs from the summit of Everest. But this time it was images that Gustavo should have had and didn't, rather than those that he possessed but shouldn't have. Aside from the few seconds of video Gustavo had shot of Nils, there were no images of the doctor on top. In the video Nils doesn't look crazy, as Big Dorjee had described. He isn't tearing off his oxygen mask or walking off the summit or lying on his back and refusing to get up. He stands as still as a mannequin. It takes him a few seconds to wave when Gustavo introduces him to the camera, but there is nothing else to indicate that he is having a problem. Why were there no photos of her father on the summit? Fabiola wondered. Getting a client to the top of the world is perhaps the greatest success a mountain guide can claim—like coaching a college basketball team in an NCAA final. Not making the photographic evidence that, had Nils survived, would be a linchpin in the guide's success seemed like yet another blunder. Or perhaps it was something worse, Fabiola thought. Something that Gustavo didn't want anyone to see.

Elizabeth Hawley packed up, and Fabiola and Davide took her place for their own interview with Gustavo. Music began to pour from the lounge's piano. Nepal's slow decline seemed to have dragged the instrument down with it, leaving it badly out of tune. Friends familiar with how Nils Antezana kept music playing throughout his house every moment he was in it would have thought the doctor would cringe at such discord, but Fabiola knew her father's love of the bittersweet souvenirs of the British empire would have drawn him to listen to it anyway. Then she remembered Pat Falvey's minidisc recorder hidden in her backpack. She wanted a record of the dissonance in Gustavo's story, not an out-of-tune piano. Fabiola waved a waiter over and handed him a few bills.

"Please, could you have the piano player stop and come back a little later?"

Damian leaned forward to talk directly with Gustavo. The four parties in this interview would speak only Spanish.

"Gustavo, from a professional point of view, certain things you did . . . morally, ethically, were incorrect," Damian said.

"For example?" Gustavo asked in a voice worn ragged by the cold and exhaustion.

"You took two days to inform the family," Damian responded.

"Look, Damian," Gustavo said. "I will explain something to you. I believe I don't even have to explain it to you. I did not have a satellite telephone."

"Nevertheless, you called from Camp Four."

"No, they called me."

"Oh, yes, they called you. OK, perfect. Then you had a satellite telephone or they [contacted you] by radio?"

"No, no. I had my satellite telephone. First, I didn't have my notebook at the South Col, second, I did not have a battery, because when they called me I could not make calls from my telephone. . . . And I was dead, dead, dead. I fell. They had to look for me."

"Pat Falvey, the Irish, [said] when he went looking for you [the morning after the accident], you were on the phone," Damian responded.

"That's when I [received a call]," Gustavo explained. "And I didn't have Nils's home telephone number. And I could not send information the next day not knowing what had happened."

If he couldn't make calls, how did he notify his Web site that he had summited? Fabiola wondered.

"It would have been better for you not to inform your Web page of anything," Damian said.

"No, no," Gustavo protested. "What I informed my Web page—"

Damian didn't let him finish.

"[You said] you made the summit," he said, trying to stem the flow of outrage in his voice. "*A person died on you.*"

Gustavo couldn't go a sentence without contradicting himself. He didn't have a satellite phone and then he did. He didn't have a battery for the phone, but then it rang with a call. He got down at nine p.m.; he got down at eleven thirty. When Gustavo denied that he had claimed to have summited Everest in 2000 and Cho Oyu in 1995, and that he had told Nils that he hadn't made it to the summit of Everest in 2000, Damian pointed to a printout of Gustavo's Web page.

"Right here, it's quite clear. It says you made it to the summit. In this page, your page under 'Experience,' it says you made it to the summit," Damian said. "Look, Gustavo, we are going in circles here."

He pushed Gustavo about his decisions during the summit bid.

"I'm sorry, Gustavo," Damian said, "but you all should have [turned around] . . . Because if you left at eight and you arrived at ten a.m., it's fourteen hours to make the summit."

"Damian, I did not know he was sixty years old," Gustavo said.

"He was sixty-nine years old," Damian corrected. "All the more reason."

Gustavo's voice began to rise. "He was walking very fine during the entire expedition."

"You were seen going too slowly," Damian responded.

"You know something? A lot of people see you on the mountain," Gustavo responded.

Damian asked why Gustavo didn't have Nils using oxygen lower on the mountain.

"Damian, I can't put a knife to his throat," Gustavo responded. "I asked him if he wanted to put it on and he said no."

Fabiola had managed to stay quiet as long as she could. She demanded to know why Gustavo hadn't notified other climbers that he had left his client behind, why he hadn't tried to send someone up to rescue him.

"That night I came down at eleven o'clock," Gustavo said. "I was dead tired."

"But you were not unconscious," Fabiola said.

"No, Fabiola, I was not unconscious," Gustavo said. "But I was dead tired . . ."

Davide was seething.

"*You* were tired," he snapped.

"Coming down I suffered a fall. . . . Look, I have the marks from the bumps.

"The day we were bringing your father down," Gustavo said, "when I arrived at the Balcony, I remained there, waiting. They were fifty to seventy meters farther up. They were helping Nils because Nils could no longer do anything by himself. He could not stand, could not walk, could not talk, nothing."

"Could not talk?" a skeptical Fabiola said. "Nevertheless, [you said] he told you, 'The mountain is my home. Leave me here.'"

"He told me that farther up there, before I came down to the Balcony."

Gustavo said that Nils's request to be left on the mountain came two rope lengths up from the Balcony. But Gustavo had already said he hadn't been within speaking distance of Nils since they were on the South Summit, far higher up the mountain.

"I'm not going to lie to you . . . ," Gustavo said. "I was dead tired. It didn't occur to me [to notify people at Camp Four], don't ask me why, I don't know what happened. . . . When I woke up, the first thing I did was ask Dorjee and Mingma what we were going to do about Nils. The weather was horrible. . . ."

Fabiola pointed out that Gustavo had managed to call for help for himself.

"It is not that I was unconscious or in bad shape," he said.

"Then you could have informed [someone] that my father was still up there if you were not unconscious or in bad shape; you needed to tell somebody, 'My companion is up there' or send someone . . ."

Gustavo said he didn't let anyone know that he had left his client on the Balcony because Dorjee and Mingma had made it to camp before him, so he believed they had let other teams know that a stranded climber needed a rescue.

"But you are the guide," Fabiola said. "That is your responsibility. . . . You were well enough to shout for help to rescue you at the place where you had fallen. You could have said to someone that my father was left up there."

"Dorjee and Mingma were on that," Gustavo responded. "Dorjee said to me, 'We are waiting for the weather conditions to improve, in order to go up and get him.'

"You have to find who is at fault," he said. "I know the story."

"I hope you question your career," Damian said. "Because, personally, I am going to make sure no one else will have you as a guide."

The comforts of the Yak and Yeti were appealing to me and Carolyn, but mostly we checked in because the hotel had security. Perhaps we were being overly cautious, but we didn't want to lose our notes, computers, or digital images to a hotel-room break-in. I knew Damian Benegas only by reputation when he approached me in the lobby.

"You were on Everest?" he asked, but quickly lost interest when he learned I was on the other side of the mountain from his brother, Nils, and Gustavo.

Later, as I sat in a gazebo in the hotel's gardens to transmit photos to the newspaper that would show my own expedition blowing up, I saw Damian sitting with a beautiful and exotic woman and a handsome but somber man. They looked shocked and grief-stricken and I realized that despite how horribly my trip to Everest had ended, my teammates and I had walked away with our lives. There were people who had it far worse.

While Fabiola was discovering unsavory facts about Gustavo Lisi's history in the mountains, other climbers warned me that the man who had invited me to Everest had a complicated past as well.

David Neacsu had worked for seven years to put together the first Romanian expedition to Everest in 2003. George Dijmarescu's previous successes on Everest as well as his Romanian heritage prompted Neacsu to pay his and Lhakpa's expenses to join the team, and also those of Lhakpa's young sister, Doni. When I sought David out during the summer of 2004 to ask him about his expedition, my only surprise was how familiar the story sounded.

"The person whom I had been e-mailing for more than 6 months proved to be somebody else in the mountains," he wrote back in an e-mail. George told the Sherpas and other expeditions that he was the expedition's leader, David wrote, "telling the people other things than what I had asked . . . turning my people against me."

When David developed heart trouble in Advanced Base Camp, forcing him to descend to Base Camp and climb no higher, George stepped in.

"Dijmarescu sent to some journalists in Romania an e-mail . . . telling many untrue things about me (that I did not want the expedition to succeed, that I was sending people to death, that I was a liar and a thief . . .)," David wrote. "All the newspapers were talking only about the Romanians that were fighting on Everest."

The e-mail in question, which was published in a Romanian magazine, has George saying he wrote it on a handheld computer with a toothpick. But when David confronted him, he said, George denied writing it at all.

"George was acting like the tyrannical leader," Sebastian Koga, the team's doctor, told me.

Coco Galescu, the Romanians' strongest climber, questioned George's authority in Advanced Base Camp, Sebastian recalled, and George lunged over the dining-tent table at him. Coco fell onto the rocky ground with George on top of him.

Coco was injured but hid it, hoping he could still make the summit.

"He was wheezing badly and basically breathing out of one lung," said Sebastian, who climbed with Coco until the injuries forced him to descend from 24,000 feet.

In Kathmandu, an X-ray revealed two broken ribs had caused fluid to fill one of Coco's lungs. In a telephone call and an e-mail exchanged with me during the summer of 2004, Coco confirmed Sebastian's recollection of the events.

Sebastian recalled George threatening others who might stand against him. "You don't know what happens at night and I have this ice ax," he quoted George as saying. He remembered thinking to himself, "These tents have very thin walls. What if he does come after me?"

Lhakpa's sister Doni was fifteen and had no mountaineering experience when George led her into the death zone on Everest in May of 2003.

"It took one and a half hours to take her over the Second Step," Russell Brice said. "Thirty to forty people had to turn around. That is incredibly selfish."

Other climbers and guides reported that George prowled at the base of the Second Step with his ice ax to make sure nobody else could climb it while Doni was there. In the end George joined the retreating climbers, reporting alternately that he had had problems with his oxygen mask, was turned back by the weather, or was troubled by the crowd. But the family of Sherpas continued upward. That morning Doni became the youngest person to climb Everest. Lhakpa set the record for ascents by a woman. With Mingma Gelu, they were the first trio of siblings to summit together. But when they returned to Camp Two that afternoon, George was less than congratulatory, Sebastian Koga said.

Doni, exhausted and inexperienced, stepped over a piece of George's down gear with her crampons on, Sebastian said.

"[George] hit Doni right in front of me. It was a backhanded, nasty slap," said Sebastian, a neurologist who has worked with head trauma patients at a Kathmandu hospital, studied the effects of abuse in Romanian orphanages, and conducted research at Tulane University's medical school in New Orleans.

While I was on Everest with the Connecticut team, Sherpas for other expeditions told me about George hitting Doni. After my team returned to the States, Chuck Boyd said that George had admitted to him early in our expedition that he had hit Doni. He had done it, Chuck said, because the girl belittled him for retreating during the climb. In late October 2004, when I asked for his side of the story, George denied hitting Doni or injuring Coco Galescu. But a month later, in an e-mail to MountEverest.net defending his actions,

George said that he had struck the fifteen-year-old because, after climbing to the summit of Everest and returning, she had tried to hit him with a rock.

Sebastian cited other parallels to the Connecticut expedition.

"The Sherpas demanded more money off us after having behaved really horribly," he said. "Dijmarescu and his Sherpas abused the hell out of us."

After they were paid, Sebastian said, the Sherpas climbed with George and Lhakpa and left behind members of the Romanian team who had paid them but didn't keep up.

Later, George asked Sebastian to join him for another attempt at the summit.

"I was honestly afraid that if something went wrong, he could turn homicidal," Sebastian said.

In the meantime, Lhakpa asked David Neacsu to take her and her sister away from Everest and her husband, the expedition leader reported. "On the same day, I received a phone call from Dijmarescu asking for my help. He needed money for his second attempt. I gave him money and let him use the oxygen that remained . . . many of them he sold to Russell Brice—in order to get money to pay the Sherpas."

Russell said he doesn't know if his team bought oxygen from George, but said the value of oxygen has made the bottles so popular with thieves that he no longer purchases secondhand tanks.

As George began his second attempt on the mountain in 2003, his wife, her siblings, and the rest of the Romanian expedition and Sherpas were making their way back to Kathmandu. On the day George made his way to Camp Three, Lhakpa and Doni had their photo taken with Sir Edmund Hillary at a party commemorating the fiftieth anniversary of the first ascent of the mountain. But the Romanian team's successes were overshadowed in their homeland by the tensions on the team.

"It was the first attempt by the Romanian government to fully sponsor an expedition. We [had] met the president and the prime minister. We were doing it right," Sebastian Koga said. "It kind of destroyed climbing in Romania, all this negative press."

"[George] is a menace . . . a real sadist with delusions of grandeur, intemperate ambition, poor judgment and endless egotism," Sebastian wrote to me in an e-mail. "He is the very embodiment of everything that is unacceptable and dangerous in a mountaineering teammate. He uses intrigue, rumor-spreading, and manipulation to divide a group and take power over them."

Nineteen

The morning after Gustavo told Fabiola about leaving her father to die on Everest, she ran into him as he was walking out of the hotel's breakfast buffet.

"Have you seen the Sherpas?" he asked. "I need them as witnesses to get my summit certificate."

Fabiola looked at the fork on a nearby table and wondered what it would feel like to stab him with it.

"But if I lose my composure with him," she thought to herself, "none of these climbers will ever take me seriously, and I'll never get to the bottom of what happened to my dad."

"No, I haven't seen them," she said calmly, and walked to the other side of the restaurant, where she sat down with Andres Delgado, the leader of the Mexican climbers whose permit Gustavo and Nils had shared, and his uncle, José Luis Abreu.

"Lisi is here?" Andres said, a sudden fury igniting his mountain-weary voice as he got up from the table. "Where is he? He owes me money."

Gustavo was gone when he went to look for him.

Two days after Gustavo, Big Dorjee, and Mingma made it back to Kathmandu, the duffel bag with Nils's equipment arrived on a flight from the mountains and was delivered to the Yak and Yeti. Fabiola was suspicious as soon as she saw it. There was no way all her father's equipment could fit in it. She and Davide had the concierge open the hotel's luggage room, where they found blue expedition barrels with Gustavo's name written on them. Fabiola wondered how the man who had paid for the expedition could have so little and the man working for him have so much. Gustavo had told Fabiola that he had a few of her father's things in his barrels and said he would handle sending all of Nils's gear back to Washington. But the American Embassy required an inventory of a dead climber's personal effects and took care of returning them to the family. Fabiola called the Embassy and they sent a truck to pick up her father's duffel and Gustavo's barrels. Then she left a message for Gustavo telling him where he could find his gear and headed out with Davide and Damian.

When Fabiola unzipped her father's bag at the Embassy, the stench told her that this wasn't his equipment. Nils bought all new, top-of-the-line gear for his Everest climb, but the first thing Fabiola pulled out of his duffel was a reeking sleeping bag that was old, worn, and stained.

"That's a Sherpa's sleeping bag," Damian said.

At the bottom of the bag she found the date book her father had used as a diary during the expedition. She set it aside while she rummaged through the bags and barrels to find his wallet, where he must have kept the cash his family had wired him. Nils had told both Fabiola and Gladys that on top of what other cash he carried to the mountain, he was bringing $10,000 to give as tips to his guide and Sherpas—$5,000 for Gustavo, and $2,500 each for Big Dorjee and Mingma. Gladys had wired him the money in Kathmandu, and he had told her he planned to stash it in a secure place in one of his tents when he was on his summit bid. It had to be somewhere in the gear he had left in the camps, but it didn't show up in what had come back from the mountain. Fabiola coaxed one of the U.S. Marines who worked at the Embassy to get bolt cutters and chop the locks off Gustavo's barrels. Inside them she found the sleeping bags and equipment that matched the receipts Fabiola had for the gear Nils had purchased for the climb. She also found a flag from Gustavo's hometown in Argentina on which he had written that in the year 2000 he became the first resident of Salta to reach the summit of Everest. But she found none of the cash.

Gustavo arrived at the Embassy a few minutes later with Big Dorjee and Mingma. When Fabiola confronted him, he insisted that the Sherpas must have blundered and put her father's gear in his barrels. He said he had no idea where his client's wallet or the $10,000 ended up. Damian angrily brandished the flag on which Gustavo was continuing to promote his false claim of climbing Everest in 2000.

"What are you doing with this?" he demanded. "What are you using this for?"

Gustavo said he was confused when he wrote it—it was just a misunderstanding.

The Embassy's Steven Brault was concerned enough to sit Fabiola, Davide, and Damian down with Gustavo to talk about how the guide ended up with most of his dead client's gear in barrels he was sending home to Argentina.

Afterward, Fabiola and Davide met with Big Dorjee and Mingma at a café across the street from the Embassy. The Sherpas asked about their tips for leading her father to the top of Everest. Their agreement through Manuel Lugli promised them payments running between $15 and $120 for each trip between the high camps on the mountain, along with a $900 bonus for each of them if they got to the summit with Nils and Gustavo. They got her father to the summit of Everest, the Sherpas pointed out, and were due their bonuses. Fabiola was dumbfounded. The men who had left her father to die on the mountain wanted gratuity for their services.

"I'll think about it," she said. "Let's meet for dinner tonight, and I'll let you know."

That night at the Yak and Yeti, Fabiola sat down with the Sherpas and gave them each around $300. They were visibly crestfallen but nodded their thanks to her, rose from the table, and walked away.

"You're never going to see them again," Davide told his wife.

Gustavo also approached Fabiola for money. Although he was staying in one of the most expensive hotels in Kathmandu, he said he didn't have enough money to get back to Argentina. Nils had promised him a bonus as well, but Fabiola didn't need to think about whether she was giving any money to Gustavo.

The next night, Fabiola remembered her father's diary. She lay in the hotel bed, reading key passages out loud to her husband. As measured by the datebook, Nils Antezana's expedition began on March 15, 2004, with the listings of a bank wire, deposit, and purchase of a thermos and cushions. He landed in Milan on April 3, and first mentions his guide the same day.

"Gustavo is late."

On April 5, they arrived in Kathmandu, where Nils described the architecture, filth, demonstrations for the restoration of Parliament, and strike-emptied streets. Flying to Lukla to begin the trek to Base Camp on April 9, he noted the flowers, food, and stony path. They arrived in Phakding at 2:20 that afternoon and in Namche Bazaar at the same time the following day. On Monday, April 12, the noise in the two-story lodge in Tengboche where they stayed made it impossible to sleep, and on April 13, in Pheriche, he went to the Himalayan Rescue Association's altitude illness lecture and had his oxygen saturation tested at 86 percent—a bit low, but not a problem. He did, however, have a worrisome cough. On April 14, he slept only half the night due to "persistent nightmares of suffocation and desperate thirst." He reached Base Camp on April 16 with a GI infection and diarrhea, and on April 17, wrote only, "Gastroenteritis terrible. No food. Dehydrated, Weak, Miserable."

Despite his illness and diminishing strength, Nils continued up the mountain. On April 19, his stomach bug again kept him from eating anything, but on April 20, he made his first trip through the Icefall anyway. "Exhausted. Shouldn't have done it," he wrote.

By the time he made his next trip through the Icefall, he felt better, but he was still moving very slowly. On Sunday, April 25, Nils took seven hours to climb from Base Camp to Camp One through the Icefall's "glass skyscrapers," and across twenty or thirty crevasses bridged by up to seven ladders lashed together. On April 26, they continued to Camp Two through the "Valley of Silence," and returned to Base Camp the following day. Gustavo left Nils behind both days and "complained that it was too taxing on him to come down slower." They argued that night and the following day, Nils noting that he had a "Serious talk about [Gustavo] not staying with me whenever we go snow or ice climbing or training."

As she read, Fabiola could see her father's expedition falling apart right on the page in front of her.

"I almost fired him," her father wrote. "He is not very reliable. He is immature at 32 yr. He does not have a good sense of responsibility and confuses it with . . . (Servitude, humiliating.) He is pretty selfish deep inside."

They rested for two days and on Friday, April 30, Nils celebrated his sixty-ninth birthday with a better meal than usual, *chang* (rice beer) and whiskey. Food, however, was becoming a constant source of frustration. On May 4 and 5, they had only tea and crackers for breakfast and dinner because Gustavo didn't like the dehydrated food they had brought for their return to Camp One. Their stove quit working, so Swiss climbers nearby made them tea.

"Gus—always too much ahead of me. (Not a very good companion.)," Nils wrote. "In retrospect, reviewing the 4 days of BC–C1–C2–C3–C2–we made horrible mistakes of feeding and hydrating ourselves adequately. I suppose I assumed Gus would take care of it, and apparently he trusted that the Sherpas would

take care of it. I'll leave open the answers for the final responsibility?"

On Sunday, May 9, the team returned to Base Camp for their final
rest before making their summit bid, and although Nils had marked
out spaces for journal entries through May 14, by Wednesday, May 12,
he was no longer writing in his diary.

When the Connecticut team returned to Kathmandu, more bad news
was coming from Everest. Russell Brice, fed up with climbers helping themselves to his equipment and supplies, had sent his Sherpas
to strip his ropes and ladders from the mountain as soon as his
clients came down from the summit. Dozens of other climbers and
Sherpas were stranded in high camps or endangered in their summit bids. No injuries, however, resulted.

When our luggage from the mountain arrived at our hotel, Carolyn and I discovered the locks had been pried off the barrels and
duffel bags. A tent and a bag of unused film were taken. In all, nine
of the Connecticut team's thirteen tents, which retail for $500 each,
were missing. In addition, all ten bottles of oxygen Anne and I had
planned to use high on the mountain, which cost $410 each, were
unaccounted for. Anne calmly listed the thousands of dollars of
missing gear and the expedition's troubles to Dawa Sherpa at Asian
Trekking. But Anne trembled with anger when she saw the banner
honoring George and Lhakpa, and associating the team she had
worked so hard to bring to the Himalaya with the man whose
volatility she believed had shattered it.

She wasn't much happier with Chuck and Dave when they explained to Dawa that they were rounding up money for their Sherpas, the tips they had implied they had already paid when they were
convincing Anne and me to pay our Sherpas early.

"You told me you paid your Sherpas!" Anne snapped.

A few days later, Carolyn and I ran into Lhakpa at the Nepali
Department of Immigration, where she was trying to arrange travel
papers for Mingma Gelu, her brother, to accompany her and George

to Pakistan for the K2 climb. But the climb wouldn't come off, she admitted, if she couldn't convince the king, or someone else in the Nepali government, to fund it.

"George says I must push harder," she said.

Most of the climbers on our permit, even those who summited, had fallen short of their dreams.

Guillermo's descent on oxygen should have deprived him of credit for climbing to the summit without it. But despite the fact that George, Dave, and Ang Mingma all said that Guillermo was on oxygen all the way from Camp Three to ABC, and I had seen Guillermo asleep with an oxygen mask and tank beside him in the Connecticut team's dining tent, he has claimed to be the second Mexican to summit Everest without using oxygen on EverestNews .com, in interviews with South American media, and on the Mexican Web site of the automobile manufacturer Audi.

Dan Lochner had just turned twenty-two when he successfully climbed Everest. He needed only to reach the summit of Mount Vinson in Antarctica to fulfill his quest to be the youngest person to climb the Seven Summits. But another climber, also from Connecticut's "Gold Coast," spoiled his dream. Britton Keeshan, of Greenwich, was also twenty-two, albeit several months older than Dan. The grandson of the children's television personality Captain Kangaroo, he completed his climbs to the continental high points when he summited Everest from the south a few days after Lochner. For Lochner to take the record, he would have to climb Vinson before any expeditions were flying into Antarctica. But, he told me in Kathmandu, he had a plan.

"I'm going to try and skydive into the mountain," he said.

He'd done one tandem skydive in the past, he pointed out.

In the end Keeshan won out, but held the record for barely a year: In 2005, an Australian woman was twenty-one when she finished the Seven Summits. Although he still claimed to be raising a million dollars for prostate cancer research as well as to pay for his climbs, the Web site Lochner created to raise money to fight cancer, Oath7.com, was no longer functioning in 2006.

Lochner's partner, Dan Meggitt, was also crestfallen. "I thought it would be more glamorous," said Meggitt, who had once sailed solo around the world. "I thought there would be more climbing involved."

"Maybe I'll finish this Seven Summits thing," he said when I asked what was next for him. "It's something to do."

It took the better part of a month for the fractured team, traveling alone or in pairs, to make their way back to Connecticut.

Twenty

Fabiola was in touch with Tom and Tina Sjogren, at Explorers-Web in New York, soon after she returned to London from Nepal. She wouldn't be home long, she told them, because she hoped some of her questions about her father's death in the Himalaya would be answered in the country of his birth in the Andes. They weren't surprised. Tom and Tina knew well how a remote mountain could send its visitors on to unexpected corners of the globe.

In 1999, two weeks after Michael Matthews had vanished and after four years trying to climb the mountain that had killed him, Tom and Tina made it to the top of Everest. They had decided to go to Russia before they even made it back down to Base Camp.

In the loads their Sherpas carried on the mountain were satellite phones, solar panels, and camcorders. Yet while Tom and Tina's high-tech communications from the summit of Everest to the rest of the world worked flawlessly, they realized that malfunctioning oxygen systems put many climbers and climbs at risk. Although they had only a few problems with their own oxygen that year, they'd had faulty oxygen gear in the past, and had seen how many of their peers on the mountain turned back from their climbs when their systems failed. What's more, they noted, the trade in bottled O_2 on Everest was growing into a multimillion-dollar business that was concentrated in just a few hands—most notably in those of their pal Henry Todd.

Henry had made all the arrangements for Tom and Tina's first climbs on Everest. They had grown disenchanted enough with his organizational style to take over their own logistics, but after four years on the mountain together, they considered him a friend. And, they say, Henry had told them that they had no choice but to purchase their oxygen from him: He claimed to hold exclusive rights to sell coveted Poisk oxygen in Nepal. Tom wanted to visit Poisk, in Russia, to break Henry's monopoly. Tina wanted to know why so many of their rigs had failed that spring.

In Saint Petersburg, the Sjogrens toured Poisk's warehouse and testing facility—a huge steel chamber filled with seats from jet fighters, which could depressurize to imitate the atmosphere of 30,000 feet and drop the temperature below zero.

"Of course you can buy oxygen directly from us," the sales rep responded when Tom made his pitch. Henry not only didn't have an exclusive relationship with Poisk for oxygen on Everest, they said, he hadn't bought any oxygen from them in two years.

"They ran for their books," Tina says.

" 'Here he's buying and here he's buying,' " she recalls the employee telling her as he showed their records. " 'And here it stops.' "

The Poisk representatives were upset by the reports of high rates of failure in their equipment on Everest that spring.

" 'That is not Poisk,' " the Sjogrens say the reps told them. " 'That is something else.' "

Henry had visited Tom and Tina in their hotel room in Kathmandu before they all headed to the mountain that spring. He was exhausted, they recall, and said he had spent the previous night riding atop a truck from India. A few weeks later, on the mountain, the Sjogrens' *sirdar*, Babu Chiri, had joked with them about some of the Poisk oxygen other teams were using. The tanks may be Russian, he said, but it's "Indian oxygen."

For several years, Henry had been paying Sherpas to carry empty oxygen bottles off Everest—one of many lauded efforts to clean up the mountain. The Sjogrens suspected he was refilling the empty tanks in India and hawking them as new bottles from Russia.

"They were marketed as straight-up Poisk oxygen," Tina said.

By October 1999, Tom and Tina had turned the Web site they had created to follow their climb of Everest into what would eventually become ExplorersWeb. Their investigations of their old friend would prove the site's most explosive content:

Oxygen is expensive to manufacture. The bottles must go through rigorous testing for their structural integrity, fittings, and the oxygen itself. The procedure takes three weeks for every single bottle. A failing system high up on a mountain can easily kill a climber not acclimatized to go without oxygen. The brain clouds up and vertigo enters in minutes. In bad cases, the climber either sits down in the snow to die, or when trying to descend—falls to his death.

Soon enough, Todd was collecting empty Poisk bottles. Poisk is currently the leading brand of oxygen on Everest. Manufactured initially for Russian fighter pilots, now the oxygen is made with a license of quality for climbing. Todd had a better idea. How about refilling the bottles for a very low cost in India instead? Said and done. Poisk bottles found their way to Todd's new lab for refills. Forget the tests, forget the licenses—it was Indian oxygen sold in Russian brand packages.

Then the problems started. Expedition after expedition reported failing oxygen bottles. "I tried six bottles before I found one that worked," reported one client in a 1999 expedition. "One in three failed," reported another climber that

same year, but in another expedition. A third expedition filed
a report of oxygen fraud to the Ministry, followed by another
one. And then someone died . . . Initially one of the strongest,
he suddenly slowed, and then fell off the mountain. "Our oxy-
gen didn't work," said the fellow clients. "Keep it quiet," or-
dered the leader. He had gotten his oxygen from Todd, and
Todd had been best man at his wedding.

ExplorersWeb visited the Russian plant for proof. The
proof was right there, in their books. Poisk bottles sold on
Everest with Todd as the main supplier, but in the book, there
were no sales from Poisk to Todd in the past two years.

An oxygen molecule from India is identical to one from Russia,
and a climber desperate for a breath won't care what country it
comes from. The problem, in fact, is often not with air, but with
water. Part of the process of refilling an oxygen tank is making sure
that the gas is dry, which can be difficult in the humid air of India.
A tank filled with oxygen that is too moist will often work fine
when a climber tests it low on a mountain, but in the subzero,
middle-of-the-night temperatures high on Everest, the water in the
gas can freeze, clogging the system with ice.

It's one of any number of potential malfunctions that show a
dangerous irony, namely that many problems with oxygen systems
don't manifest themselves until the equipment is at an altitude
where lives depend on it. And problems aren't exclusive to the refilled Poisk bottles. In 2004, a new company, Summit Oxygen, introduced a revolutionary system that would allow climbers to cut the
weight of their oxygen system in half by providing the gas when the
user is breathing in, but not when they are exhaling. A British Army
expedition had tested the system in 2003, and in 2004, expeditions
on both sides of Everest eagerly took to it. But Will Cross, attempting to become the first diabetic to climb Everest, reported that he
was forced to turn back from his summit bid when the battery-
powered system, which had worked perfectly up to the South Col,
stopped providing gas. On the north side of the mountain, I sat with
Dan Mazur's SummitClimb team as they went about fixing the sys-

tem with whatever tools they could find. Another team abandoned the rigs altogether in favor of Poisk setups.

Summit Oxygen was back on Everest in 2005, this time with even more problems. A British climber reported that his system barely delivered any gas. An Indian Army climber turned back with suspected trouble with the system's O-rings, and a Sherpa with a Norwegian team sealed leaks in the system by pouring water on them and letting it freeze. Xavi Arias, a climber with a Catalan team, turned back above 8,000 meters when his Summit system failed. His hypoxia caused him to fall during his descent, injuring his leg so badly that Sherpas had to carry him down.

"All the [Summit Oxygen] bottles they had have failed except for four," reported a team from Valencia, Spain. Two of that team's climbers continued up with the working cylinders, but two hours later an update on their Web site reported, "The four remaining O2 bottles have failed as well."

Summit Oxygen confirmed the problems and, on MountEverest .net, reported that 25 percent of the oxygen bottles and 50 percent of the delivery systems malfunctioned.

For the last week or so we have sadly received emails and telephone calls from various expeditions stating that there are certain failures with our system . . .

I have been in contact with the majority of the users, however some I have not been able to reach.

In 2006, there were more innovations, although some companies were not as forthright about their problems as Summit had been. Valentine Bozhukov, a seventy-two-year-old Russian climber, registered Russian Oxygen, LTD, in Nepal and patented equipment to refill tanks with liquid oxygen to a pressure 20 percent higher than the tanks normally hold—a service he would provide not only in Kathmandu but in Everest Base Camp as well. Russian expedition leader Alex Abramov reported that his countryman came to his camp peddling oxygen at a substantial savings compared with other systems.

"Valentine Bozhukov visited us today—he came to talk us into using his invention—liquid oxygen," Alex reported. "It is poured into bottles, evaporated, thus creating the pressure of 300 atmospheres. But I consider this to be dangerous and don't trust it."

George Dijmarescu and Dave Watson were back on Everest in 2006 as well. Bozhukov signed on as the "oxygen sponsor" for their small Fantasy Ridge Expedition and joined them at a Kathmandu restaurant.

"Tonight at dinner Valentine and [his wife] Victoria had a special treat for us, a liquid oxygen cocktail!" Dave Watson wrote on EverestNews.com on March 22, 2006. "In the middle of the restaurant, they poured glasses of apple juice and then added the O2. It looked like dry ice with the 'smoke' pouring over the rim of the glass and rolling across the table.... We drank it and it was great."

Few other climbers were so eager to drink the "cool aid," and many of Valentine's business relationships were not so amicable.

When I spoke with Andrey Maximov at Poisk, he had no complaints about Henry Todd, who openly sells Poisk bottles that he now acknowledges refilling himself in his own lab as well as new tanks from the factory. Henry, in fact, remains at the top of Poisk's client list. But Maximov had serious concerns about Valentine, who he claims defrauded another Russian oxygen company, Zvezda, which had a service center in Kathmandu.

"His newly established commercial activity was built on fraud, theft and false documents," Maximov wrote in an e-mail to ExplorersWeb.

In 2003, according to Maximov, Valentine, while posing as the director of the Russian Service Center and as an educational consultant for Zvezda, had used homemade equipment to refill oxygen bottles and issued certificates of their authenticity. Zvezda had repeatedly warned Valentine against issuing certificates in their name guaranteeing the oxygen tanks he had refilled in Kathmandu using methods and equipment that didn't meet the standards required in Russia. Eventually the company took legal action against him.

"When he came to Poisk office in [St.] Petersburg three years ago, he asked for a photograph with its Director and then used it in Kathmandu and in Everest Base Camp as actual proof of being our official representative. He also claimed that Poisk had granted him the permission to refill its cylinders. . . . In our opinion, it is not possible for anybody to be engaged in the enterprise of this kind without sufficient qualification and special equipment. Deliberate disregard of which can bring about grave consequences."

In March 2004, according to the Russian Service Center, a cylinder with an expired working life that Valentine Bozhukov was refilling exploded, leaving the entrepreneur with a scar on his face advertising that gravity.

But desperate situations and cutting-edge innovation often climb together. Ted Adkins, a lieutenant with the Royal Air Force, ran out of oxygen during his summit bid on the Nepal side of Everest in 2004. He fell unconscious on the South Summit. A descending Sherpa found him, hooked him up to a tank of oxygen, and left Adkins to regain consciousness and make his way back to Camp Four.

After his near-death experience, Ted distributed an oxygen mask he'd invented. He had designed it while sitting in front of his tent in Base Camp with a pilot's mask and some unusual bits and pieces.

"It was a condom opened and dropped inside a 500ml coke bottle and the lip folded over the bottle neck. Then a rubber hose sealed over this and led up to the mask," he wrote of his invention. Oxygen flowing while Ted exhaled inflated the condom, which acted as a reservoir to deliver the gas with the next inhalation. It was an oxygen-on-demand system akin to what Summit Oxygen was striving for. Climbers tested it in 2004 and a commercial team provided it for many of their clients in 2005. All of them have reported that the mask is a major advancement. Will Cross, who failed to reach the summit of Everest in 2004 and 2005 with Summit Oxygen, successfully summited in 2006 with one of Ted's Top Out masks.

In the eight decades that climbers have attempted to reach the top of Everest, every type of mountaineering equipment and clothing has undergone major advancements—titanium replacing iron, Polartec instead of wool. Yet while every other piece of garb and gear undergoes rigorous testing on other mountains around the world before arriving at the bottom of Everest, the technologies that are virtually unique to the world's tallest mountain—the systems that deliver oxygen to climbers' lungs—have always made their first trips up the peak, to some degree, as experiments. Above 8,000 meters, the lines between ingenious innovation and reckless research, between capitalism and profiteering, are as thin as the climbing ropes. But with well over a million dollars' worth of oxygen arriving on the mountain every spring, there are plenty of business incentives and black market opportunities.

Homebrewed refills—once seen as back-alley, bootleg bottles of oxygen—are now commonly and openly used by most Everest teams. Many commercial expeditions acknowledge providing them for their clients, although most say they use the refills low on the mountain and reserve new bottles from Poisk for their summit days. Today, Henry Todd is proud of his refilling operation.

"Most of the expeditions on this mountain are using refilled O_2 bottles and most of the bottles are coming from me," he told me in 2006 during his annual expedition to Everest's Nepali side.

When asked for further details, he demurred. "Why would I show the henhouse where I get the golden egg?"

Golden eggs and their hidden henhouses are something Henry has a bit of experience with. In November of 1974, Dick Lee, head of the drug squad at England's Thames Valley Police headquarters, noticed an unusual number of arrests involving LSD. Three years later more than 800 detectives arrested 120 suspects in dawn raids throughout England, Wales, and France and unearthed 20,000,000 doses of acid worth more than £100,000,000 as well as £800,000 stashed away in Swiss bank accounts. It was, the police claimed, the "greatest haul of drugs anywhere in the world"—enough acid to supply half the users on the planet. The targets of the lengthy and laborious undercover operation, codenamed Operation Julie, stretched all the way from acid guru Timothy Leary and the Brotherhood of Eternal Love to Angry Brigade, a terrorist organization responsible for several bombings in Britain and suspected of using funds from the drug sales to finance their activities. At the heart of the acid ring the police identified four people, one of whom remained a mystery for months. Some acquaintances knew him as George, others as Jim, and a few as Henry. Nobody knew where he lived.

An informant told Lee that Henry was "a great, bearlike man, imposing both in size and in personality, who ran his part of the organization with an iron hand," and bragged that he would " 'hammer any coppers with an iron bar.' "

Eventually police files showed that Henry was born in Scotland, schooled in Singapore and Malaysia, worked as a freelance photographer in Paris, and served two years in jail after a conviction for theft and false pretenses in what a judge in Oxford in 1966 called an "orgy of crime."

Under the heading Characteristics, the file stated:

Large man, full of energy, secretive, fast driver, intelligent, good organizer, suspected violent temper, outgoing, rugby player (London Scottish), interested in climbing, keen on traveling, good food and attractive women.

Detectives tracked Henry, tapping his phones, digging up buried garbage, and watching as he connected with other members of the operation in various countries. He used several aliases and front companies to make purchases from a variety of vendors so that nobody would be able to add up the intended use of the equipment and chemicals. When one of Henry's climbing partners visited Yosemite National Park to scope out some potential climbs, police tailed his friend all the way to the American climbing Mecca.

On March 25, 1977, when fourteen officers smashed their way into Henry's flat, he seemed neither anxious nor shocked. Nearly a year later, Henry pleaded guilty to a variety of charges and was sentenced to thirteen years in prison, then "bounded from the court still full of energy." Henry was released from prison after seven years and threw himself into mountaineering.

In 1988, he was on Annapurna, one of the most difficult and deadly 8,000-meter peaks, with the legendary Polish climber Jerzy Kukuczka. In 1989, he made his first trip to Everest with another group of Polish climbers. The climb was a debacle and Henry decided that if he was a part of any more big expeditions, he was going to be in charge.

Henry's expeditions are bare-bones affairs, best for climbers who can take care of themselves—although he'll take just about anybody who can pony up the price, so he has plenty of novices along as well. And that price—$30,000 or less for a trip up the south side of Everest—is less than half what the high-end commercial expeditions charge. His clients eat lots of lentils. Henry provides the climbing permit, base-camp facilities, tents in each of the high camps, cooks, a small team of Sherpas and, of course, oxygen equipment. And he still draws a colorful cast of characters, many with impressive pedigrees: Among the climbers who joined his 2006 expedition were three doctors, a United Nations security officer, and a British diplomat.

While running his expeditions, Henry's side deals in oxygen, ropes, and weather reports earned him the nickname the "Mayor of Base Camp." But most climbers know him better as "Seven-year Henry," or "The Toddfather." No figure in the history of the mountain has inspired so much loyalty and acrimony. As Henry's problems in the press and the courts have mounted, many returning clients, perennial Everest guides, and veteran climbers have gathered in his defense. Others point fingers. But whether his neighbors in Everest Base Camp see Henry as a hustler or a hero, most recognize that he has found his place in the world, a spot where his particular business acumen fits in well.

A well-regarded guide told me, "If I had to pick three people I could trust my life with in the mountains, Henry would be at the top of the list."

"You know where he learned how to do all this, don't you?" another respected veteran guide asked. "In prison."

"I'm a flawed character," Henry told me when I went to speak with him in Base Camp early in the 2006 Everest season, "and flawed characters are easy to dismiss."

For a few people, however, Henry has proven decidedly difficult to dismiss.

I first met Henry a dozen miles south of Everest on the stunning peak called Ama Dablam—Mother's Jewel Purse, in the Sherpa tongue. Henry had stopped at Advanced Base Camp with a young woman from Colorado, whom he was guiding down from the summit while my team was on its way up. His reputation had preceded him, largely because he had preceded the other climbers on the mountain that year. Henry had made his way up Ama Dablam a few days before the date allowed by his permit, and when other teams arrived at the mountain, Henry's colleagues informed them that because his ropes were already fixed on the peak, they would have to pay him fees that added up to hundreds of dollars to make the climb—even if they had brought their own ropes and had no plans to use Henry's. He had effectively built a toll road in the roadless Khumbu Valley, a fundraising technique he had also employed in the late 1990s through the Khumbu Icefall on Everest, and other mountains. The expense and intrusion angered many climbers who were on Ama Dablam when I was there, as well as others around the world. When I descended from the summit, a liaison officer with the Nepali government questioned my team about whether Henry's team was on the mountain before the date allowed by their permit.

Henry initially agreed to a more in-depth interview for this book. But citing advice from his attorneys, whom he said feared further legal difficulty, he never spoke with me again. He coaxed friends and sources who had provided me with photos of him to withdraw their permission to use the images, and would answer no detailed questions about his oxygen business, except to say that his refilling operation is overseen by the top American gas company.

Even Henry's most ardent defenders admit that he is no saint, just as many of his detractors acknowledge that some of the accusations against him are almost impossible to believe. To me, his rope tricks seemed a small irritation. But I remain troubled by the fact that he allows no transparency of his oxygen business—a significant portion of a multimillion-dollar industry. Particularly given that he had graduated from manufacturing an illegal drug in a secret laboratory to producing a substance that lives depend on in a place that is effectively beyond the law. Certainly in any mountain range in the developed world, the manufacturing processes and business practices surrounding an enterprise like Henry's would be subject to intense scrutiny.

Twenty-one

Some 400 people had attended Nils Antezana's memorial service on June 12, 2004, at Our Lady of Victory Church in Washington, D.C. The program for the event carried a black-and-white portrait of Nils as a young doctor on the front and a color picture of him in Everest Base Camp nearly forty years later on the back. A flyer that was passed out with the program had more photos of Nils in the mountains, along with pictures of him skydiving, scuba diving, and with his family. In the testimonials, Dave Okonsky wrote about their adventures jumping into the ocean and sky together, Nick Ellyn described their hikes in the Appalachians and Italy, and Dr. Luanne Freer told of Nils's offers of assistance at Everest's Base Camp medical facility.

Although it didn't come until nine months later, in a strange way the letter Fabiola received from Bob Metler telling of Nils's flying partners' plans to sell their Cessna seemed a similar tribute. Bob cited maintenance and fuel prices and the difficulty of finding time to fly, but by the fourth paragraph he got to the heart of what had really grounded him.

> *In truth I feel that we all miss your Dad a lot more than we thought we would, and the group just isn't the same without him. He could miss two months of flying, meetings, and still keep us going with his great adventures and continued friendship.*

For the people who had shared Nils's adventures, the sky, the sea, and the peaks in between them would never look the same. But there were other admirers from surprisingly high places.

The day before the memorial service, Fabiola's phone rang with a call from Tuto Quiroga, the former president of Bolivia. He had never met Nils, but had read the report on the front page of a paper in La Paz about the second Bolivian to climb Everest and how he had died during the descent. Quiroga told Fabiola that he had once dreamed of climbing Everest himself.

"If there's anything I can do," he said.

Late that summer, the Antezanas held another memorial service, this one in Cochabamba, Bolivia, for Nils's family and friends there. But Fabiola spent much of her time in La Paz, walking between the hotels where guides hung their flyers, the adventure travel agencies that hired them, even the street corners where they hung out between jobs. She tried to learn everything she could about Gustavo Lisi and how he had met her father. Fabiola visited Quiroga, who connected her with the ministers of tourism and sports, and with Bernardo Guarachi, the first Bolivian to reach Everest's summit. Nils had hired Bernardo to lead him up some climbs in South America and visited the offices of the guide he trusted as a friend whenever he was in La Paz.

"What do you think about me climbing Everest?" Nils had asked Bernardo during a visit a few years before he headed to Nepal.

"Look, Nils," Bernardo recalls telling him, "I really wouldn't do it."

Nils pointed out that he had just climbed Aconcagua.

"Aconcagua is a completely different mountain," Bernardo said, convinced that Nils was just making conversation.

Bernardo also knew Gustavo Lisi, and although he denies Gustavo's claim that he introduced Nils and Gustavo, he acknowledges that it is likely that they met at his guiding company. Several years earlier, Gustavo had worked for Bernardo's agency for a few months until a series of complaints, including the one from Dave Morton of Alpine Ascents, prompted his firing. Clients came back from trips with Gustavo claiming he treated them like they were working for him rather than the other way around, and several complained that he left them behind on mountains. Then, on a trip where Bernardo was leading a group on the same mountain as Gustavo, he got back to camp after summiting and looked back up the mountain to see Gustavo's group struggling to make their way down the mountain without their guide. He looked through the camp and found the guide chatting with some of the other climbers there. Bernardo fired Gustavo then and there. But after letting him go, Bernardo discovered thousands of dollars' worth of equipment was missing, including at least one piece of gear that was priceless—the ice ax Bernardo had used to get to the top of Everest. He sent an e-mail to his former employee questioning him about the missing gear.

"Your wife probably sold it," Gustavo responded to Bernardo.

Aldo Riveros, President of the Bolivian Association of Mountain Guides Associations, also had concerns about Gustavo. Aldo had worked hard to get the Bolivian guides recognized by the International Federation of Mountain Guides. He divided his time as a guide between Bolivia and Chamonix, France, where guiding without IFMGA-recognized credentials is a crime. He had seen how imposing strict international standards had made the mountains in Europe safer, and he hoped to see those kinds of improvements in Bolivia, too.

In 2003, as the Bolivian organization was completing the process to join the IFMGA, Aldo ran into an Argentinean guide in La Paz—Gustavo Lisi. The first thing he noticed was the patch on Gustavo's jacket with the IFMGA logo. Aldo asked where Gustavo had completed his training to gain the certification, and the Argentinean said that he had studied in Tuscany.

"That's strange," Aldo thought to himself. "Tuscany doesn't have an IFMGA program."

Aldo sent an e-mail to the organization in Italy, and they checked their records and reported that Gustavo Lisi had never studied with them and was not certified as a mountain guide in Italy. Aldo questioned Gustavo about his Italian credentials the next time he saw him, and Gustavo said he had studied with the Italian Alpine Club. But the club doesn't train or certify guides, Aldo responded. He let the Tourist Police know about the irregularities with Gustavo's credentials, but he didn't cross paths with him again. Bernardo and Aldo didn't know that Nils was actually pursuing his dream of climbing Everest, or that he had taken on Gustavo as his guide, until they read the newspaper reports about the doctor's death.

A few months after Aldo had begun looking into Gustavo's background, Theresita Quevado also met Gustavo. She was far more impressed with the Argentinean guide than Aldo was.

Maria "Theresita" Quevedo is Gladys Antezana's niece, but she felt especially close to Nils after living with the Antezana family in Washington, D.C., for six months in 1980. Theresita and Nils always had a special connection. She admired his polish and focus, and was charmed by how interested he was in her life. Nils dropped in on her and her family whenever he came to Bolivia from the United States to climb. She was so thrilled to hear from him when he came to Bolivia for some warm-up climbs a few months before his Everest expedition that she invited him and Gustavo to come to her spacious home in La Zona Sur of La Paz for a luncheon. Theresita would be the only member of the Antezana family, prior to Nils's death, to meet his companion for his Himalayan adventure. She recalled that Nils and his guide had just climbed Huayna Potosi, a mountain overlooking La Paz and one of the country's most popular ascents. They were headed for Illampu, another of the country's high-altitude trade routes, the next day. Gustavo, she recalls, was charming. Nils showed confidence in his guide, pointing out that he was highly trained and had already been to the top of Everest. Gustavo bolstered his client's trust by entertaining Theresita and her husband with stories about his climb to summit Everest in 2000 with the Basque team, while Nils sat back and smiled. Theresita was happy for Nils—she knew he was a bit old to be climbing Everest, but he had always been so fit and organized and determined. She couldn't think of anything he had set out to achieve in which he had failed. And he had an ace in the hole—a guide who had already been to the top of the mountain.

Theresita never saw Nils again. But a year after her uncle died, she saw his guide several times around La Paz during the climbing season. Gladys had called her often to pass on what Fabiola was learning during her investigations into her father's death. So when she saw Gustavo, sitting alone in cafés in La Paz, she recalled his regaling her family with stories of his climbs. And that's all they were, she realized—just stories. It broke her heart to think of how eagerly she had believed them. There was so much she could say to the man who she believed had led her uncle to his death, but she just turned and walked away.

Five hundred miles south of La Paz, in Salta, Argentina, Irene Meninato read in the newspaper about Gustavo's climb and Nils Antezana's death. Four years earlier, she had seen other news stories reporting that Gustavo had climbed Mount Everest and rescued a Basque climber, Juan Carlos Gonzalez. She had been suspicious then about Gustavo's Everest climb, and her doubts were borne out later in *Desnivel*, the Spanish climbing magazine. But even before that, Irene had been wary of Gustavo. She had climbed with his cousin, and knew enough about Gustavo to make her want to track down Fabiola.

Nine years earlier, in Salta, at the weekly meeting of Club Amigos de las Montañas—the Friends of the Mountains Club—Gustavo Lisi sat facing the club president, his cousin, Flavio Lisi. It was July 10, 1995, and the board of directors was preparing to vote. They had three options for Gustavo's punishment—censure, suspension, or expulsion from the club.

The scandal that had provoked the meeting was impossible to completely untangle. The "shopping affair," as it was called in the club's minutes, was named for the Nuevo Norte Shopping Center, which was one of Gustavo's sponsors for his first trip to the Himalaya—the expedition to Cho Oyu with Hector Ponce de Leon and Andres Delgado in 1995. To fund the trip, Gustavo surreptitiously solicited thousands of dollars from local companies, claiming the money was for a club-sponsored expedition, when in reality he was keeping it for his own trip. When Gustavo's fraud was exposed, the club was embarrassed, and its relations with the local businesses, which members had hoped would sponsor an actual club trip to the Himalaya, were strained. In meetings with club leaders, Gustavo was evasive and never accounted for the money. The leadership of the fifty-year-old club with the motto "The Best for Your Companion" had to do something.

A decade earlier than that, Flavio Lisi had been proud to introduce his cousin to mountaineering and the venerable club of about 100 members. At age thirteen Gustavo had moved through his first trips up mountains with strength and confidence. Flavio had signed waivers to take his cousin, at sixteen, on his first climbing trip to Bolivia.

Gustavo couldn't have found a better mentor. Flavio was on the first Argentinean expedition to climb an 8,000-meter peak, an ascent of Shishipangma in Tibet, and was seen as one of the strongest climbers in the region. But he is best remembered for his devotion to the club, and his belief that mountaineers are defined not by whether they stood on a peak's summit but by how they behaved on its flanks.

"He loved the club," Irene says of her climbing partner. "More than mountaineering, the club was his life."

After a few years, however, it was clear that Gustavo didn't feel the same way. He appeared interested in the club only when it could bring him some money or get him on a trip. By the time he was eighteen, Gustavo had been accused of theft by some of his climbing partners, according to Emilio Gonzalez Turu, who climbed with

Gustavo at the time. Flavio was increasingly concerned about his cousin's behavior.

He's a great athlete, one of the directors pointed out during his hearings, "but his human face leaves much to be desired."

Gustavo had supporters, both in the club and among the companies where he raised his funding. So when the directors voted, in 1995, after six weeks of meetings, they tied—four for expulsion and four against. Breaking the draw fell to the president. It would drive a wedge through the Lisi family forever, and drive Gustavo to threaten to rip Flavio's head off, but Flavio didn't hesitate to throw his cousin out of the club he loved. Gustavo Lisi was no longer a "Friend of the Mountains."

A year later, Gustavo joined another mountaineering club in Salta—Janajman—and was included in a Himalayan expedition they were planning; but according to documents filed with the secretary of tourism in Salta, before another year had passed, the club was investigating seven cases of Gustavo "habitually subtracting goods and money from other people." In October of 1997, he was thrown off the expedition and out of his second alpine club.

"Something bad is going to come of him," Flavio told Irene.

But fate got to Flavio first.

In 2000, as Gustavo prepared for his first trip to Everest with Juan Carlos Gonzalez and the Basque climbers, Flavio was on Aconcagua with Irene, who awoke in the night to a gurgling in her tentmate's throat. Two hours later, Flavio was dead of pulmonary edema.

By then, Gustavo was guiding in the Andes. His company, Alpamayo Expeditions, offered climbing, trekking, mountain biking, paragliding, and four-wheel-drive expeditions out of Salta. His posters advertised his Union of International Mountain Guide Associations certification, and Gustavo had a stack of documents to back up his credentials. But inspectors for the secretary of tourism in Salta contacted the organizations that gave his certifications in November of 1999.

The Association of Mountain Guides of Peru, in which Gustavo claimed membership, responded:

Gustavo Lisi is not a mountain guide, is not tenured in the Association of Mountain Guides of Peru and in as much, is not a member of the [UIMGA].

The secretary of the UIMGA in Italy, responding to the certificate that Gustavo provided to prove his membership in the organization, wrote that not only was he not a member of the UIMGA in Italy, but the organization had no certificate like the one Gustavo had provided. The president's signature that it displayed, they wrote, was a forgery.

The same day that they received the fax from Italy, the secretary of tourism notified Gustavo that his application to be registered as a provider of alternative tourism in Salta was denied due to the falsification of his credentials and the forgery.

Yet five years later, Fabiola saw that Gustavo noted his UIMGA certification in the materials that he had sent her father. Davide wrote to the organization in his native Italy, and they again reported that Gustavo Lisi was not on the list of UIMGA guides certified in Italy.

Fortunately for most guides working on Mount Everest, the highest mountain in the world requires the lowest guiding certifications in the world—that is, none. The government of Nepal, where Gustavo Lisi led Nils Antezana, doesn't recognize anyone as a mountain guide. Consequently anyone, regardless of training, experience, or criminal record, can call themselves a mountain guide on Everest. The only requirement is a client willing to pay them for the service. Certainly the mountain draws some of the best-trained and most-experienced guides in the business, but others show up with no knowledge of crevasse rescue, certification in avalanche safety, or even basic first aid training. And the Nepali and Chinese governments' lack of resources to monitor the mountains ensures that neither a lack of climbing experience, nor a history of irresponsible or illegal acts in the mountains, is likely to preclude any guide or independent climber from returning to the Himalaya year after year.

Irene told Fabiola what she knew of Gustavo's history in Argentina, and the two women corresponded often over the summer and fall of 2004. By then, Michael Leahy, a writer at the *Washington Post*'s Sunday magazine, had contacted Fabiola and was working on a cover story detailing Nils's troubled climb.

"Tell me the minute it's published," said Irene, who, after Nils's death, was determined to continue Flavio's efforts to prevent Gustavo working as a guide. "So I can translate it."

In February 2005, Fabiola, David, and Gladys were back in Bolivia for the annual meeting of the Bolivian American Medical Association, where Nils had been scheduled to speak. This time Fabiola brought dozens of copies of the *Washington Post* Sunday magazine story and Irene's translation of it in her suitcase. She passed out a number of them at the conference, but held on to most of them to distribute as she retraced her steps from a few months earlier through the hostels and agencies popular with guides in La Paz. She hadn't seen Gustavo since he had gotten his summit certificate and left Kathmandu. But she knew Bolivia was Gustavo's bread and butter, and was certain he was leading climbers into the mountains of her father's homeland.

Fabiola left a stack of the stories about her father's death at Aldo Riveros's and Bernardo Guarachi's offices. Then she walked up the street to the Hotel Naira, an eighteenth-century colonial house converted to an inn that is popular with climbers. Gustavo, Bernardo told Fabiola, was a friend of the owner's son, and used that connection to market his services at the hotel. Fabiola gave a copy of the *Washington Post* report to the owner, who listened intently as she told her story.

"Is this really the kind of person you want associated with your hotel?" she asked.

HARTFORD, CONNECTICUT—SUMMER 2004

George and Lhakpa's K2 climb never got off the ground. They returned to Hartford together in mid-June after the Connecticut Everest expedition. Lhakpa didn't comment for my final story on the expedition. And I knew she would never read it.

She, George, Chuck, and Dave dropped in on Connecticut's new governor, M. Jodi Rell, during a stop the official made in the town of Bristol that summer. Although the governor's appearance was just a few miles from Anne's home, they didn't invite her, Bill, or me to the event. Chuck, however, did invite us to the photo session they had arranged for the following week with Rell, where they planned to give the governor the Connecticut flag George had carried to the summit. Two days later, Chuck called Anne, furious that an anonymous caller had tipped the governor's staff to the expedition's troubles, and the photo op was off. But Anne's call to the capital was far from anonymous. She had left her name and phone number in case anyone there had any questions about what had happened to us in the Himalaya.

"For me, it was just another route," Dave said when I spoke with him in October of 2004. Like the other climbers who had reached the summit, he was eager to put the expedition's problems behind him. "The mountain does strange things to people."

"I just don't have the money," he responded when I asked if he was going to pay back the thousands of dollars that Bill had paid for the Sherpa Dave had ended up using.

Three days later, in *The Burlington* (Vermont) *Free Press*, Dave said his own sponsors had provided him with more than $16,000 for his Everest climb. Although in our interview he had told me that he hadn't spoken with George in months, in the *Free Press* he announced that he was planning to return to Everest with George to attempt the last unclimbed ridge on the mountain's eastern side—the Fantasy Ridge, so named because George Mallory had once opined that the ridge could be climbed only in a dream.

Bill had also decided to return to Everest. He didn't like unfinished business, and had spoken with Anne and me about returning to Tibet together to do Everest right.

Anne had trouble sleeping during the summer, but had a new field hockey team at Trinity to occupy her in the fall. Her once-close friendship with Chuck was beyond repair. Considering the turmoil of our last night in Base Camp, she said, "That he is willing to set himself up to profit by turning a blind eye to somebody else's suffering is unconscionable."

Sitting on my porch the day a worker was installing a security system in my home, Chuck said that Sherpas had told him that Lhakpa deserved the beating she received in Base Camp. Women in Nepal don't speak to their men like that.

Chuck tried to turn his success on the mountain into financial success for his guiding business and slideshows, which he and Dave marketed under the name "The Connecticut Everest Experience." George was a guest at some of the shows. None of the funds Chuck and Dave garnered from their presentations and sponsors made it into the Connecticut Everest Expedition's coffers.

"I just want to bask in the glory of this happening and make some of my money back," Chuck told me after returning home. That would be difficult, he said, if the expedition's troubles came out.

With the expedition's total cost running more than $100,000, money was bound to breed resentment. The four expedition members who summited had raised less than 5 percent of what got the team there. Nonetheless, George threatened to sue for more of the team's money in a lengthy e-mail he sent us in early June.

But that was the least of his threats. The night before her departure from Kathmandu, Anne referred to Dan Lochner and Guillermo as the "Hitler youth" for their loyalty to George despite his volatility. Although George's hostility toward the woman he had named as leader of the expedition had been building for months, his belief that she had called him "Hitler" was the grievance he latched on to.

"I will make you regret those comments," he addressed her in the e-mail to the team, "you better believe I know how I can do it to harm your career."

His threats to "hunt this bitch down, like a hiena [sic]," and gender-based taunts would have been enough to qualify any physical act he took against Anne for prosecution as a "hate crime" under Connecticut law.

Two weeks after Carolyn and I had returned from the Himalaya, as we jogged up our street, George watched us from one of my neighbors' yards, where he was visiting a customer of his home-improvement company. I realized that much of the peril that had turned me back from my climb of Mount Everest had followed me home.

For much of the summer, I was mired in the same struggles that I had been in in the Himalaya. Chuck visited mutual friends to tell his side of a story I had yet to publish. Acquaintances in the local climbing community picked sides. The publisher of a mountaineering Web site requested that the *Courant* take me off the story, claiming he had veteran mountaineers to discredit my reporting.

But most disturbing were the phone messages Anne and I received from a woman who had met Lhakpa at George's slideshow at Yale, forty-eight hours before the Connecticut expedition's departure to Nepal. Lhakpa had told her that she was organizing an all-women Connecticut expedition in the coming year. George would work for them as a Sherpa. The caller wanted us to reconnect her with George and Lhakpa. She was ready to sign up. And I remembered George's final words on EverestNews.com describing the Connecticut Everest Expedition's climb to the summit.

"Six summits in six consecutive attempts," he wrote at the end of his report, before offering his services. "Do you need a guide for Mount Everest?"

Twenty-two

After Nils's death, Fabiola and Davide decided to move from London to New York as soon as Davide could find a position with an investment bank there. They wanted to be closer to Gladys, at least for a year or two, until she adjusted to life without her husband. Once they arrived in Manhattan in late 2004, they quickly grew close with Tom and Tina Sjogren. And they learned that Nils's last trip and the Connecticut expedition were far from the first to have controversy and recrimination avalanche from the Himalaya back into the developed world. In fact, the most enduring scandal in mountaincering had been growing for five years in the city they had just left.

Tom and Tina told Fabiola how, soon after they had gotten home from their visit to the Poisk facility in Russia in 1999, they had called David Matthews and told him their suspicions about the oxygen his son Michael, the young British climber, had been breathing when he died on Everest that year. John Crellin, another client on the OTT expedition, had already contacted David Matthews with his concerns about the oxygen, and Dave Rodney,

Michael Matthews's best friend on the climb, also came forward with allegations about the gas, OTT expedition leader Nick Kekus's violent outbursts, and the team's disorganization.

Michael's death haunted *Back to Everest,* Rodney's documentary about his two Everest climbs. Dutch OTT client Katya Staartjes detailed the expedition's problems in a book. Most damning was the docudrama *Lost in Everest's Death Zone,* broadcast in England, which combined reenactments of the troubled expedition with Dave Rodney's footage from the climb. By then OTT had changed its name to Alpine Mountaineering, but the company would soon go into liquidation.

In June of 2002, the executors of Michael Matthews's estate filed suit against OTT, Jon Tinker, Mike Smith, and Henry Todd, asking for a total of more than £150,000 in damages. Jon Tinker and OTT admitted that there were problems with the oxygen equipment, but maintained that they were corrected by the time the climbers headed for the top of the mountain. Dozens of mountaineers rallied to support the defendants. Many feared the suit could spark a trend of disgruntled clients and grief-stricken families hauling guides into court.

Ripples from the legal action even threatened to spoil the anniversary celebrations of Everest's first ascent. As part of the Golden Jubilee celebration in 2003, David Matthews had offered £300,000 in sponsorship for an exhibition of memorabilia collected by the Royal Geographic Society from Sir Edmund Hillary and George Mallory's climbs. However, Jon Tinker, one of the men Matthews was then suing, sat on the board of the Mount Everest Foundation, which pressured the Royal Geographic Society to refuse lending anything to the exhibition unless Matthews dropped his suit or his sponsorship. In May 2003, the month of the anniversary, Jon Tinker and Mike Smith reached a settlement with the Matthews family, but accepted no liability.

Henry did not settle, but he had other problems to deal with, most notably that he had been banned from Nepal, where he ran his Everest expeditions, in 2001 and 2002. His new round of troubles had started with a journalist named Finn-Olaf Jones, who had pitched climbing Mount Everest for a series of stories for Discovery

.com, and a film for the Travel Channel, which is also part of Discovery. Finn, searching for someone to take him up Everest, contacted Himalayan Guides, Henry Todd's outfit. A week later a tall, hardy man with a Scottish accent, a beard, and a huge down coat showed up on Finn's doorstep in Washington, D.C.

"A very posh accent. I liked him," Finn recalls. "He really could not have been more charming."

Six months later, when Finn was sprawled out on the rocks of Everest Base Camp, bleeding from his face, with his expedition leader looming over him and hurling threats, Henry didn't seem so charming.

The expedition had had its troubles from the beginning. Many of Henry's clients found him elusive. Climbers on the expedition's first summit bid had had to bail out when they found their high camp wasn't set up. Instead of heading up the mountain to assist his clients, Henry's Sherpas were carrying empty oxygen bottles down to sell in Base Camp. When the disgruntled summit team got back to Base Camp themselves, Henry had vanished again. And, Finn was learning, Base Camp had a dark side. An expedition leader had several thousand dollars stolen from her tent, and a journalist working with another team had his phone, laptop, and camera taken. As Finn sharpened his reporting, his irreverent tone got on a few climbers' nerves. A teammate who had grown increasingly vulgar and abusive snatched Finn's video camera out of his hands, hid it, and refused to give it back. Finn eventually punched the man he dubbed "psychoclimber," and the camera turned up on his sleeping bag later that day.

But the real problems started in a different camp. According to Finn, Henry spent a lot of time with an old friend, Bob Hoffman, who was leading the 2000 Everest Environmental Expedition—a huge and lavish operation. The environmental expedition claimed to have raised at least $600,000 to clean up the mountain and boasted several high-profile sponsors, including the companies Inventa, Gateway, and Verde. But one sponsor they boasted of surprised Finn—the Discovery Channel.

"I'm with Discovery, too," Finn said when he approached the

team for an interview with Hoffman, "and nobody told me anything about you guys."

Tensions escalated fast. Members of the environmental team visited other expeditions to inform them that Finn-Olaf Jones was an imposter and didn't work for Discovery himself. A number of other climbers Finn spoke with expressed suspicions that the "environmental" climbers were putting their resources into an extravagant expedition rather than cleaning up the mountain. In fact, skepticism about environmental climbs had been building on Everest for a few years—I had heard many of the same criticisms Finn did during my own trip to the Himalaya a few months earlier. Finn sent an e-mail to Discovery asking if it had anything to do with the environmental expedition and, if it didn't, expressing his desire to investigate the expedition's claims of cleaning up Everest. His editors confirmed that Hoffman's expedition was not sponsored by Discovery, but Finn's e-mail detailing his suspicions was leaked back to the environmental team. Finn was resting in a village with Henry and several other teammates when what was reported to be twenty-one members of the environmental expedition surrounded his tent in Base Camp and shouted for him to come out. According to Finn, when he and Henry returned to Base Camp, Henry headed to the environmental camp to try to calm things down. But climbers there showed him what Finn had written about Henry, including a reference to him as an "Everest caterer." It seemed a small slight for the rage that followed.

Finn was having a cup of tea outside his tent when the man he had paid to bring him to Everest stomped out of the Inventa camp. Finn asserts that Henry landed a blow on the right side of his face that sent him sprawling onto the moraine.

"You get the fuck out of Base Camp, or I'm going to fucking kill you," Finn says Henry shouted at him while sitting on his chest and punching him in the face until Sherpas and Henry's Base Camp manager pulled him off.

Other witnesses—friends of Henry's—reported that he forcefully shook Finn, but did not punch him. Finn's injuries, they said, occurred when he fell onto the moraine while running away. Dan said nothing, determined over time to even the score with Henry through simply informing people about what a trip with him is really like!!!!"

Henry's problems continued to grow when he got off the mountain.

In Kathmandu, Finn filed a complaint at the Ministry of Tourism and Civil Aviation. Six months later, the ministry announced that due to the assault and other incidents, they were banning Henry from Nepal until February of 2002. The Nepal Mountaineering Association, which represents the Sherpas and local mountaineers, lauded the ban in a November 15, 2000, press release. Not that being thrown out of Nepal prevented Henry from running his climbs there. During his time as persona non grata in the country, he led his annual Everest expedition there via radio from Tibet.

Forbes published Finn's account of his expedition under the headline INTO FINN AIR. But his last dispatch to Discovery.com best summed up his vision of Everest.

There are certain things that can't bear too much scrutiny there, and I think the key to success is keeping a certain distance from the overwhelming dissonance of the human anthill that is base camp. I have stayed at many base camps throughout the world, but Everest's is much different. The money, for starters. There's way too much of it floating around like a cloud on the mountain, and that attracts some people who are more focused on cash than climbing. Then there's the mania that comes with breathing thin air for too long. And the oversized egos and bruised personalities seeking some kind of completion amidst this soaring scenery.

To some, however, Henry's flamboyance got him more attention than he merited, while the other group that complained about Finn's scrutiny wasn't getting enough. The 2000 Everest Environmental Expedition's claim of Discovery sponsorship was not the only thing about them that didn't add up.

In 1963, during the first American ascent of the mountain, Barry

Morrison, who was writing for Quokka.com, did not see the assault but reported that Finn had gashes in his face and was truly afraid for his life. Morrison also signed an affidavit stating that Henry's Base Camp manager, Melissa Kade, and another member of the expedition told him they would lie to protect their relationships with Henry and would not cooperate with investigations into the incident.

After the altercation, Henry headed back into the environmental team's camp, where Finn says his assailant was met with applause and a cigar. Meanwhile, Henry's expedition doctor swabbed the blood from the wounds on Finn's face and head, then advised him to get out of camp. Finn took his media equipment and moved into a tent at the camp of Alpine Ascents commercial team to hide from members of the environmental team who he was told were still looking for him in camp.

When I asked Bob Hoffman, he said Finn's impression that the environmental team was claiming sponsorship by Discovery was just a mix-up. The media people who came along with his expedition had some connections with Discovery and hoped to get some coverage, but had never claimed actual sponsorship, according to Bob. He also claimed that the environmental team's climbers were in a higher camp on the mountain when Henry and Finn had their run-in, and that he and his team hardly knew Henry, much less hosted him in their tent after the altercation. But lawyers investigating the incident on behalf of Discovery determined that "Mr. Hoffman caused Mr. Todd . . . to become enraged and assault Mr. Jones." And climbers with other expeditions distinctly recall the environmental climbers being in Base Camp both before and after Finn was injured there.

"That was my first year working at Base Camp, and I would not have believed it. What a crazy place!" Ellie Henke, Alpine Ascents' Base Camp Manager, said. "Oh my God! Finn's face! He was all just torn up and bloody and it's like, OK: number one, get him some medical attention; number two, let's get a liaison officer up here. You need to make a statement. We tucked him in at our camp, and by that time it was not safe to be letting it be known around

Base Camp that he was even up at our camp. We kind of shuffled him around up there."

Later she heard Henry's claim that Finn was injured when he fell on the talus.

"You'd think if somebody had slipped and fallen down, they'd have scrapes on their hands and holes in their knees. This was just on his face. He did not fall down. No way."

During the two days that Finn waited for a helicopter to evacuate him, he says sympathetic Sherpas armed with ice axes protected him from the climbers with the environmental expedition.

"You are in great danger here," he recalls Melissa, Henry's Base Camp manager, warning him when he came back to gather his remaining gear.

There were no further attacks, but both Bob Hoffman and the environmental team's media coordinator promised legal action against Finn for his negative coverage of their expedition. The lawsuits never materialized, and Finn ended up thankful that he didn't make it any higher on the mountain with Henry than he did.

Finn's teammates Mike and Kristy Woodmansee didn't witness the fight, but they had their own problems with Henry, which they described in a journal of their climb distributed via e-mail. On May 18, the day of Henry's row with Finn, Mike wrote:

The weather is sketchy and Henry has stretched himself awfully thin. Food, tent space, oxygen and Sherpa support are in short supply, especially with the Sherpas being complete slackers these days. Add to this the fact that Henry had an insane outburst and beat Finn up over remarks he made about Henry on his website and you have the picture of an extremely dysfunctional leader.

On May 21, two days after Finn left, the Woodmansees hadn't seen Henry in more than two weeks.

"Henry skulked into camp around lunchtime, ate with the Sherpas instead of us, dove into his tent and avoided all contact with his team. What a jerk!!!" Mike wrote.

When food Henry had left in an unmarked bag disappeared, Mike reported that Henry threatened to "slit the throat" of whoever had eaten it.

The Woodmansees planned to leave for the summit from high camp at ten o'clock a few nights later, but despite the fact that Henry was the biggest oxygen dealer on the mountain and his clients' lives would soon depend on the bottled gas, they still hadn't been provided the oxygen or regulators they would use on their summit bid. When they did get their setups, they were cobbled together with parts from three different countries. Four out of seven regulators they tested before going up high didn't work. Within ninety minutes of starting for the summit, both Mike and Kristy were forced to turn back because of malfunctioning oxygen equipment.

"I was soon stricken with a claustrophobic panic attack!!" Mike wrote. "It took me a minute to realize I was getting no oxygen!! I literally ripped the mask off and tried to catch my breath in the thin air above the col . . ."

With their oxygen systems busted, the Woodmansees had no choice but to descend to Camp Four to try to find replacements. Two other team members also turned back from their summit bids due to faulty oxygen systems. One found another regulator and started back up, only to have the system fail again. Henry was sleeping in his tent when the Woodmansees returned to look for new regulators, but despite their repeated shouts and visits to him in his tent, he refused to get up and assist them. The expedition leader told Mike that it was his own fault he had poor equipment, because he hadn't given their regulators to a Sherpa when Henry wanted to test them.

"Henry went on to say that because I had not given my regulators to the Sherpa who first came and asked, that he had given [other climbers] higher quality oxygen systems he would have otherwise given us and in turn had given us inferior equipment and too bad about that!!!" Mike wrote. "By this point my contempt for Henry had grown toward hatred and dragging his tent with him in it off the Lhotse Face seemed justified . . . Instead,

Bishop dubbed the Everest's South Col "the world's highest junkyard." Sir Edmund Hillary once advocated closing the mountain for five years to let the environment recover. The Nepalese government instead chose to charge a $4,000 environmental deposit, which was refunded when expeditions removed their garbage. Thirty-one years after Barry's ascent, his son, Brent Bishop, helped organize the cleanup expedition with the most lasting impact on the mountain. Brent's wasn't the first effort to clean up the mountain, and after climbers around the world realized how effective a poster child a dirty mountain could be for fundraising, it certainly wouldn't be the last.

Using the Nepali name for Everest, the 1994 Sagarmatha Environmental Expedition that Brent helped organize removed more than five thousand pounds of garbage, including two hundred empty oxygen tanks. Most significantly, the expedition instituted an incentive system that paid Sherpas for each oxygen bottle or load of trash they carried down. The system is now employed all over the mountain. Within a few years, the South Col was void of almost all the recyclable oxygen bottles that had once been strewn there. But the media still presented Everest as a dirty mountain, and every year "environmental expeditions" stepped forward to solve the problem or, according to their critics, cash in on it.

"I believe that if you can't get off the plane in Kathmandu, and in the first fifteen minutes come up with a list of twenty more pressing issues than trash in the mountains, you are blind," Brent Bishop wrote to a *Climbing Magazine* editor just a few years after his cleanup climbs on Everest. "Anybody picking up trash in the mountains and telling the world that they are accomplishing something really significant is delusional."

One way or another, however, environmental expeditions were cleaning up.

Bob Hoffman, leader and organizer of the 2000 Everest Environmental Expedition that concerned Finn, had been on Everest three times before—in 1992, 1995, and 1998—and brought down empty oxygen bottles from the mountain each time. Hoffman, a New Yorker living in California, had stepped on plenty of toes during his journeys up Everest. Some climbers were wary of Bob's 2000 expedition because of their previous experiences with him. Others were offended that hundreds of thousands of dollars were dedicated to clean up a place that only mountaineers see, while villages nearby were desperate for basic environmental improvements like sanitation and clean water. But several climbers oblivious to Hoffman's history or the needs of the nation said they needed only to look at the 2000 Everest Environmental Team's matching coats, spacious tents, and gourmet meals to wonder how much of the up to $750,000 they claimed in sponsorship was put into cleaning the mountain and how much was funding a luxury cruise to the top of the world.

An accounting of the work Bob's team had done in 1998 hinted at the answer to that question. According to the team's Web site and Bob's statements to the press, his 1998 team removed 157 oxygen bottles, 211 fuel canisters, 546 used batteries, 3,200 pounds of trash, and 535 pounds of human waste. But according to one of the team's environmental coordinators, they had brought 132 oxygen bottles to the mountain for their own climb, so they would have removed only 25 tanks that were on the mountain before they arrived. Almost all of the batteries collected by the team as trash also came with them to the mountain. And about half the trash collected would have been generated by the team itself. More than one "environmental expedition" has been witnessed photographing their own trash and putting it up on their Web sites as evidence of the garbage they had collected.

Brent Bishop, using the going incentive rates to Sherpas, calculated that the team would have spent $375 to bring the oxygen bottles down, $218 to carry the trash off the mountain, and about $1,200 to haul it all away. To many on Everest, the $1,800 total seemed a paltry investment in the environment for a ten-member team with budget of at least $300,000. Bob, however, claims that the environmental investment was much higher, partially due to the helicopter he says the team hired to haul out trash. And both detractors and supporters of environmental climbs have pointed out that the system the 1998 team put in place to manage human waste—toilet tents with large plastic buckets that can be sealed and hauled away—was a major improvement that is now used all over the mountain.

Still, many mountaineers were growing suspicious of cleanup climbs. Wally Berg, a veteran guide, was on the mountain in 1998 with a grant of a few thousand dollars from Nike to pay Sherpas to bring down trash. Although commercial operations have an incentive to spruce up the mountain to improve the experience of their clients, Wally has never attached the word "environmental" to his expeditions. He believes every climber should work at cleaning things up without expecting any pats on the back. Late in his expedition, climbers from Hoffman's group approached him, demanding that he turn over the oxygen bottles his Sherpas had carried down the mountain. The environmentalists had presold oxygen bottles for between $150 and $300 each to raise funds and didn't carry enough bottles off the mountain themselves to fulfill those obligations. Wally's Sherpas were making only $15 or $25 per bottle, but he hung on to the bottles his Sherpas had collected anyway.

Several members of the 1998 Everest Environmental Expedition were openly critical of Bob Hoffman as a climber, a leader, and an environmentalist.

"In reality we feel that Hoffman used the environmental twist merely as a way to get the permit and sponsorship," Pasquale Scaturro, the climbing leader for the expedition, wrote to the American Alpine Club, which sponsored Bob's team and provided nonprofit status to help many expeditions raise funds. "Hoffman recently informed one of our base camp managers that the entire cleanup was a 'joke.'"

Another of Bob's teammates also wrote the AAC: "Hoffman tried to order us to 'only pick up batteries and empty fuel cylinders.... 'That trash looks good on the news! Don't pick up anything else,'" he quoted Bob as saying.

According to the two letters, the expedition had a less than environmentally friendly finish.

Some of his teammates reported that Bob had commandeered all the team gear for himself and shipped it back with the recyclable trash and the empty oxygen bottles they had brought back from the mountain, as well as the team's twenty-four two-way radios. He also included flammable items like the team generator, dozens of full canisters of stove fuel, and several partially full oxygen bottles. Although as an airline employee he should have known better, he sent the flammable cargo on a Thai Airlines flight to Bangkok. Fortunately, it didn't explode until it was on the docks in Thailand, but the fire left several members of the team out thousands of dollars, and prompted an investigation by Thai authorities. Despite repeated requests from several of his teammates, Bob never provided a final accounting of the expedition's finances.

"I consider his handling of the finances fraudulent," one of his teammate's letters to the AAC reported.

In their notes to the club, expedition members cited several instances where Bob's blunders, negligence, and selfishness put team members at risk. He failed to help a friend severely injured in a fall or to participate in a search-and-rescue operation for a teammate gone missing. His overbearing, caustic personality alienated both his teammates and other teams. Pasquale, who would later gain fame for leading the expedition that put blind climber Erik Weihenmayer on the summit of Everest, wrote that Bob Hoffman's leadership "led to a very dangerous and life threatening atmosphere high up on the mountain.

"His behavior is an embarrassment to not only our team and the AAC, but to western climbers in general."

The other letter to the AAC was even more blunt:

My primary concern is that Hoffman never has the chance to lead an expedition again. In my view, he is a danger to himself and anyone around him. Especially emboldened as he is now with his questionable success on Everest.

The fact that Hoffman is representing himself as an environmentalist is galling. He should not be allowed to dupe any more corporate sponsors into simply paying for his guided vacations in the Himalayas. By doing so, he is siphoning

scarce funds away from truly worthwhile projects, making it
harder for real environmentalists to find support.

Despite the criticism of his earlier effort, for his part, Bob told
me that the 1998 team hadn't accepted any sponsorship money to
clean up the mountain, so any investment they made in the environment was charity on their part. The fact that they had included
the word "environmental" in their name didn't commit them to any
level of investment in the environment. He told me his problems
with Pasquale Scaturro had started when he prevented the climbing
leader from taking food and ropes dedicated to the Everest ascent
to use in a different climb.

In 2000, Bob was again leading an environmental expedition to
Everest, this time with well over half a million dollars in corporate
support and a documentary team in tow. *Beyond the Summit—The*
2000 Everest Environmental Expedition would be narrated by
Sharon Stone and appear on the Outdoor Life Network and National Geographic International. What the expedition didn't have,
after Bob's former teammates' letters to the American Alpine Club
and a subsequent investigation by the organization, was an endorse-
ment from the club, which had supported Bob's previous endeavors on the mountain and virtually every other American expedition
to Everest.

The 2000 team claimed they dedicated at least $600,000 exclu-
sively to the cleanup effort, which removed 1,000 pounds of
garbage and 632 oxygen bottles from the mountain. At that rate,
they spent nearly $1,000 for each oxygen bottle they carried off
Everest—about fifty times the going rate of between $15 and $25
that Sherpas were already being paid to remove spent oxygen tanks
from the mountain.

At least on Everest, there has been less interest in climbs promoted
as cleanups since the 2000 Everest Environmental Expedition. But
mountaineering to promote causes and raise money for charities
has become so popular that it's hard to find an expedition that

oesn't have at least one climber touting a philanthropic mission on the mountain and soliciting donations for it. Among the people trekking only as far as Base Camp, the number of people raising money for charities is staggering. "Charity challenges" are effectively walkathons on steroids. Participants raise a certain amount of money for a charity, with a portion of their fundraising paying the cost of an exotic adventure such as climbing Kilimanjaro or walking to Machu Picchu. The trek to Everest Base Camp in Nepal is probably the most popular destination for the adventuring philanthropist.

In Britain the challenges have become so popular and effective a method of fundraising that a number of adventure travel agencies now specialize in them exclusively. In 2006, one agency alone organized eight charity treks to Everest Base Camp, each with up to twenty-five participants. In all, there were at least fifty climbs and treks on Everest that year with several hundred participants claiming to use their endeavor to raise money for charitable causes.

Ironically, charity treks to Everest, which were in part born of the success of the environmental expeditions, are now cited as an ecological burden. Prakash Sharma, director of Friends of the Earth Nepal, stated in 2006 that charitable organizations are ignoring the environmental consequences of the heavy traffic they bring to the mountain, which include overdevelopment in exceedingly sensitive alpine areas, demand for fuel to keep visitors in hot food and showers, and a problem that the environmental expeditions had largely cured—litter.

But at least charity challenges organized in Britain, the United States, and elsewhere in the first world are subject to the laws of those countries, to some degree ensuring that the funds raised make it where the donor intended. Philanthropic efforts in the developing world, however, are exceedingly vulnerable to fraud. One climber headed to Everest in 2006 sought me out to solicit coverage of his climb and the charity he was supporting. He claimed his charitable effort for an internationally known organization was more legitimate than many on the mountain, and a better investment for donors because he wasn't using any of the funds he raised to pay for his climb.

"I'm paying for the entire climb out of my pocket," he said. "So all of the money I raise is going to [the charity]."

Two months later, after he successfully reached the summit, I ran into the climber at a party in Kathmandu. He said he had raised about $20,000.

"A lot of people say 'Just keep it and pay for your climb. You did a lot to raise public awareness,'" he said. "I'm thinking maybe I'll split it with them fifty-fifty. Half to [charity] and half to pay for my climb."

Another climber in 2006 claimed on the Web that all the funds donated to her were going to a children's charity, but in a subsequent news story she stated that more than two thirds of the money raised was used to pay for the climb.

Certainly there are hundreds of thousands of dollars raised on Mount Everest for worthy causes. But it is just as certain that there are plenty of scams as well. Charities are unlikely to complain that some of the money raised in their names is paying for climbing trips. Something is better than nothing, and criticism might cost them what donations they might have received, not to mention alienate other supporters with bad publicity. Donors, on the other hand, might be surprised when a charitable donation pays for a relatively wealthy mountaineer's down suit rather than to put a few hundred poor children in shoes.

George Dijmarescu jumped on the charity bandwagon during his 2005 expedition. On April 27, he filed a report to EverestNews.com telling of a Tibetan yak man who brought him cheese and then wept when George gave him thirty dollars. Touched by the encounter, George announced plans to cross the Nangpa La Pass from Chinese Tibet into Nepal, accompanying the caravan led by the man, to show how hard the Tibetans' lives were. But those weren't his only plans, he wrote:

As I lay down inside my sleeping bag I came up with an idea: Poverty Alleviation in Tibet, in short PAT. Upon my return to

Connecticut I will try to register this as a non profit organization, unlike others. All funds received and I mean 100% will go to the needy Tibetan families and my starting point is at the bottom of Mt Everest. With your generous help needy Tibetans can raise to a level of acceptable poverty, a time when they can provide vegetables for their children and who knows, maybe even send them to school . . .

Please help these people by writing a check to Poverty Alleviation in Tibet (PAT) along with your address and contact number. I will let you know what happens with your Dollars. This is my promise.

To date, PAT has not been registered as a nonprofit, and there has been no further word of George's efforts to reduce poverty in Tibet or to document the difficult lives of the Tibetan people.

Mountaineers on the Chinese side of Everest climb to Camp One on the North Col during the first day that the ropes were fixed to the camp in 2004. (Photo by Michael Kodas/*The Hartford Courant*)

Juan Carlos Gonzalez lost seven fingers on Everest, and the photos he took on the summit were stolen from him.

(Photo by Michael Kodas)

Gladys, Nils, and Fabiola Antezana during a family vacation.

(Photo courtesy the Antezana family)

Tom and Tina Sjogren and the Sherpas who joined them as part of the Everest Internet Expedition transmit photos, video, and audio from the top of the mountain on May 26, 1999.

(Photo courtesy Tom and Tina Sjogren/ExplorersWeb)

Sherpas work their way up the headwall of the North Col of Mount Everest during the 2004 spring climbing season.

(Photo by Michael Kodas/*The Hartford Courant*)

George Dijmarescu, *bottom right;* Lhakpa Sherpa, *top right;* Ang Dawa Sherpa, *top left;* and Dawa Nuru Sherpa pray before heading out on their summit bid during the 2004 spring climbing season on Everest.
(Photo by Michael Kodas/*The Hartford Courant*)

Anne Parmenter struggles up the North Ridge of Everest just below
Camp Two. (Photo by Michael Kodas/*The Hartford Courant*)

(Photo by Michael Kodas/*The Hartford Courant*)

(Photo by Anne Parmenter)

Anne Parmenter, *top*, and Michael Kodas recover in Camp One after turning back from their summit bid due to the conspiracies and threats of other climbers.

George Dijmarescu sits in a tent dubbed "The Pleasure Dome" while trying to coax Sherpas with the Connecticut Everest Expedition to rescue Guillermo Carro. (Photo by Michael Kodas/*The Hartford Courant*)

Lhakpa Sherpa is rescued by Carolyn Moreau, *top,* Anne Parmenter, *center,* and Chuck Boyd, *left,* after she was in a domestic dispute with her husband, George Dijmarescu, in Mount Everest's Chinese Base Camp. Lhakpa was thrown from the team's dining tent and left unconscious outside it. (Photo by Michael Kodas/*The Hartford Courant*)

LEFT: David Sharp during his attempt to climb Mount Everest in 2003. David perished on the mountain in 2006. (Photo by Jamie McGuinness)

ABOVE: In May 2006, Lincoln Hall was left for dead near the Second Step on Mount Everest, but he survived the night and was rescued the following day. (Photo by Jamie McGuinness)

Mark Inglis, who lost both his legs to frostbite on a climb in New Zealand twenty years before, rides a yak down to Chinese Base Camp from ABC on Mount Everest. His summit bid in 2006 left him with badly frostbitten hands and leg stumps. (Photo by Michael Kodas)

Twenty-three

The link on EverestNews.com was irresistible.

"Lakpa Sherpa wants to take Oprah to the Summit of Mt. Everest!"

I clicked it and found that, in fact, Lhakpa had already taken Oprah to the top of the mountain. A photo showed Lhakpa, my neighbor in Hartford, posing on top of Everest with a copy of *O*, the magazine devoted to the talk-show host, with the shadow of Everest's summit pyramid stretching out onto the horizon behind them. Lhakpa is in a red down coat. Oprah is in a yellow pantsuit. For the first time in any summit photo that I had seen of Lhakpa, she appeared to be smiling behind her oxygen mask.

"CLIMB LIKE A SHERPA!!" the link on EverestNews.com read. "CLIMB WITH A SHERPA!"

My own grin faded as I read further.

Lakpa Sherpa, successful 5 time summiter of Everest, announces the creation of her new guide service, Sunny Mountain Guides . . .

Visit Lakpa's website sunnymountainguides.com for information and a description of the many ways Sunny Mountain Guides and Lakpa can help you plan an exciting visit to the top of the world!

A year earlier, Lhakpa, as a co-leader of my team, had sequestered herself in the cook tent to avoid climbing or working with her teammates, and wouldn't so much as share a meal with the people she was allegedly leading. She denied food to a member of her group, failed to provide the shelters she had promised to her teammates in a storm-bound wilderness, and finished her own expedition lying unconscious on the stony ground outside the team's dining tent. The Sherpani she led in the 2000 Women's Climb complained that Lhakpa refused to climb with them or work as part of the team, ensuring that she was the only member to reach the summit. Now Lhakpa—or Lakpa— was hawking her services to guide others up the mountain? I followed the link to her Web site and read of her offer to take the inexperienced on a stroll in the death zone.

"Have you ever taken a walk and wished you were climbing Mt Everest?" the home page read. "Perhaps you can! I have summited Mt Everest for the past five years—more than any woman on earth! Now I am willing to share my experience with others. . . . Imagine yourself arriving in Kathmandu, an exotic city and gateway to the Himalayas. I will meet you, get you settled in your lodgings, arrange transportation to Base Camp at Everest and lead you up the magnificent mountain."

The Web site was more polished than most, with a slideshow displaying photos of Lhakpa, her family, and the Himalaya scrolling across the top; links to bios of the family and friends that made up her Sherpa staff; sample itineraries; a photo gallery; and a form, consisting of just ten questions, to book her services.

"Sherpas are brave, unbelievably strong companions on your climb. Their knowledge of the mountain is vast . . .

"I 'climb like a Sherpa' because I am one. . . . I am Lakpa Sherpa, Director of Sunny Mountain Guides . . ."

No matter how hard she might have worked to remedy her illiteracy since I had been on Everest with her the year before, I couldn't imagine Lhakpa was capable of even speaking the words that were attributed to her, much less writing them. But more worrisome than who had written the Web site was the question of who would read those booking forms. At the time, the site made no mention of Lhakpa's husband, George Dijmarescu, and the only hint that she was married came under the heading "About Us."

Our daughter, Sunny, is the inspiration for the name of the business. It . . . also reflects my positive attitude toward the mountains.

In any new business, as in any new climb, the first steps are uncertain. A climber who wishes to attempt more complex climbing, but hasn't the experience to arrange the many complicated details, can leave the planning and execution of a full scale high altitude expedition to Sunny Mountain Guides.

We look forward to serving as your guide.

The means by which someone with the wealth and notoriety of Oprah could reach the summit of Everest were multiplying by the year, and not all of them involved walking there. A few months earlier, at the height of that year's spring climbing season, a number of climbers watched as the "Mystery Chopper" landed on the summit of Everest—nearly a mile higher in the atmosphere than any helicopter had previously flown. The accomplishment wasn't met with the kind of accolades that most people receive for getting to the summit, despite the fact that the French pilot of Eurocopter's high-altitude prototype showed far more skill and daring than any climber who reached the summit that year. Nepali aviation authorities not only denied that the accomplishment had taken place but also levied fines against the company, which had a permit to test the chopper in the Everest region but not to land on the summit. Many climbers, as well as EverestNews.com, tried to debunk the flight, as though being able to fly to Everest's summit diminished the accomplishment of climbing there. But within two years, many climbers, as well as *Outside* magazine, were touting high-altitude choppers as a potential new level of security on Everest. Few pointed out the fact that a helicopter requires far better weather to ascend a mountain than a climber does, and most people who need a rescue at high altitude are in unstable conditions that would prevent a chopper from flying. But rescue flights are just one type of false security luring the unwary up Everest.

I was still reading the Sunny Mountain Guides site when Fabiola called me. I met her and Davide a year after I first saw them at the Yak and Yeti, and as we had followed our own paths through Everest's underworld, we had become close. Like Lhakpa Sherpa, Fabiola was about to start a new career, she told me. Her investigation into her father's death had led her to leave the world of finance and take a job as a journalist at ExplorersWeb, Tom and Tina Sjogren's company, where she would be the only employee with them in their New York office. Among the Web sites she would write for was MountEverest.net, which was increasingly crusading against corruption in the mountains, and was the archrival of Lhakpa's patron, EverestNews.com. Fabiola, whose father had clutched at the legs of his Sherpas as they left him to die on Everest, knew how few Westerners could "climb like a Sherpa" and survive.

In her new job, Fabiola soon learned that the media was as pervasive a force on Everest as the weather, and, in its own way, was just as volatile. Tom and Tina have many critics, many of whom like to point out that the couple has climbed only one significant mountain in their careers—although that mountain was Everest, and they visited it six times, giving them a certain expertise. Their archrival, however, George Martin, owner and general manager of EverestNews.com, says that he has never climbed anything. He has never set eyes on his Web site's namesake mountain. When they were first starting their own Web site, Tom and Tina considered purchasing EverestNews.com from Martin. When they visited him in Ohio to check out the business, the corpulent man in overalls who met them at the airport could not have seemed less like a mountaineer. Martin boasted to them that he had been out of the plains of Ohio only once in his life. Nonetheless, he claimed to publish "the largest mountaineering publication in the world"—"Where Everest Climbers Come for News." With the hundreds of pages of blogs and commentary from dozens of expeditions that Martin's Web site published, the Everest Speakers Bureau he promoted, and the Everest-Gear he sold, Martin had appointed himself one of the foremost experts on the mountain. But during their meeting, as Martin doodled in a legal tablet, the Swedes decided that EverestNews.com was not the business opportunity they had thought it was. So instead of purchasing Martin's Web site, they became his competitor.

ExplorersWeb's Manhattan offices were a half-hour cab ride from Fabiola and Davide's Upper West Side apartment. In the office, Fabiola quickly learned as much about Michael Matthews's and Henry Todd's experiences on Everest as she had about her father's. Hardly a day went by that Tom and Tina didn't bring up the case that was continuing to haunt Everest and the man they believed was at the heart of the mountain's troubles. Fabiola was usually fascinated, but sometimes Tom and Tina seemed obsessed. That's an easy malady to pick up on Everest.

Since my first trip to the mountain, I had sat in front of a laptop perched on my coffee table as if it were a crystal ball conjuring images of an angry goddess of a mountain on the other side of the world. A few hours away, in New York, Fabiola Antezana was doing the same thing. We spoke often about the troubled expeditions that had brought both of us to Nepal and the continued turmoil we were witnessing from afar. A few times Fabiola talked about trying to get a closer view of the mountain that had taken her father from her, and visiting Everest herself. By the time she started her job at Explorers-Web, Carolyn and I were well into our plans to go back ourselves.

Even when we wanted to, we couldn't seem to get away from the mountain. Not a day went by when I didn't encounter the Everest metaphor—someone conquering "the Mount Everest of wreck diving," "the Mount Everest of violin concertos," "the Mount Everest of math problems," even "the Mount Everest of inebriation." Dozens of businesses, from a bottled water company to an online poker site, took the name of the mountain. My mother's e-mails from Kansas arrived via EverestKC.net. In a New Paltz, New York, antique shop that Carolyn and I visited with Fabiola, her husband, and the Sjogrens, Davide pulled out a book containing 100 years of *New York Times* front pages. By chance, he cracked it open to the page announcing Hillary's first ascent of Everest. Fabiola hungrily clutched the book and read the story aloud to us.

On Christmas Eve, the Antezana family welcomed Tom and Tina to their holiday festivities in Washington with the same enthusiasm that the Sjogrens had when they embraced Fabiola as their employee. Tom and Tina said they needed some time in Gladys's guest room to prepare their gifts—the ice axes they had brought for Fabiola and Davide would be a challenge to wrap—but Fabiola first showed them around the house. She pointed out an icon of Saint Peter, Russian plates, and an ancient painting of the holy family. The doll portraying Jesus in their crèche had been in the family for more than a century. Photos from Nils's climbs hung on walls and sat on shelves in almost every room. Fabiola stopped at a table in the formal living room that was set up like a shrine, with photos of Nils as a young man and from his climbs of Everest and Illimani after he retired—all arranged around a crystal cross. She opened a small box amid the pictures, and on the underside of the lid, the Sjogrens immediately recognized the photo they had put up on their Web site when Nils was missing. Inside the box sat a ceramic heart, kneaded and glazed by an artist friend of the family's to look as though it were pounded from bronze, atop a stack of two-inch squares of parchment, each bearing a line from a poem. Fabiola read them out loud to her guests.

" 'Because of him, you are loved,' " she began.

Her daughter had read only a few stanzas when Gladys rushed into the room from the small study beside it.

"Fabiola, Fabiola, I must show you something," she said, but her daughter kept reading.

" 'And at the top of the world . . . his thoughts were of you.' "

In the next room over, Gladys had been overseeing a worker who was running a cable to Nils's desk. The pathologist hadn't liked computers, but his son, the neurosurgeon, needed a high-speed connection when he was visiting from Oregon. When the worker pulled back a rug to hide the cable, he discovered two leaves—each nearly fifteen inches long and eight inches wide. Nils had often brought back interesting leaves from his adventures. These were just too big to press into a book as he had with the others. Without their father to explain their significance, the family would never know what kind of tree they had come from, or where in the world he had found them.

"Oh, I have every day surprises," Gladys said, throwing her hands in the air and laughing. "Surprises and surprises and surprises."

On Christmas Eve 2005, Nils Antezana had been dead for more than nineteen months, but he was still giving his wife presents. Gladys stepped back to the living room to again ask her daughter to come see her discovery, but Fabiola, brought to tears by her reading, had her face buried in Tina Sjogren's shoulder.

I showed up at the Antezanas' home with a Christmas Eve surprise as well— news. The day before, in London's Southwark Crown Court, David Matthews, unsatisfied by the civil settlement he had made with the men who had led his son up Everest, brought manslaughter charges against Jon Tinker, Mike Smith, and Henry Todd. District Judge Martin Walker listened to four hours of arguments, and issued summonses for the defendants who the case argued breached their "duty of care" to Michael Matthews by providing him with faulty oxygen equipment, neglecting to assign someone to follow him down from the summit, not discussing safety procedures, and failing to call off the climb when it became obvious that the oxygen equipment was unreliable. David Matthews supported the charges with some new evidence, including a letter that Henry Todd had written to the manufacturer of his oxygen tanks a year before Michael Matthews's expedition. Henry acknowledges in the letter that he had had problems with the valves in his oxygen cylinders in the past and complained that the company was still not confident in the competence of the equipment that he was reselling on Everest. Malfunctioning oxygen equipment, Henry wrote, could put some of his customers' lives at risk, and that would not be very good for his business.

It was a rare private prosecution—in Britain individuals can file criminal charges that, if a judge can be convinced to sign off on them, are tried before the Crown. But mostly it was novel for the scene of the alleged crimes. It was the kind of case that was certain to draw attention around the world—one British tabloid referred to the "Everest Murder Trial" in a headline.

No media would be as close as the Sjogrens, who were both covering the case for their Web site, and witnesses quoted in court documents. Tom provided what is perhaps the case's most astonishing testimony: that Henry Todd, who had never summited Everest, climbed nearly to the top of the mountain after Michael disappeared in what Tom and Tina believe was an effort to dispose of evidence—Michael's corpse and his oxygen equipment. Henry's plan to remove the ropes and ladders he had installed in the Khumbu Icefall after he came back down, the Sjogrens claimed, was an attempt to prevent rescuers from finding Michael's body.

For many mountaineers, the Sjogrens' statements were evidence not of a cover-up but of the madness of the entire affair, and the lengths Henry's enemies would go to to have their vengeance. Henry's actions were consistent with many scenarios, other climbers pointed out, most of them more likely than climbing into the death zone to search for the body of a man he didn't know in order to destroy evidence.

"Six people tried to turn Matthews around," Henry told me when I asked about the suit. "Then he disappears in the storm, and it's suddenly the oxygen and I'm supposed to have climbed up the mountain and thrown his body off. It's ludicrous.

"Tom and Tina are farcical," he ranted. "But they have a Web site."

That was something they regularly reminded Henry of.

Two weeks before David Matthews began his private prosecution, their three-part special report on oxygen on Everest ran on ExplorersWeb under the headline THE HIGHEST DEATH LAB IN THE WORLD. Henry appeared in the first paragraph of the first story and figured prominently below. ExWeb had already run a series about Henry, which began, appropriately, on April Fools' Day 2003, and was entitled EVEREST'S MOST DANGEROUS PERSON. For most of the decade, Henry had been on trial, either in the courts or in the press.

Seven months after he brought the criminal charges, David Matthews sat in London's Southwark Crown Court with his head in his hands. Although the judge who had heard the case at Christmas time believed David had presented adequate evidence to pursue charges, the next judge to hear the case, Geoffrey Rivlin QC, found that while the OTT Everest expedition was beset by problems, the prosecution lacked proof that they had caused Michael Matthews's death. He would not put the case before a jury.

As for Henry Todd, Rivlin stated that there was "not one scrap of worthwhile evidence" to prove that Michael's oxygen equipment had failed and the prosecution's case in that regard depended on "pure and wholly impermissible speculation."

Judge Rivlin dismissed all of the charges against the defendants.

"It is not the purpose of the criminal law to stifle the spirit of adventure, or inhibit personal ambition and endeavour," he said. "It would be most regrettable if the serious crime of manslaughter might be seen as a cloud, constantly hanging over those old enough to decide how they wish to live their lives."

Outside the court David Matthews said he was "shell-shocked" by the ruling.

"This means it is open season for guiding standards to remain slipshod on Everest," he said. "Our purpose was to try and help other families not to go through what we have had to go through."

Back in New York, at ExplorersWeb, Fabiola's new career in online journalism was hectic, stressful, and often fun. She interviewed climbers, ocean rowers, and polar explorers, and received satellite phone calls and e-mails from adventurers in the most remote corners of the planet. But as the 2006 Everest season heated up, reports of revolution in Nepal and madness on the mountain rubbed on some still-open wounds. Sometimes she was outraged by the madness, mendacity, and malfeasance she saw spreading on the mountain where her father had died, but mostly she felt numb and confused. On our arrival in Kathmandu, Carolyn and I had much the same reaction, knowing that among the old friends we were reuniting with and the climbers we were just meeting, somebody we knew probably wouldn't be coming back from the mountains.

Twenty-four

In 2004, David Sharp and I had each vowed that we wouldn't return to Everest. But two years later we were both in Sam's Bar in Kathmandu on our way back to the mountain.

Although almost nobody was on Everest yet, with the deteriorating political situation in Nepal, the climbing season already seemed to be spinning into a fiasco. A nationwide strike slated to begin in early April would last for weeks, shutting down businesses and transportation. As many as 300,000 pro-democracy activists filled the streets of Kathmandu in protests against King Gyanendra and his dismissal of Nepal's parliament a year earlier. The demonstrations grew larger and more violent by the day. Mountaineers out after dark in Lukla were kept from their lodges by razor wire and cadres of soldiers. Two groups of climbers, traveling by bus to Tibet, were caught in firefights between government soldiers and rebels. Flights in and out of the mountains were delayed for days by the turmoil, and Maoist insurgents enforced weeklong bans on travel by road in the countryside.

Since the genesis of the Maoist revolution known as the Nepalese

People's War in 1996—the same year as the infamous disaster on Everest—the political situation had gradually gone from being a backdrop to the climbing season to a position center stage. The murder in 2000 of Nepal's king, queen, and most of the royal family by the heir to the throne, who then took his own life, sent the country spinning into turmoil that ratcheted up annually. Initially the chaos was rarely more than an inconvenience to climbers and trekkers, but each year the Maoists became bolder in their demands of payments from tourists. They took to calling the forced donations a "revolutionary tax" and gave receipts to the victims of their extortion. At Base Camp on the 8,000-meter peak Makalu, the Maoists hung a banner welcoming climbers and trekkers, and listing the price for a safe visit. Then, in 2005, a Russian climber headed to Everest during a strike had part of a foot blown off by a grenade that was thrown into the car he was riding in.

Sam's Bar was a welcome haven from the pro-democracy demonstrators demanding that the king abdicate the throne; the Maoist insurgency in the countryside; and a country that seemed poised on the brink of revolution. The walls were covered with encouraging notes—graffiti scrawled by trekkers and climbers returning from their adventures. Reggae, David Sharp's favorite music, poured from the stereo onto the patio. At the bar, David and I each had plans to meet up with Jamie McGuinness, a New Zealand expatriate living in Kathmandu and the proprietor of the trekking and mountaineering company Project Himalaya. Carolyn and I sat with David as we waited. Jamie was putting together the expedition I was headed back to Everest with, and had led the expedition to Cho Oyu in 2002 that was David's first taste of an 8,000-meter summit. David and Jamie had spent a glorious half hour together atop the world's sixth-tallest mountain, eating lunch and taking in the view, which was dominated by Everest.

They were on the tallest mountain together in 2003, when David first failed to reach the top. David returned to Everest in 2004, and when he failed again, he told friends that he wasn't going back.

Then, a few days before Christmas 2005, Jamie received an e-mail from David.

"I'm (stupidly) contemplating a final (final) attempt on Everest."

Jamie wasn't surprised that David had reconsidered. Every year the mountain is full of climbers who have sworn they wouldn't return.

David Sharp had started climbing with the mountaineering club at Nottingham University, which he attended in the early 1990s. In 2001, he signed on for his first Himalayan climb—a guided trip to Pakistan's Gasherbrum II, the thirteenth-highest mountain, with Henry Todd. Henry later recalled David as a shy loner and was worried that he wasn't as careful as he needed to be at altitude and didn't always make good decisions.

Richard Dougan met David when they were both climbing Cho Oyu in 2002 and found that, although David was difficult to get close to, he was smart and charming once you did. But while David and Jamie had had success on Cho Oyu, Richard's climb ended with tragedy: One of his teammates perished in a crevasse. Richard had planned to climb Everest with the man who died, and offered David the vacant spot on his team. His new friend jumped at the opportunity.

They climbed the Tibetan trade route on the mountain. David seemed strong as he started their summit bid, but, nearing the Second Step, he realized he was getting frostbite on his nose and cheeks. He urged Richard to continue without him, but they both ended up retreating. That night David took off the plastic mountaineering boots he had worn to avoid paying $350 more for the far warmer Millet boots that most climbers wear on 8,000-meter peaks. He found his left big toe was frostbitten badly enough to require amputation. Part of the second toe on his right foot also would have to be removed.

"My toes are worth more than $35 apiece," he said to Jamie, lamenting his decision to save money on footwear.

For his 2006 expedition, David signed on with Asian Trekking, the company whose bargain price had drawn me as a customer two years earlier. He was a member of what is known as an "international" expedition—a mix-and-match cluster of climbers, most of whom haven't met before they arrive in Base Camp, and can hardly be considered teams. They often do little together other than eat in the shared dining tent. David, however, appeared to have other motives besides cost for how he selected his outfitter. Jamie had offered David a spot on his 2006 Project Himalaya expedition for $1,000 more than he was paying Asian Trekking. But although David recognized that Jamie was offering an incredible bargain for a far-better-provisioned expedition, he declined the offer. Committing to a team would prevent him from doing things independently, he told Jamie, and he wanted to climb on his own. With two previous Everest expeditions under his belt, along with visits to Cho Oyu and Gasherbrum II, he believed he understood the high-altitude game well enough to play it solo.

When we met at Sam's Bar, David opened up quickly. He talked of his hopes of starting a family and cautioned against taking unnecessary risks in the mountains. He had made many of his climbs in the Alps solo, and looking back, he told Carolyn, he regretted his recklessness. Nonetheless, he said he was planning on climbing Everest alone.

I worried that he might again suffer for his thrift. He had purchased only two bottles of oxygen, barely enough gas to get through his summit day, and only then if he made good time and nothing went wrong. And he still hadn't decided whether he was going to use supplemental oxygen at all. At times, he said, he felt that using bottled gas was cheating. He debated using it with an Austrian guide sharing his camp who considered using supplemental oxygen a form of doping. David said he was going to carry his two tanks of oxygen with him, but would break them out only in an emergency. That struck me as a dangerous plan—a hypoxic climber might not recognize that he has a problem or remember his emergency oxygen supply. In the end, it appears David decided to use his bottled oxygen.

At Chinese Base Camp, David moved into an Asian Trekking site with more than two dozen other climbers and Sherpas—including George Dijmarescu, Dave Watson, and Lhakpa Sherpa from the troubled Connecticut Everest Expedition I had climbed with two years earlier. Asian Trekking's international team also had two other Americans, another Brit, four Brazilians, four Austrians, an Ecuadorian, and a Malaysian. David spent a couple of weeks acclimatizing and equipping high camps he called "British" Camps One, Two, and Three—a homage, like the Shakespeare he carried to the mountain, to George Mallory's fatal climb on the same route eighty-two years before. He didn't inform anyone when he was heading up to prepare his camps or make his summit bid. He carried no radio or sat phone. On May 11 he arrived at Camp One, at 7,000 meters—23,000 feet—along with dozens of other mountaineers who were dashing for an unusually early weather window. Temperatures in the coming days would be brutally cold—nearly 40 degrees below zero at night—but the winds would be light and there was little chance of snow.

By midnight on the morning of May 14, David had climbed above Camp Three on his way to the top of the mountain. Most climbers hope to complete the ascent to the summit within eight hours and allow about four to return to camp. Nobody recognized David on the way up, but Bill Crouse, a guide with Russell Brice's Himalayan Experience expedition, realized from descriptions later that he had seen him. The first time was early in the morning at the Exit Cracks that lead to the mountain's northeast ridge. Then, at eleven thirty a.m., as Bill was on his way down from the summit, he had to lead his clients around David, who was sitting in the path of their descending boots on the Third Step—the last of the technical obstacles guarding the summit. An hour later Bill looked back up the mountain as he rappelled down the Second Step and noticed that David had moved only 100 meters higher up the peak.

Bill radioed Russell, who was monitoring his climbers with a spotting scope from Camp One, and noted that it was late in the day for a climber still heading up. There are no witnesses to David's final steps onto the mountaintop, but at that rate, he probably reached the summit at about two thirty, after at least fifteen hours of climbing. The sun set at about six p.m., so it was probably already dark when, during his descent from the top, David sat down next to the corpse with green boots that already occupied the cave some 800 vertical feet above high camp.

The next climbers to see David, about twelve hours later, were also with Russell's operation. Max Chaya, on his way to becoming the first Lebanese climber to summit Everest, was the first HimEx client out of Camp Three. Max didn't notice David as he passed Green Boots Cave.

"After we went by, David must have heard us," Max said later, "and clipped into the rope. I would have noticed if I had to unclip from the rope . . . to go around him."

Half an hour later the next climbers to reach the cave, also from HimEx, had to unclip to get past David. The group included Mark Inglis, who was climbing on two prosthetic legs; guide Mark "Woody" Woodward; Mark Whetu, a cameraman for the Discovery documentary; and Wayne Alexander. In all, Russell had at least fifteen mountaineers headed to the summit that day. Behind them was a twelve-person Turkish team, a number of independent climbers, and at least one other expedition.

When Woody reached the cave, he was shocked to see a pair of red boots next to the green ones he had seen there before. In the bubble of light from his headlamp he saw a figure seated with his arms wrapped around his knees, ice crystals on his eyelids, and his nose already black with frostbite. He wasn't wearing an oxygen mask and had only thin, blue liner gloves on his hands. Woodward shouted "Hello?" and shined his light into David's eyes, but got no response.

"Oh, this poor guy," Woody recalls thinking at the time. "He's stuffed."

Mark Whetu, the cameraman, had also been up Everest a few times before. He shouted for the figure in the cave to get moving, not realizing how bad off David actually was.

Wayne Alexander, at the back of the line, watched David from a distance, but never considered whether he might be alive. Then, as he neared the cave, Wayne saw David's head move. He leaned on the rocky outcrop so he could peer in at David's face.

"He was stricken," Wayne remembers. "It was horrific."

His first instinct was to give David a hug—just a tiny bit of human contact to ease the loneliest moments of a man's life.

But when he looked up, his teammates had moved ahead and

Wayne, not wanting to stop long enough for the cold to dig into him or to lose his place in line, moved on as well. Like Woody, Wayne was certain that David was beyond help. Seeing the dying climber, however, affected him far more deeply than reaching the summit of Everest, and he would regret not stopping long enough for that embrace. None of the ascending HimEx climbers discussed trying to rescue David, although Woody, Mark Whetu, and Mark Inglis all reported trying to radio their teammates in lower camps about him.

When the first climbers with the Turkish expedition arrived a few minutes later, David seemed to be fidgeting with his rucksack. A Sherpa prodded him to get up and get going, and he waved them off. They continued up, believing he was just resting, but the next group of Turkish climbers found David lying motionless, and thought he was dead.

"We completely had no doubt," Serhan Poçan, the leader of the team, wrote in a report. "He was a dead body for us while we were climbing up."

The next time Serhan saw what he had been certain was a corpse, some seven hours later, he was terrified to see David's arm move.

"We made him upright and tried to give him some hot drink but he couldn't drink it," Serhan wrote. "His nose was completely frozen deep inside. His hand was frozen as a rock. He was able to open his eyes but couldn't say anything."

Serhan found David's oxygen bottles were empty.

And Serhan already had his hands full. Around sunrise his wife, Burçak Poçan, on her way to becoming the first Turkish woman to summit Everest, had fallen unconscious and hung from the ropes on the Second Step. Sherpas rescued her and, after she came to, were assisting her descent just below Serhan. They had also noticed that there was a new body in Green Boots Cave, and stopped. Their *sirdar* broke icicles off David's nose and saw life in David's eyes, but got no response when he spoke to him. Others with the team put him on oxygen and tried to get him on his feet, but he couldn't stand or speak.

Max Chaya, the Lebanese mountaineer climbing with HimEx,

was the first climber to top out that day, reaching the summit around sunrise. As he passed David again, during his descent, he also noticed him moving. David was lying on his back with his knees up "like he was doing sit-ups."

"He was much closer to death than he was to life," Max recalled. "His arms were extended in front of him and curled like he was holding a big basketball. He was wearing light blue liner gloves. You could see that his fingers were frozen—they were crooked as well as bent . . . His nose was black and the sides of his face were turning purple."

At nine thirty a.m. Max called down to Russell Brice, described David's condition, and asked what to do. According to Russell, that was the first he had heard of David Sharp's predicament.

"I established that David was still alive but unconscious, and that his arms were frozen to the elbow and his legs were frozen to the knees, and he had frostbite to the nose," Russell said in a statement a month later. And, like the Turkish, Russell had other problems. Twenty-four years earlier, Mark Inglis had had his legs amputated below the knee as a result of the frostbite he got while trapped for two weeks in an ice cave on Mount Cook. The trapped climbers and their rescue had been big news in New Zealand, homeland to both Mark and Russell. Now, as a member of Russell's expedition, Mark had become the first double amputee to summit Everest, and the Discovery cameras promised to make it another media event. But he was coming down from the summit with his hands seriously frostbitten and the stumps of his legs so badly frozen and battered that he had to ride makeshift sleds and yaks off the mountain. Two other HimEx clients had stubbornly tried to continue to the summit when Russell ordered them to turn back. They eventually did retreat, but with bad frostbite as well.

"I've got two clients in a very bad way coming down the mountain," Russell reported after the expedition. "I have to look after those people, and I don't have the manpower or the oxygen or anything to be able to help another man at that time of day."

David was only a two-hour hike from high camp, but it would take perhaps a dozen fresh climbers to carry him down and through the awkward Exit Cracks. A few days later it took nearly twenty Sherpas to rescue another badly frostbitten but conscious climber who collapsed near the summit and had to be carried to ABC in a stretcher. And during most of that rescue, the stricken climber could walk, which David could not.

Max Chaya and his Sherpa spent an hour giving David oxygen and trying to get him on his feet, until Russell radioed Max, who was weeping, and coaxed him to get a move on before his own oxygen tanks were exhausted. Max recited the Lord's Prayer in French to the dying climber, then headed down. When he got back to camp, Max, who had just achieved his years-long dream of climbing the Seven Summits, wasn't in the mood to celebrate. He zipped himself into his tent and cried for two hours.

Phurba, Russell's *sirdar*, was a ways behind Max. He also put David on oxygen, and tried to get him on his feet. But David collapsed under any part of his own weight. He did, however, seem to have come out of his coma, perhaps from the oxygen or the warmth of the daylight. Phurba was wearing a helmet camera, shooting video for the Discovery documentary, and recorded David speaking.

"My name is David Sharp, I'm with Asian Trekking and I just want to sleep," he was reported to say. (One of the HimEx climbers who saw the raw tape told me that the only words David spoke that he could understand were "I'm with Asian Trekking.")

They moved him into the sun, hoping to make his final hours more comfortable, then continued down to Camp Three. The following day, May 16, Sherpas climbing with a Korean expedition confirmed that David was dead. A year later, when other climbers carried David's pack down from Green Boots Cave, they found his heavy mittens, an injection of dex, and other supplies that, although they wouldn't have made him much more likely to survive, would have been a few more weapons in his fight against the brutal cold and hypoxia that killed him. Like the oxygen tanks he told us he had forgotten about during his climb in 2004, David apparently hadn't remembered some of his most critical supplies.

Word of David's death got out on the blog of Vitor Negrete, a Brazilian climber who shared David's camp and was making his way to the summit the day after David died. And there were other horrors in Vitor's report. His own tent and food had been stolen from Camp Two.

"All these events have affected me deeply—I even considered calling the attempt off," Vitor reported via satellite telephone to his Web site in Brazil. "At C3 we have left another cache with food and gear—I hope we can find that one intact. Otherwise the summit bid will be seriously jeopardized."

Ang Dawa, the Sherpa climbing with Vitor, visited friends in Camp Two to replace the supplies that had been stolen and arrange a tent for the night. But in Camp Three, Vitor ordered Ang Dawa to stay in camp. The Brazilian headed for the summit without oxygen, his Sherpa, or his satellite phone. Vitor summited about noon, but he tired on his descent and collapsed near the Second Step. He managed to radio Ang Dawa, who climbed up to Vitor and helped him back to camp. But while the Sherpa was heating drinks in their tent, his client took three loud gasps and fell dead.

Three days later, Igor Plyushkin, a climber honored as a "Snow Leopard" in Russia for climbing all the former Soviet Union's 7,000-meter peaks, reached the summit of Everest from the north as part of the huge 7 Summits Club Expedition. He made it back to Camp Three and was strong enough to continue down to Camp Two with his teammates before his summit day was over. But the next day Igor barely made it fifty feet from camp before he was having trouble breathing. Guides hooked him up to oxygen and injected him with dex, but ninety minutes later he was dead. His teammates wrapped him in a sleeping bag and covered him with stones.

By late May 2006, the carnage had left Everest fans desperate for some good news. The first bit they got was when the king of Nepal announced that he was reinstituting the country's parliament and relinquishing most of his control of the government. Then, in Tibet, they got another dose just as the sun hit the mountain's northeast ridge on May 26. Dan Mazur, the American owner of the huge SummitClimb guiding operation, was headed for the summit with clients

Myles Osborne and Andrew Brash. Just before the Second Step, sitting a few feet from a 10,000-foot precipice, they saw a dead man coming back to life.

"He had his down suit unzipped to the waist, his arms out of the sleeves, was wearing no hat, no gloves, no sunglasses, had no oxygen mask, regulator, ice axe, oxygen, no sleeping bag, no mattress, no food nor water bottle," Myles wrote on their team's blog of their discovery of a man who had survived a night out in the open in Everest's death zone. "His fingers looked like ten waxy candle sticks. His head wagged and jerked around, his beady eyes embedded in a frosty face, trying to focus on something, anything."

Although there were steep, thousand-foot drops on either side of him, the climber was not tied into the mountain.

"This looks like an execution," Dan said to his clients, although he couldn't really believe that someone had attempted to murder the climber before him.

As Dan, Myles, and Andrew approached, the climber uttered what, during the 2006 season on Everest, would be as famous as Mallory's "Because it's there" quip.

"I imagine you're surprised to see me here," he said.

Dan asked if he could tell them his name.

"Yeah, I can tell you my name," he replied. "My name is Lincoln Hall. . . . Can you tell me how I got here?"

Lincoln, an Australian climber, was shivering violently. He kept removing his hat and gloves, believing that he was hot, rather than cold—a sign of severe hypothermia. Delusional and hallucinating, Lincoln was convinced he was on a boat rather than a mountain. He wanted to jump overboard, and the other climbers held him back from the edge, tying him to the peak to keep him from throwing himself off it. They hooked him up to their own oxygen, fed him snacks, and gave him hot drinks. On his coat they noticed a patch for the 7 Summits Club Expedition. Dan radioed his staff in ABC, and they rousted the climbers at Lincoln's camp, who required some convincing that their client was still alive. So certain were they of Lincoln's death that they had already notified his wife and sent out a press release. Dan, Myles, and Andrew watched their own chance for the summit fade away while they waited with Lincoln for his rescuers to arrive, four hours later. As 7 Summits Sherpas slowly led the stricken climber down the peak, the men who had found him climbed down fast, their elation at saving a life mixing with the disappointment of giving up their chance to stand atop the mountain.

The 7 Summits expedition was the largest on the mountain in 2006, with thirty-three climbers and four guides planning to climb Everest. The sheer size of the crew was bound to lead to confusion, which was further complicated by the fact that there were really two commercial guiding operations called "7 Summits" running their expeditions together. Alex Abramov, a veteran Russian guide, ran 7 Summits Club and had been growing his Everest operation fast in recent years. Harry Kikstra, a young Dutch guide, photographer, and author, owned and operated 7Summits.com, the other commercial operation in the huge camp. Charismatic, with long blond hair and a business background, Harry's guiding service is impressive online: His site is full of his photographs, information about the seven continental high points and trips he is offering to climb them, along with forums, blogs, podcasts, and mountaineering merchandise. Harry, however, had first climbed Everest himself only a year earlier, and he had developed a deadly cerebral edema near the summit. With help from a Sherpa, he managed to climb down under his own steam, but had to be carried the last few hundred meters into ABC. His team's doctor told him he was lucky to have survived. Now he was back on the mountain and running his own guiding operation there. He had brought fifteen clients onto the expedition, but would be leading only one. Harry, perhaps the least experienced Everest guide of 2006, was leading a climber who would need the greatest care in the history of the mountain—Thomas Weber, a German mountaineer who was inspired to climb Everest after having a tumor removed from his brain. Since then, Thomas's eyesight had deteriorated as the air pressure around him had decreased, such as when he climbed high peaks. As he neared the summit of Everest, Thomas would be effectively blind. And there was no telling what other ways his wounded brain would respond to the exertion, cold, and hypoxia. Harry and Thomas had ice-climbed blindfolded before the expedition, but otherwise they did little to prepare for the unusual challenges Thomas's disability would present during the ascent. Thomas, who was using his climb to raise money for two Himalayan charities, had created an elaborate Web site and was accompanied by a pair of cameramen to make a documentary about the climb.

Lincoln Hall, best known as a climber and author, was also making a film. He was on Alex Abramov's 7 Summits Club's expedition as a cameraman to document a fifteen-year-old Australian's attempt to set the youth record on Everest. Lincoln had been on plenty of expeditions, including a first ascent in Antarctica and an expedition to Everest in 1984, during which he had climbed high, but failed to summit.

The night before he left Kathmandu for Everest in 2006, he had beers with a friend with whom he had once written a book and who was also headed to the mountains the following day—Sue Fear. Sue's achievements in the mountains had earned her the Order of Australia medal and the "Adventurer of the Year" title from the Australian Geographic Society. She had summited Everest in 2003. In 2006, she was headed to Manaslu, a treacherous 8,000-meter peak in western Nepal. When I met up with Lincoln myself in Kathmandu, two months later, his memories of his meeting with Sue were foggy—like many of his recollections of his 2006 climb. But he recalled her telling him that Everest had changed a lot in the twenty-two years since he was last there. The place wasn't very pleasant anymore. Watch out for thieves, she had warned, especially in the high camps

Lincoln had started his summit bid on May 22, the same day that Thomas and Harry had set out. When the teenager he was filming gave up just a short way out of Advanced Base Camp, Lincoln and the team's three Sherpas decided to try for the top anyway. At midnight on May 24, Lincoln and his Sherpas left Camp Three with Thomas Weber; his guide, Harry Kikstra; and their two Sherpas. The night, for an 8,000-meter peak, was warm and windless. They passed the cave where David Sharp's new red boots poked out beside an old pair of green ones, much the same way they had walked past the day-old stack of rocks with two boots sticking out of it in Camp

Two—the grave of their teammate Igor. Lincoln and his Sherpas moved ahead of the others at the Second Step and reached the top around nine a.m., where they made a joyous radio call to ABC.

But an hour into his descent, Lincoln sat down in the snow and couldn't get up on his own. Sherpas struggled for nine hours to get him down the mountain, but Lincoln didn't make their work easy. He thrashed deliriously, kicking at them with his spiked boots and cursing. Another Sherpa came up to help, but by four p.m., when they reported that Lincoln had lost consciousness, the Sherpas had managed to move him only 150 meters down from the summit—to just below the Second Step, near another fresh corpse. By the time the sun had set, Lincoln was showing no signs of life. One of the Sherpas poked him in the eye, but got no response. At seven twenty that night, with their expedition leader urging them to save their own lives, the Sherpas declared Lincoln dead and made a hasty descent to Camp Three. Twelve hours later, three climbers on the northeast ridge—Dan Mazur and his clients—found the mountaineer half dressed and half alive. And amid the worldwide attention garnered by Lincoln Hall's rescue, the story of Thomas Weber was almost lost.

When Lincoln was standing on the summit at nine a.m., Thomas, his eyesight so weakened that he could only roughly make out the forms around him, was approaching the Third Step. To the climbers nearby, Thomas appeared delirious. He staggered toward the edge of the mountain as if he intended to jump off it, and his companions had to grab the ropes to hold him back. Harry and the Sherpas discovered a hole in their client's oxygen mask, so one of the Sherpas gave his own mask to Thomas and replaced it with a mask he pulled off a nearby corpse—a French climber who had died a few days earlier. Thomas seemed to move and see better after they replaced the damaged mask.

Anne Parmenter, my climbing partner from Connecticut, was back on the mountain with the Project Himalaya team. As she and five of her teammates climbed past Thomas and Harry at the Third Step, Anne noticed that, during the thirty minutes that she was in sight of him, Thomas's oxygen mask was pushed off to the side of his face so that he was getting little supplemental gas. He was wearing no goggles or sunglasses, having told his guide that he could see better without them.

Harry says he was impressed with how strongly Thomas had climbed up to that point, noting that they had kept up with many of the climbers on the mountain and had passed a number of them. But to Chris Klinke and Fredrik Strang, also with Project Himalaya, Thomas was moving like a zombie—badly uncoordinated, swaying back and forth, and holding the rope to keep his balance. He struggled to switch his equipment from one rope to the next. Neither of the climbers knew of Thomas's failing eyesight or the lack of coordination brought on by his brain surgery, and they feared he had a deadly case of cerebral edema. They were also concerned that Harry was some twenty feet in front of his struggling client.

"Your client does not look well," Chris told Harry as he passed him. "Have you thought about giving him any dex?"

"No, no, no, he is always like this," Harry responded.

When Fred approached Harry, he found him asking advice over a two-way radio.

"Hey, this guy needs dex, he needs water, he needs to get down *now*," Fred told Thomas's guide.

Harry didn't respond to Fred's plea. He had, however, noticed that his client seemed suddenly weak and off balance, and had become concerned that Thomas wasn't responding to his instructions. Thomas told him he wanted to continue up, but admitted that he was now totally blind. Harry turned Thomas around at nine fifteen a.m., just fifty meters below the summit. The Project Himalaya climbers continued to the top, passing Lincoln Hall on the way up and again on the way back down.

Harry and Pemba Sherpa short-roped Thomas back down the mountain. At the Second Step, during their descent, the Project Himalaya climbers waited more than thirty minutes for Thomas—with Harry's and a Sherpa's help—to rappel down in front of them. At the bottom, he struggled for a long time to get past the rocks overhanging the abyss, got his crampons tangled in some old ropes, and began to panic. One of the Sherpas cut Thomas's boot free and was preparing a new oxygen bottle for him when Thomas, with a terrified expression, looked right at Harry's face, as if he had completely regained his sight.

"I am dying," he said.

Then he fell onto the slope of snow below him and slid toward the void. Harry says he was completely surprised by his client's sudden collapse, and grabbed him, but could not hold on. Thomas ended up hanging from the fixed rope, with his head pointing down the mountain and his face down in the snow—a position that prevented him from breathing. Anne looked down from the top of the Second Step to see Thomas's leg shaking violently. Then she saw it stop. When she got down, she found one of Thomas's Sherpas hiding behind the rocks to avoid the crisis. Chris was surprised to see that Harry was again more than twenty feet away from his stricken client, talking on the radio again. He asked if Harry had any dex to inject into Thomas to revive him. Harry said he didn't, so Chris gave the guide a syringe of the drug, but never saw him inject it. Scott Woolums, leader of the Project Himalaya team, was assisting a client who was having difficulty descending the Second Step. He headed down as fast as he could, but it still took fifteen minutes to reach the bottom. Scott lassoed a cord around Thomas's pack, and Harry helped hoist his client up to them, which ate up even more precious time.

Six months earlier, Thomas had sent a note to Scott in Oregon inquiring whether he was interested in guiding him up Everest, and Scott had quoted him a price. Thomas had hired Harry instead, but his still-warm body ended up in Scott's lap anyway. By the time the two guides could start CPR, he was gone.

Just then Harry heard that another 7 Summits climber, Lincoln Hall, had collapsed above the Second Step. He sent Pemba, the strongest of Thomas's Sherpas, up to assist Lincoln.

Beyond the e-mails that Scott had exchanged with Thomas, none of the Project Himalaya climbers knew him. Nonetheless, his death haunted them.

"The guide failed in his duty," Chris said.

Fred Strang was also upset by Harry's passivity toward the crisis.

"He did absolutely nothing for the whole time I was climbing down," Fred said of Harry's reaction to his client's collapse.

That afternoon, Harry shut off his radio for several hours. But two days later, Fred went to see him in the 7 Summits site at ABC, where climbers were monitoring Lincoln's rescue. Neither the uncertain survival of a member of his summit team nor the death of the man he was personally responsible for appeared to dampen Harry's mood.

"They took it so lightly; Harry was in a pretty good mood," Fred said. "He was laughing and trying to sell me some trips."

When Fred made it back to his own camp, Chris pulled him aside.

"You know you don't want to go on a trip with that guy," he said. "He just killed his client."

Harry, however, claims he did everything he could for Thomas, and that he was blindsided by the criticism of the Project Himalaya climbers. If they were so concerned, he asked, why was Scott the only one to help?

Even Lincoln's rescue had a dark side, but he didn't talk about it in the interviews he gave to Australian newspapers, or during his appearances on the *Today* show and *Dateline* in New York.

After Dan Mazur and his clients discovered Lincoln alive below the Second Step, the 7 Summits team sent as many Sherpas as they could find to climb up and get him. A dozen Sherpas and fifty bottles of oxygen were dedicated to the effort to bring Lincoln down. In the meantime, two Sherpas in Camp Three, the closest camp to where he was found, were sent up to the Second Step to get him started on his descent. They didn't seem very happy to see him alive, and were further angered by his stubborn, slow caution. Even afterward, Lincoln had trouble separating his hallucinations from reality, but he is sure that at least one part of the nightmare was real—when one of those first two Sherpas to reach him took his ice ax from him and beat him with it. Two Italian climbers reported seeing a Sherpa striking Lincoln with the ax at the First Step. Lincoln also remembers them threatening him and demanding money and equipment in return for his life, but he admitted when I saw him in Kathmandu that he had trouble determining which of his memories were delusions. Regardless, he found himself as afraid of those first Sherpas who came to help as he was of the crisis they were rescuing him from.

"I thought they were going to throw me off the north side of the mountain," he said.

When another Sherpa showed up, one whom Lincoln was friendly with from previous expeditions, the ones who had been abusing him gave back his ice ax. Lincoln asked his old friend to stay with him— to protect him from his rescuers. At the Exit Cracks, Lincoln met up with the Sherpas sent from lower camps. The news that Lincoln was alive got out before he got off the mountain, but soon after he descended to Base Camp, there was more bad news. Sue Fear, the friend who had warned him of Everest's troubles, had died in a crevasse fall on Manaslu.

In the twelve days between David Sharp's death and Lincoln Hall's rescue, those left behind by the calamitous season on Everest visited my teammates and me at our dinner tables. Swedish climber Tomas Olsson had attempted to ski down Everest's Norton Couloir the day after David died in his cave. When one of Tomas's skis broke, he was forced to rappel down the couloir. But the snow anchor he hung his rope from failed, and he tumbled thousands of feet down the mountain. When Tomas's body was found several days later, his partner, Tormod Granheim, came to our dining tent in Base Camp and used our radio to pass on the news.

Caroline, the wife of French climber Jacques Hugues-Letrange, came to our tent in ABC just after we had finished breakfast, looking for any information we might have about her husband. The couple had climbed the northeast ridge to the top together, but had become separated during their descent. Caroline had been trying to learn her husband's fate since she had gotten down without him the day before. She stood outside our dining tent weeping while one of my teammates tried to comfort her. Later, she learned her husband had collapsed of exhaustion near the Third Step.

With the four Sherpas who had died early in the season preparing the climbing routes, the season closed with eleven fatalities on Everest. There were twelve if you counted Pavel Kalny, a Czech climbing Lhotse who died on May 5 after falling at a point where Everest and Lhotse share the same route. Although his partner made it back to camp, Pavel spent the night out in the open after his fall. He was still alive when Sherpas found him the next day, but died a short while later, despite the efforts of a Chilean doctor to save him.

"The 'Everest Circus' was becoming an 'Everest Graveyard,'" blogged Pauline Sanderson, a member of the EverestMax Expedition and half of the first married British couple to summit. The 2006 death toll on Everest was second only to that of ten years earlier, when twelve climbers perished during the disastrous 1996 season.

And there were plenty of other notable problems. One climber had all her climbing gear stolen from Base Camp. She borrowed enough to contine her ascent, but the Sherpa she had hired sexually harassed her in her tent, threatened to abandon her in the death zone, and finally stole all of her oxygen. Two climbers with a climb promoting peace had much of their gear stolen in Base Camp after they descended from the top. Another climber with that team collapsed below the summit, precipitating a thirty-six-hour rescue involving two dozen other climbers.

Russell Brice was just finishing the rugged, daylong hike down from ABC to Base Camp, and we had just started on our way up. Even after thirteen miles at 20,000 feet, Russell, who has hiked this trail more than any other Westerner, moved at twice the speed we did. Carolyn and I were resting on a boulder; she whispered to me how thankful she was that he couldn't see how slowly we'd been walking. He looked at his feet and kicked absentmindedly at the stony ground, then raised his eyes to the trail ahead.

"I hate this part," he said.

I had expected Russell to be elated. He had gotten a legless man onto the summit along with several other clients, and had a television crew finishing a six-part documentary on his expedition. But he didn't seem very happy. Russell is renowned for his patience on the mountain: In most of his expeditions to Everest he has waited until the end of the season, when a late weather window almost invariably rewards his faith with warmer temperatures, longer days, and a less-crowded climbing route. But in 2006, he, like many other climbers, had jumped at an early stretch of weather that was stable and clear, albeit some twenty degrees colder than what he usually sent his teams into. Many of his clients came down with frostbite, and a few would lose fingers. Mark Inglis would not only have most of several fingers amputated, but several centimeters would be cut off his already half-size legs. Russell said he didn't consider an expedition a success if everyone didn't come down unscathed.

As opposed to the deadly season ten years earlier, when most of the climbers were killed in a sudden storm, Russell pointed out that all of the fatalities of the 2006 season happened in unusually fine weather. Climbers continued up alone and late, pushing themselves in a very bad place to step beyond one's limits. Changing weather might have turned them around or kept them from heading up in the first place. In a way, the 2006 victims were killed by good weather. Other climbers noted another difference from the 1996 season, when most of the fatalities were climbers with expensive, high-end guided expeditions. In 2006, half of the fatalities were either clients or employees of the king of the discount Everest climb—Asian Trekking.

On the trail outside Base Camp, Russell told me of David Sharp and how his people had found him with his arms and legs wooden with frostbite, unable to stand or speak, and how they had given him oxygen and moved him into the sun, but couldn't revive him. Despite the forty or more climbers who witnessed the disastrous end to David's climb, he remained unidentified for two days. When Russell descended to ABC, he asked around to find out which expedition was missing a member. He initially thought David was Russian because his clients had misunderstood the few words they heard David speak. Russell didn't yet know about the video in which David identified himself. George Dijmarescu said that one of his campmates was unaccounted for, and Dave Watson retrieved David's backpack from his tent. In the pack Russell found David's passport, a wallet with £2.30, and a ziplock bag with about $2,500—enough money to purchase more oxygen or pay a Sherpa to aid his ascent. Russell also found David's receipt from Asian Trekking. Not counting oxygen, David had paid just $6,400 for his expedition. According to Russell, George and Dave declined to contact their friend's family with word of his death. So although Russell had never met David, he called David's parents with the terrible news. It's a task that's fallen to him often in the past, despite the fact that he himself has had only one client perish.

For many in the madhouse of crowds and carnage on Everest, avoiding responsibility is one of the keys to success. Russell mentioned that a Tibetan who worked for a commercial expedition had come down with his face covered in blood a few days earlier. The leader of the expedition walked right past his injured employee, so Russell and his team's doctor had stitched up the man's head.

Farther up the trail from where I had chatted with Russell, I ran into Dave Watson and asked him about David Sharp.

"That's what you get for being proud and not using Sherpas or oxygen," he said. "He wasn't part of our team. We weren't responsible for him."

In interviews with the Associated Press, *Men's Journal*, and other media outlets, Dave would lament the death of the climber he claimed was a friend.

"It's too bad that none of the people who cared about David knew he was in trouble," Dave told the AP, touting his and George's paying for the "rescue" of Guillermo Carro Blaizac in 2004. "Because the outcome would have been a lot different."

Later in our hike, Carolyn and I passed George, who throughout his 2006 expedition could be recognized from a hundred feet away by the large, laminated photo of his daughter that he wore around his neck like a rapper's gold medallion. George gave us the same greeting he had given Anne when he met her in Camp One. He spat at us.

While David Sharp died in what, for Everest, was beautiful weather, in the weeks to come his passing stirred up a storm that Russell couldn't escape. More than anyone else on the mountain, the guide who never saw David alive would bear not only the responsibilities that came with his death, but also the blame for it.

It started when Russell's client Wayne Alexander gave a television interview from the mountain and told of passing the dying climber, and continued when Mark Inglis, the double amputee who had summited with Wayne, arrived in Kathmandu to a hero's welcome. In the media spotlight, some began to present Mark and Russell as villains.

"On that morning, over forty people went past this young Briton," Mark told a television crew from New Zealand, describing David's death. "Trouble is, at 8,500 meters it's extremely difficult to keep yourself alive—let alone keep anyone else alive."

He claimed that the HimEx climbers were the only ones who had tried to help David, which angered other climbers who knew that wasn't the case. But the real bombshell was Mark's claim that he had radioed Russell as soon as they had found the stricken climber— while the team was ascending.

"Look, mate, you can't do anything," Mark claimed Russell had told him. "You know, he's been there X number of hours, been there without oxygen, you know, he's effectively dead."

If what Mark said were true, then eight hours before the first descending climbers tried to help David, Russell had his team continue to the summit rather than pull themselves together to try to save the fallen climber. HimEx had more than a dozen fresh climbers who could have worked on the rescue—perhaps enough to get David down to Camp Three. But even if they had managed to bring David to the high camp, the end result might not have been any different. Keeping the badly frostbitten and severely altitude-sick climber alive in a tent in the death zone would have been extremely difficult, and it would have taken a large team at least another day to get David down to ABC, the closest place with any real medical resources. In all, three team members initially said that they contacted their leader while they were ascending. Mark Woodward recalls calling down when they found the stricken climber, but says he received no response. Mark Whetu, the cameraman and guide, told the New Zealand magazine *North and South* that he radioed his sighting of

David back to Camp One, where Russell and team doctor Terry O'Connor instructed the team to continue their ascent but to assign Sherpas to check on David on their way down.

Russell steadfastly denies hearing anything about David from his ascending climbers. He claims that he was out of contact with his climbers in the early morning because he took the wrong radio to his tent with him, and that the first he heard of the dying climber was the radio call from Max Chaya at nine thirty a.m.—at least eight hours later than when Mark Inglis said he called Russell.

After Mark's press conference, Russell put out a six-page press release describing his various good deeds on Everest and detailing his team's actions with David Sharp. Logs of his own radio calls, as well as those of the documentary makers who were filming Russell for the duration of his teams' attempts to reach the summit, support his claims that none of the climbers who passed David Sharp in the morning called Russell. Three weeks later, in a statement to the Associated Press, Mark Inglis recanted his claim of contacting Russell during the ascent, claiming hypoxia, frigid temperatures, and stress caused him to confuse the facts.

"I was sure that I heard radio traffic at the time," Mark said. "I also thought I had called myself and received a reply, but like all things in that early part of the day, my focus was on my hands and the challenges to come . . . that combined with the difficulties with the oxygen mask meant that I may be mistaken. . . . My recollection is unclear."

Mark continues to hold an image in his mind of making the radio call, but to several climbers who saw him after his summit bid, it seemed unlikely that the call he thought he made was anything but a delusion. The frigid, gritty air had given Mark laryngitis. When I spoke to Mark as he descended from Advanced Base Camp, his voice was barely a whisper and he could hardly get a sentence out.

But his statement to the press in Kathmandu a week later was loud and clear. And the damage was done.

Media around the world, and especially EverestNews.com and ExplorersWeb, jumped on the story of the veteran expedition leader who told his climbers to leave a man to die. Never mind that of the two climbers most criticized for not saving David's life—Mark Inglis and Russell Brice—one had no legs and the other wasn't even there.

"For years, ExplorersWeb have been fighting the silence surrounding some deaths in the mountains. Each time, we have been told that the secrecy is only a concern for the victims' families and we have no respect. Time after time, it has turned out that the hush has served much less noble agendas: To cover up foul play in mountains without law," ExplorersWeb wrote in an editorial.

EverestNews.com also condemned Russell and the Himlayan Experience climbers and eventually announced its own "investigation into the death of David Sharp," which it said would take between six and twelve months.

"So who is brave enough to talk?" the story asked.

Both Web sites requested that the video Russell's Sherpas made of David Sharp dying be released, despite his family's request that it not be shown. Russell's critics pointed out that, while the leader said he didn't have the manpower to help out David Sharp due to exhaustion and emergencies among his own climbers, he gave one of his guides permission to break away from his team and tag the summit solo at the height of the crisis.

The New York Times, the *Times* of London, and dozens of other newspapers, broadcast outlets, and blogs around the globe wrote about David's abandonment as a sign of the rotting ethics on Everest and Lincoln's rescue as a rare glimpse of heroism. Many used Tom and Tina as sources. Back in Russell and Mark's homeland, Sir Edmund Hillary told the New Zealand Press Association, "It was wrong, if there was a man suffering altitude problems and huddled under a rock, just to lift your hat, say 'good morning' and pass on by."

Sports Illustrated of June 12 promoted Rick Reilly's column on the cover with the headline DOWN WITH EVEREST.

"Many of them are not true mountaineers. They're trophy hunters," he wrote. "They spend up to $100,000 each to be guided to the summit, another checkmark on their to-do list of life, right behind *Run with the bulls* and *Play Augusta.* You think they're going to spend all this money and not make it all the way? Over your dead body. . . . Climbing Everest used to be the pinnacle of human achievement, a rare feat. Now it's like making the white pages."

"Of course [some group] could've gotten [Sharp] down," Ed Viesturs, the best-known mountaineer in the United States, said.

"That mountain became a circus years ago," Juanito Oiarzabal, the most famous Spanish mountaineer, said. "And it's getting worse."

Guides, climbers, doctors, and clergy around the world commented on the possibility that David Sharp could have been saved. Many pointed to Lincoln Hall's rescue as evidence that David could have been rescued, without noting some key differences in the conditions of the two men, most notably that Lincoln could walk and David could not even stand.

A few weeks after he got off the mountain, Lincoln Hall came from Australia to New York to appear on the *Today* show and *Dateline* with Dan Mazur, the man who found him. Although they didn't summit Everest, Dan and his clients—Myles Osborne and Andrew Brash—were welcomed as heroes when they returned home. However, Dan told me his two clients were "pissed" at having to turn around, and he didn't think they would hire him as a guide again.

But beneath the hype of ruthlessness and heroism was a powerful irony. Russell Brice has an enviable safety record on Everest and the rest of the Himalaya: In twenty-three expeditions, he has put 270 people onto the summit of 8,000-meter peaks, with only two fatalities. Russell runs a tight ship that is both more comfortable and stricter than anything else on the Chinese side of Everest. He's almost universally respected among the guiding community. Dan Mazur, on the other hand, runs an inexpensive, seat-of-your-pants operation. Although his company has many loyal customers, Dan's large operations and laissez-faire attitude grate on some of his clients and many other guides, Russell among them. In 2005 alone, three clients died on Dan's expeditions to Everest and Pumori, the big mountain's daughter peak.

Russell regularly accused SummitClimb of being one of the expeditions that never contributes to fixing the ropes on the mountain, and told me he removed all his rope from the mountain in

2004 specifically because he felt Dan was taking advantage of him. Dan, in response, told me that Russell owes him money from a previous year.

I have found both Russell and Dan to be generous in the mountains, and they both helped me when the Connecticut expedition was falling apart. But at the end of the spring 2006 climbing season, I saw the tables turned. Russell was attacked in the press as a villain and Dan was anointed as a hero. Dan and his clients discovered Lincoln Hall and, by all accounts, did the right thing, which was to give up on reaching the summit to help the stricken climber any way they could. They called for a rescue and waited with Lincoln until the arrival of the Sherpas, who did the actual rescuing.

"We were rescuing people right and left," one of Dan's guides said while recounting their climb. "Himalayan Baywatch—that's what we do."

During the last meeting of his team in Base Camp, however, Russell choked up as he listed his team's casualties. More than ten fingers would be lost to frostbite, Mark Inglis's legs would have to undergo additional amputations, and a Sherpa was dead.

A few days after he returned from Everest, I saw Russell at Tom and Jerry's, a large, loud Kathmandu bar, where he was letting off steam with several other Everest guides and a few clients. Most of the city was celebrating Nepal's returning democracy. But Russell was again fighting back tears—both furious about and devastated by the storm of criticism that was falling on him.

"Don't I help people?" he asked me as we discussed what had been written about him and his climbers after David Sharp's death. "Haven't I saved people?"

While fingers around the world pointed at the famed guide and his celebrated client, most of the climbers in Kathmandu saw it as an example of the tall-poppy syndrome. Russell, several climbers told me, was bound to get blamed simply because he had a big operation in the limelight. Mark Inglis hadn't let his shortened legs keep him from rising above the crowd—he has eagerly pursued media attention for his climbs and his work with various charities—so he too was an easy target. In 2006, to his chagrin, he would get far more attention for his candor about a climber he couldn't possibly have saved than he would for his efforts to bring prosthetics to the legless in places like Cambodia and Nepal, or his legless climb up Everest.

In mid-June, Russell flew to Britain to visit the family of the man he had never met but was accused of leaving for dead and to return what few belongings David Sharp had brought with him that weren't lost on the mountain or pilfered after his death. Other climbers who got to know David on Everest, or who saw him during his final climb—Jamie McGuinness and Max Chaya among them—spoke with his family over the phone. David's parents have shied from the press, but his mother was inquisitive and sympathetic with the climbers she talked to. In one of the few interviews she gave after her son died, she said she didn't blame any other climbers for her son's death.

"Your only responsibility," she said, "is to save yourself—not to try to save anyone else."

David Sharp's death probably wouldn't have turned into the pin that burst the balloon of nobility surrounding Everest were it not for the notable climbers who witnessed his struggle, or the number of people involved. Many other dying climbers have been passed by on Everest. In fact, the Indian climber known as Green Boots was passed as he was dying by a team of Japanese climbers ten years before David sat down in the same spot.

In 1998, the American climber Frances Distefano-Arsentiev summited Everest from the north with her husband, Sergei Arsentiev, but became separated from Sergei during her descent, faltered, and collapsed near the First Step. Sergei tried to rescue his wife the following day but vanished, leaving his ice ax and rope near his wife. Frances survived for two days, with climbers from Uzbekistan and South Africa, as well as a number of Sherpas, stopping to try to assist her as she pleaded for help, but the other climbers were unable to drag her down.

When I was on Everest in 2004, climbers from Africa, Europe,

Asia, and the Americas reported leaving dying Korean, Bulgarian, and American mountaineers behind. Including, of course, Nils Antezana.

In fact, with adventurers who don't speak the same languages struggling to help the people who fall beside them as they climb to the Earth's high point, Everest, in a very real way, has become the Tower of Babel.

I had hoped to touch the heavens myself in 2006, but neither my work nor my health would allow me to make a summit bid. For me, the greatest joy of the Everest season was hearing that my climbing partner, Anne, had made it to the top. Back in Kathmandu, Carolyn and I embraced upon seeing our expedition's Web site with a photo of our friend standing on the summit with her gloves off and a fist raised in victory. But, as with many Everest climbers, Anne's triumph didn't bring transcendence. Her success blunted none of her outrage over the betrayals two years before, and afterward she was more likely to talk of the team that exploded than the one that got her on top of the mountain. Nonetheless, seeing her standing on the summit was one of the few bright patches in the darkness coming off the peak.

Epilogue

Soon after I sat down to talk with Gustavo Lisi, the power failed. It seemed appropriate. As I interviewed him by flashlight in the conference room of my Salta, Argentina, hotel, I realized that I was going to be no less in the dark when the lights came back on.

Gustavo was exuberantly earnest—animated, friendly, and convincing. He was shorter than I expected, but not short, wearing a yellow Chuck Roast fleece that matched the LiveStrong bracelet around his wrist.

He said he's still guiding, but there hasn't been much work. He repeatedly denied, however, that he was Nils Antezana's guide for their climb up Everest. He has made that claim before—to me, to *The Washington Post*, to other media outlets, and to other climbers. "We were only companions in the mountains," he told me in our interview—"*Compañeros de la montaña.*" Therefore, he said, he was not responsible for Nils's life during their ascent of Everest. But in his correspondence with Manuel Lugli, the man who made the arrangements for their expedition, Gustavo twice wrote that

Nils Antezana was his "client for Everest." When I mentioned the notes that Manuel had shared with me, Gustavo denied writing or saying anything of the sort.

"I told Manuel that I had a friend . . . he wasn't a client," Gustavo said, "with whom I'm going to go in the year 2004 to Everest."

According to Gustavo, Nils gave him $20,000 to put together the trip to Everest, but didn't pay him as a guide. However, Manuel, the nurse Rhonda Martin, and other climbers and guides whom Gustavo encountered during his trip to Nepal in 2004 recounted his proud assertions that he was an Everest guide, and Nils was the man he was leading up the mountain. Nobody who had seen them together doubted that Gustavo was Nils's guide.

They were close friends, Gustavo said, but Nils lied to him about his age, and he was unaware that his climbing partner was sixty-nine. Nonetheless, he also claimed he knew Nils's age would make the climb difficult, so he had provided him with the best of service.

"When I speak to Manuel, I tell him that it's an older person, it's a doctor," Gutstavo said. "And that he wants to go with the best that he can go with to Everest, and he didn't care how much money he had to pay [for] the best accommodations, with the best Sherpas. The best."

But if Nils was willing to pay for the best, I asked, why didn't he go with one of the $65,000 expeditions that have large staffs, luxurious accommodations, and guides famed for their repeated trips to the top of the mountain? Gustavo didn't have an answer.

Gustavo said he and Nils had been climbing together for three years before their trip to Everest, and that he had guided Nils on the Bolivian peaks Condoriri and Pequeño Alpamayo in 2003. In that time, Gustavo said, Nils grew quite confident in him.

"He told me, 'Gustavo, I want to go to Everest,'" he recalled of Nils's request that he accompany him. "And I want you to be the person who takes me to Everest because of your experience on the mountain."

Yet Gustavo insisted to me that he had clearly explained to Nils the limits of his experience on Everest—that he had retreated before reaching the top of the mountain when he attempted to climb it in 2000. But again, Rhonda Martin and others who were with Gustavo and Nils on Everest recalled the guide's claim that he had summited Everest from the north in 2000.

I asked Gustavo how he had ended up with Juan Carlos Gonzalez's photos from the summit of Everest and how those pictures had ended up in the Argentine media with stories saying that they showed Gustavo atop the mountain, not Juan Carlos. Gustavo said the photos actually belonged to him, that when he turned back during his summit attempt, he gave his own camera to the Sherpa who climbed with Juan Carlos. The Sherpa, he said, took the photos so Gustavo could have images from the top of the mountain. When I played Gustavo part of the tape that Juan Carlos made of him repeatedly admitting to the theft of the photos, he didn't flinch. He explained that he had admitted to the crime that he didn't commit to pacify the Spaniard, and had given Juan Carlos most of the photos because he felt sorry for him. He claimed that the tape actually supported his version of events, but after repeatedly listening to the tape and carefully transcribing it with a translator, I couldn't see how it did anything but incriminate Gustavo. Nowhere in the thirty-minute recording does Gustavo mention a Sherpa carrying his camera to the summit or any other aspects of his convoluted alibi. Gustavo told me the stories that reported it was him on the summit of Everest rather than Juan Carlos were the result of mistakes made by journalists in Advanced Base Camp reporting over a Web site. He denied telling any reporters that he had reached the summit. In the stories in Argentina that credited him with summiting Everest in 2000, I saw photos from the summit—the ones showing Juan Carlos—that Gustavo had provided to the papers. I read quotes from Gustavo, but found none in which he directly claimed reaching the summit. He, however, had no published corrections of the errors.

Gustavo said he didn't realize his friend Nils was in trouble until small things on the summit alerted him. Nils asked Gustavo why he hadn't taken off his headlamp, when Gustavo wasn't wearing one. Then Nils was slow to wave to Gustavo's camera.

"We needed to descend urgently, fast because Nils wasn't well," he said.

But then they had spent some forty minutes on the summit. I asked why they had dallied, if his partner was so desperately sick with an illness that can be cured only by going down.

"It was very pretty on the summit, splendid," Gustavo said. *"Fantastico!"*

The more I probed and challenged Gustavo, the friendlier and more animated he became. He said he hoped I would go climbing with him, to see how competent and safe he was, and accompany him to visit his parents.

"I have nothing to hide," Gustavo told me, eager to correct the horrible misconceptions I had about him.

As crazy as his stories seemed, he spoke with such sincerity that, but for everything I already knew, it would have been easy to suspend my disbelief.

"I think he told you the truth," the translator working for me said.

Gustavo wielded a binder of articles about his climbs to defend himself, but they didn't contradict any of the claims of his critics. He had a CD of photos and videos from his climb with Nils, which he said showed that he was never far from his partner. But Nils appears in only 28 of the 250 photographs, and in two short videos. Aside from the minute or so of time accounted for by those images, there is little to indicate that Gustavo spent much time with Nils.

In Gustavo's papers I could no longer find claims that he holds certification by the UIMGA, and he promised me that he is having his Web site changed so that it no longer implies that he reached the summit of Everest in 2000. But as of our meeting, Gustavo was still courting clients on the Internet, claiming a successful climb of Everest in 2000 that he did not make.

"Your level of experience as a mountaineer is not important," he said on the Web site in Spanish. "Only your desire to explore with me."

Gustavo eagerly told me of his apprenticeship with his cousin, the revered Argentinean mountaineer Flavio Lisi, who had died on Aconcagua. But he said nothing about Flavio, as president of the Friends of the Mountain Club, voting to have Gustavo expelled from the club, or the scandal that precipitated the club's action. When I sent notes later asking about that incident, and others with another mountaineering club and with the government of Salta, Argentina, I didn't hear back.

Gustavo put a lot of breath into attacking his critics. He says Nils Antezana's stubbornness and vanity led to his death. Juan Carlos botched his climb, he says, referring to the fingers the Spaniard lost and wielding articles with comments by other mountaineers critical of Juan Carlos's judgment during his ascent. Damian Benegas, who helped Fabiola investigate what had happened to her father, wasn't on Everest when Gustavo and Nils were there and has never been to the summit, so according to Gustavo he had no right to question Gustavo's actions. Fabiola Antezana flew halfway around the world only because she wanted to recover her father's Cartier watch, he said. The watch was never found, nor was the approximately $10,000 in cash that Nils Antezana had carried to Everest. Gustavo said he never saw the money and knew nothing about it or the watch.

Many other climbers and guides who are subjected to scrutiny for questionable actions on Everest also blame the victims of the tragedies they were involved in.

In a lengthy Q and A published on ExplorersWeb in July, Dutch guide Harry Kikstra, who led the visually impaired climber Thomas Weber on his fatal ascent, responded to the accusations of negligence against him made by witnesses to his client's death. He disputed the assertions by other climbers on the mountain that he did not stay close enough to his client or attempt to administer appropriate assistance after Thomas's collapse. As for the observation made by several climbers who saw Thomas that he was showing distinct symptoms of acute mountain sickness (AMS), or a deadly cerebral edema, Harry provided as rebuttal a note Thomas had sent him before the climb:

> *I do [cough] even on sea level, so sometimes the people has the*
> *impression that i suffered ams but it is not the case!! . . . Since*
> *I am rather tall and slim when i walk slowly with backpack*

*it sometimes looks as if i am unbalanced, again sometimes
people thought it is ams but it was never the case, guess it just
looks like it due to my physics.*

None of his accusers, Harry said, spoke to Thomas or spent
enough time with him to figure out whether his appearance of being altitude sick was simply the result of his disabilities.

"I think I did the best I could do and therefore am not responsible for his death," Harry wrote. "In the end he is himself."

A month later a photo that Harry sold to *National Geographic
Adventure* that shows his client just before he perished ran across
two pages of the magazine, along with a story describing the chaos
of the spring of 2006 on Everest.

Despite the harsh criticism he received after his climb that
spring, Harry at the time said he would be back to guide Everest
again. But when I spoke to him in March of 2007, he said he wasn't
heading back to Everest that year and wasn't sure he would ever
guide on the mountain again. He was no longer selling photos of
Thomas, at the request of the dead climber's family.

The documentary about Russell Brice's 2006 expedition began its
six-week run on the Discovery Channel in November. ExplorersWeb
welcomed that program with a rant under the headline THE MOST
SHAMEFUL ACT IN THE HISTORY OF MOUNTAINEERING.

George Dijmarescu also failed to escape Tom and Tina Sjogren's
wrath. A few weeks after my final story on the Connecticut Everest
Expedition appeared in the *Courant*'s Sunday magazine in November 2004, ExplorersWeb picked it up, exposing the ugliness of the
team's climb to the world. George demanded that they remove the
story from the site, and his pages-long e-mail exchanges with Tina
grew increasingly vitriolic. He began a note titled "My final effort,"
on December 2, 2004, with a hypothetical situation:

*Mel Gibson is **attacked** by a guy with a **deadly** weapon . . .
what he does? DEFEND HIMSELF, how? With his physical
power or his weapons . . . This is called in America . . . SELF*

DEFENSE Mel Gibson is not The Bad Guy . . . This is what happen to me in relation to Lakpa and Doni family affair.

George wrote that Lhakpa started the altercation in Base Camp on Everest by throwing rocks.

"The two women stand by me today and will stand tomorrow," he wrote. "They acknowledge **their fault** and long time ago apologized."

In another e-mail to ExplorersWeb George wrote that, in the death zone, Lhakpa's sister, a fifteen-year-old girl half his size who had just descended from the summit of Everest, the first mountain she had climbed in her life, still had enough energy to assault him when he criticized her.

I was attacked by Doni with a large rock . . . at camp two in 2003. Doni rose the rock above her and my head with the intention of hitting me on the head . . .

But despite the scrutiny of his actions in 2003 and 2004, George also continued his annual pilgrimage to the mountain. During 2005, EverestNews.com was both heavily promoting and strangely secretive about a team planning the first ascent of Everest's Fantasy Ridge. The team's goal was ambitious, as expressed in the more than twenty pages EverestNews.com published about their plans.

None of the postings, however, named the climbers involved. EverestNews.com noted that it would identify the climbers only to people who provided financial support to the team. Nonetheless, many Everest climbers had a good idea who the mountaineers were. They were finally identified on the Web site of Sunny Mountain Guides—Lhakpa Sherpa's fledgling Everest guiding business.

The American climbers Lakpa Sherpa, Dave Watson, and George Dijmarescu will join forces with their partners from Nepal. . . . These climbers plan to turn "Fantasy into Reality"!

Between them, the "American climbers" had scaled only one major Himalayan peak—although that mountain was Everest and they had climbed it a dozen times. Most mountaineers on Everest were disdainful of the project even before they knew the climbers involved.

"It's the most appropriately named expedition on the mountain," Tina told me before the climbing season started. "It's an absolute fantasy that they are even going to try to climb it."

In April, Dave, George, Lhakpa, and Dawa Nuru Sherpa walked from Advanced Base Camp on the Tibetan side of Everest to a glacier overlooking the ridge. But they turned back before they even began the hazardous series of rappels they had planned to reach the bottom of their proposed route. They never so much as touched the ridge with an ice ax, complaining that the route was "out of condition." Instead, the Fantasy Ridge team returned to ABC and climbed the same north side route they always had, giving the trio a total of fifteen summits of Everest by that route. George Dijmarescu claimed eight consecutive ascents of Everest, the most by any climber who wasn't a Himalayan native. But aside from a few brief news items, the accomplishment came with little glory.

Yet the Sjogrens' plans seem even more a fantasy. During 2006, they attended the Planetary Society Space Conference in Los Angeles and the Mars Society's conference in Washington, D.C., and met with many of the entrepreneurs who are organizing space tourism. After my return from Everest in 2006, they told me that they were looking into a private flight that would take them to Mars, which they believed they could arrange for about $5 billion within a few years. Not that they have that kind of money, but the finances don't appear to worry them any more than heading to Mount Everest with almost no high-altitude experience or making their first adventure skiing a trip to the South Pole. They're more concerned, considering what they've seen happen on a lawless mountain, with what kind of people will be drawn to the final frontier. There had already been five "space tourists" by that point, and one of the fledgling space-tour companies was offering "space walks." But, Tom and Tina said, there had also already been a few scams and ripoffs. In the meantime, they told me they hoped to climb K2 during the summer of 2007. Those plans fell through when they realized that keeping their business running and laying the foundation for their Mars flight wouldn't leave them enough time to train. They hadn't done any real mountaineering in nearly eight years, and K2 would have been only the second major summit they had reached.

Through her father, Fabiola had seen the world's high peaks as the greatest of nature's beauty and the people who climbed them as noble adventurers. But by the time she had worked for Explorers-Web for a year, she had seen more than enough madness in the mountains as well. The day Fabiola started her job in October 2005, news arrived of eighteen climbers—seven French mountaineers and eleven of their Nepali support staff —who had perished in an avalanche on Kang Guru, a mountain in northwest Nepal. It was one of the worst accidents ever in the Himalaya, but that was just the warm-up to a year of horrific carnage throughout the climbing world in 2006. Twelve climbers followed Fabiola's father's fate on Everest. Andres Delgado, one of the first climbers to contact Fabiola from Everest regarding her father's death, vanished himself on Changabang—a mountain in Indian Himalaya—late that summer. Revered American climbers Charlie Fowler and Christine Boskoff were unaccounted for for weeks in China before Charlie's body was found in the avalanche debris on a remote and obscure peak. Sue Nott, one of America's best female mountaineers, and Karen Mc-Neill, an accomplished Kiwi climber, disappeared on Mount Foraker in Alaska. Todd Skinner, one of America's most accomplished rock climbers, fell to his death when his harness broke; world champion ice climber Harald Berger was crushed when an ice cave collapsed on him; and famed American ski mountaineer Doug Coombs died when he fell off a cliff in the Alps while trying to help another extreme skier, who also fell to his death. Six climbers were killed in their tents on

Ama Dablam, the first mountain I visited in Nepal, when the hanging glacier the mountain is named for dropped house-size blocks of ice onto their camp. In December, three climbers perished on Mount Hood amid a weeklong storm on the mountain and a much longer tempest in the media. But, for Fabiola, the most troubling casualties in the mountains were not climbers. Her father's death on Everest drew her into the shadows cast by the Himalaya. Killings on Cho Oyu by the Chinese military marked the end of her inquiries there.

Those two mountains, in fact, have been the bookends for many climbers' adventures in the Himalaya. Cho Oyu, considered the easiest of the world's fourteen 8,000-meter mountains, is the most common trial before Everest. It is consequently getting record crowds similar to those that swarm the highest mountain. In September 2006, Jamie McGuinness estimated that more than 300 people filled Cho Oyu's Base Camp.

Below the peak, the Nangpa La Pass, at about 19,000 feet, leads from Chinese Tibet into Nepal. The Nangpa La—the path taken by the Sherpa people when they migrated to Nepal from Tibet five hundred years ago—is the traditional trade route between the two countries. Many of the Tibetans crossing the pass these days, however, are hoping to escape China for a new life in Nepal or India. According to the International Campaign for Tibet, some 2,500 refugees flee Tibet every year.

Early in the morning of September 30, 2006, as climbers looked out onto a line of nearly eighty Tibetans making their way to the pass, members of the People's Armed Police arrived and opened fire on the refugees. A teenage Buddhist nun, Kelsang Namtso, was leading a group of children when she was shot to death by a sniper.

"They are shooting them like, like dogs," one climber said as a cameraman with a Romanian television station filmed the attack.

About forty of the Tibetans managed to get across the pass, but thirty were captured, many of them children. The prisoners were marched back through Cho Oyu's Base Camp, which a British police officer climbing there reported was swarming with soldiers.

One climber found a Tibetan cowering in his team's toilet tent. Kelsang's body was left on the trail until the next day, when police officers dumped it in a crevasse.

But despite the scores of climbers who witnessed the attack, news of the incident was slow to emerge. First word of the atrocity came from a guide, Luis Benitez, who contacted ExplorersWeb anonymously, leading Tom and Tina to break a major international news story. In the days that followed ExplorersWeb's first story, several European climbers spoke out. Beijing reported that the Tibetans had attacked the soldiers and were shot in self-defense, but witnesses countered that the Tibetans were unarmed and running away, with their backs to the military. Then the Romanian television station PROTV broadcast their cameraman's video of the incident. Still, some climbers were not happy that the news got out. Activists for the Tibetan cause, on the other hand, were shocked at the silence of most of the mountaineers who saw the shooting. The day after he reported what he had witnessed, Luis was confronted by Russell Brice and Henry Todd, who were angry that he had broken the story. To justify their silence, Russell, Henry, and other guides cited concern for the safety of Western mountaineers who were still in Tibet and for the Tibetans that they hire, who would lose their most important source of income if the guides quit coming. But to Luis, it was simply a case of business interests clashing with human rights. To him, the guides who tried to silence witnesses to the shooting were less concerned about their clients or staffs than they were about the possibility that the news would anger the Chinese government, prompting them to restrict mountaineers' access to Tibet, and cut off guides from Cho Oyu, Shishipangma, and the north side of Everest—some of their most popular and lucrative peaks. Luis eventually went on the record, reporting that Russell had assisted the Chinese soldiers by treating them for snow blindness. Russell, however, told me that he and his clients were in a high camp during the incident and witnessed none of it.

The silent guides' fears were not unfounded. On their return to Kathmandu from Cho Oyu, several climbers reported that they were contacted by the Chinese Embassy and brought in for interviews. A few weeks later, the Chinese government announced that they were limiting the number of permits to climb Everest from Tibet and raising their price—ostensibly to calm down the Tibetan side of Everest for the Chinese government's planned ascent of the mountain with the Olympic Torch for the 2008 Beijing games, and a practice run of the torch climb planned for the 2007 Everest season. While some climbers had long hoped the Chinese would impose stricter control on the Tibetan side of Everest, many mountaineers and media wondered if the increases in restrictions and price were actually a response to the climbers who spoke out about the Nangpa La massacre. Independent climbers, Tibetan activists, and armchair mountaineers, on the other hand, raged about the silence of guides who were on the mountain at the time of the atrocity. They cited it as another example of how commercial mountaineering expeditions, already accused of overcrowding mountains and conspiring against independent climbers, were ruining the sport.

For their part, mountain guides point out that plenty of inexperienced mountaineers are on the mountain without guides or proper leadership. They increasingly feel put upon by climbers who show up on Everest lacking the skills or resources to climb the mountain on their own, but without the money to hire on with a group that can ensure their safety and that of those around them. As commercial teams began gearing up for another Everest season in 2007, guides Duncan Chessell and Jamie McGuinness were contacted by a number of climbers who were on the fence about joining their teams. But one in particular spooked them.

"It felt like it was word for word the kind of note that David [Sharp] had sent us," Duncan said.

"Asian Trekking is offering me this for $10,000," Duncan recalled the potential client writing to him and Jamie, who were offering a trip with Sherpa support, professional leadership, and Internet access, but at more than twice the price.

"What do I get for the extra money?" the man asked.

"I felt like sending him a picture of David Sharp, dead in his cave, and saying, 'Not this!'" Duncan said.

Virtually every guide on Everest has turned away clients who didn't have the skill, experience, or cash to climb the mountain, only to have them show up there anyway with whatever agency offered up Everest at a price they could afford.

"They know you're going to be there," Duncan lamented, "so they're going to be using your tents, stealing your oxygen, eating your food, and needing your help, but being completely unable to do anything to help you. When they get into trouble, they're going to expect you to save them. And if you don't, the world press is going to execute you."

For a decade, "commercial" climbers—paid guides and their clients—have taken much of the blame for the troubles on Everest. But mountain guiding is not the only kind of commerce there. The teashops, the laptops, the sat phones and solar panels; the oxygen and alcohol; the porters, prostitutes, and professional athletes; the filmmakers, the authors, and the journalists all contribute to the economy of Everest.

The mountain remains as tall as ever, but technology continues to shrink the world around it so that anybody on the planet can be a part of the peak's spectacle. And while the annual dramas in the media don't affect Everest's altitude, they certainly lower her status. Those attempting to domesticate the Goddess Mother of the Universe with ropes and satellites shouldn't be surprised that she isn't submitting gracefully to being a mere mortal's mountain.

After my own visits to Everest, the acrimony that spread from the mountain through the world seemed like a vengeful spell from a deity angered by the trespassers on her slopes. Then, a few months after my first homecoming from Tibet, a Connecticut rock climber smashed her boyfriend's skull with his own climbing hammer. Neither of them were Everest climbers. And I began to wonder how much a big mountain and its big money drives climbers to wrongdoing and how much playing on the edge inevitably leads a few people to step beyond it, regardless of where the game is played.

The diminutive cliffs of Connecticut, in fact, would be unknown but for the sabotage, vandalism, and fights that are the best-known characteristics of climbing in the state. One gifted and obsessively active climber, claiming that permanent anchors in the cliffs—bolts and pitons installed to catch falling climbers—are eyesores and a form of cheating, has waged a twenty-year crusade against the climbing community at large. He's enforced his ethics by removing or destroying hundreds of pieces of equipment—nearly every permanent climbing anchor in Connecticut—an act he admits to in his guidebooks to the area. One route had a fatal fall from the spot where gear that might have saved the climber had been removed. As the "bolt war" has escalated, climbers have found other anchors throughout New England chopped, trail work ripped out, nails strewn in driveways, and trees vandalized. The saboteur has been banned from a number of climbing areas, fined, and put on two years' probation. But so far, the legal actions haven't stopped the crimes.

To me, the "bolt war" seems less about bolts than about being at war. And in that, I see a lot of common ground between the isolated, treeless wilderness of Mount Everest and the wooded, suburban cliffs of Connecticut. Regardless of whether the mountain is 30,000 feet tall, or only thirty, some visitors are less interested in the game than in playing in a place where brute strength and ruthlessness overrule compassion, civility, and fair play. In others, the belief that they have risked their lives defying the laws of physics seems to validate defying the laws of society as well.

Certainly the percentage of people in the mountains engaged in crime and malfeasance is much smaller than in the city where I live. But in wildernesses where weather and gravity create dire consequences for the smallest of offenses, it only takes a few outlaws to bring mayhem and disaster.

In the years since I went to Everest with George Dijmarescu, I've regularly seen his big black truck in the neighborhood where we both live and work. There's a bumper sticker on the tailgate advertising SunnyMountainGuides.com, next to the large logo for his contracting business. On a couple of occasions my wife and I have run into Lhakpa in a local convenience store. Each time she has hidden before we could ask how she was.

A month after the Nangpa La shootings, Davide's position with a European investment bank in New York was eliminated. Fabiola quit her job with ExplorersWeb and prepared to resettle in London with her husband. As the movers packed up her life on the Upper West Side, she set aside one item to carry herself—the photo of her father holding the birthday card he made for her atop a mountain in the land of his birth. Just before she and Davide moved, they visited Bolivia again, this time with hopes of climbing a mountain there themselves. They hired Bernardo Guarachi, Nils's guide of choice, to lead them up Huayna Potosi, one of her father's favorite climbs. But Fabiola found the altitude sickened her when she was still a day away from the summit. And when she turned back from that peak, perhaps she left Everest behind as well.

When she and Davide arrived at their new flat in London, the photo of Nils atop Illimani was the first thing that Fabiola unpacked. Then she set out to find a position in journalism, hoping that her language skills and overseas experience would lead to work covering international affairs. By the end of the year, she had a position with ABC News. It was an entry-level job gathering faxes, researching for other people's stories, and writing up news for the Web. Most of the other people in the position were ten years younger than Fabiola. But she was confident she would move up fast, and within a few weeks she had conducted her first interviews for her own stories.

"I'm finally doing what I should have been doing my whole life," she told me.

After a few weeks learning the ropes, Fabiola was assigned to a month of overnights. The hours didn't bother her. But in the early morning, with the computer screens blank, the televisions dark, and the phones silent, she often remembered another sleepless night in

London—the night she waited for the call that never came from her father on Everest. Now she wished she could call him. To tell him what she was doing with her life. To say thanks.

"If it weren't for him and all the things that happened, I don't know if I would be here," she would think to herself. "He was my first story."

He'd be proud of the turn her life took after his death, of her doggedness in finding out as much of the truth of what had happened to him as she could. But for that, she had traded some of the regard she had once held for her father. She still saw him on a mountain's summit, but not so much on a pedestal. "How could he not have known the things I found out?" she continues to ask herself. "How could such an intelligent and educated man show so little diligence checking into the person he trusted his life to? How could his pride keep him pushing on into such an obvious disaster?"

In the last line of his diary, Nils had left open the question of who held "the final responsibilities." At least for that, Fabiola has the answer.

Acknowledgments

This book was a lot like my expeditions—many people helped put it together.

Most significant among them is my wife, Carolyn Moreau, who has accompanied me on all of my Himalayan journeys, even though she had no desire to climb to the summits I aspired to. She stayed on through the duration of endeavors that subjected her to tumult that we could never have predicted or prepared for, and overcame suffering well beyond that of most climbing trips, not to mention marriages. Without her support, faith, and courage, I could never have attempted the newspaper stories that spawned my investigations into the troubles in the Himalaya. Without her assistance as a videojournalist, researcher, editor, climber, and nurse, I would never have finished writing this book, and might not have survived it.

I have also been truly fortunate to have an agent like Wendy Strothman, who has proven an ardent advocate, a diligent and enthusiastic reader, and a good friend. Dan O'Connell, Wendy's partner at The Strothman Agency, made the chores of marketing a book fun. Leslie Wells, at Hyperion, has proven a tireless and astute editor, gently pulling me back in line when my manuscript lost the trail.

Few newspapers would have sent one of their journalists to climb Mount Everest, or continued to support such an adventure when it turned into an investigation. I've been fortunate to work at *The Hartford Courant,* which has indulged my twenty-year streak of crazy story ideas. I'm most grateful to picture editor Bruce Moyer, who unflaggingly advocated my work, and news editor Bernie Davidow, who drove me to report deeply and write with purpose. Through the darkest moments of climbing on Everest, reporting the news stories, and writing this book, Bruce and Bernie have remained stalwart friends. Cliff Teutsch, editor of the *Courant,* continued to believe in my project, even as it veered wildly off route. Among the *Courant* editors and staff who gathered to hear my breathless satellite phone calls from the mountain and helped create the series' final story in the now, sadly, defunct *Northeast Magazine,* I also wish to thank John Scanlan, Thom McGuire, Brian Toolan, Claude Albert, Jim Kuykendall, Gary Duchane, Jeni Frank, David Funkhouser, Stef Summers, David Grewe, Lynne Delucia, and Joan Dumaine. Tricia Barrett and Colette Yeich brought our story to hundreds of middle school students through the Newspapers in Education program. Dennis Yonan, Dan Corjulo, and Cassandra Corrigan provided invaluable technical support. Less tangible, but just as important, are the guidance and encouragement I have received from other journalists in the *Courant* newsroom. I want to thank all of my colleagues on *The Hartford Courant* photo staff, the most talented collection of journalists I could ever hope to work with, but especially Rich Messina, John Woike, Mark Mirko, and Michael McAndrews.

Deb Hornblow and Dan Haar gave repeated readings of my manuscript, and their generosity with their time was invaluable. Susan Campbell, Nancy Schoeffler, Deb Swift, and Daniela Altimari were also diligent and helpful readers. Matt Kaufman, Mike Swift, Rinker Buck, Tara Bray Smith, Dan Barry, and Lis Harris provided excellent guidance at crucial moments in my reporting and writing. Patrick Raycraft and Janet Fuentes Loud provided critical help with Spanish documents and translations. Jennifer Diaz, my sister-in-law, was an excellent translator and companion during my work in the Basque country.

I'm grateful to dozens of sources and subjects who opened their homes and lives to me, most notably Gladys, Fabiola, and David Antezana, and Davide Percipalle, who have been hospitable and open, even when discussing very painful events in their lives. I remain impressed by Michael Leahy's work for *The Washington Post Magazine* describing Nils Antezana's death on Everest. He set the bar high for the reporting of the Antezanas' story, and provided me with a significant head start on my own work.

A number of climbers whom I have lived with on Everest have made the tedium, suffering, and terror bearable, and the moments of joy sublime. Among those, I must first thank Anne Parmenter, whom I climbed with during all of my trips to the Himalaya and on a number of adventures closer to home. Anne's courage, strength, and convictions will always be an inspiration to me. Among my teammates on Everest I also wish to thank Bill Driggs, Iñigo De Pineda, Scott Woolums, Marnie Pearsall, Hugo Searle, Chris Klinke, Fredrik Sträng, Kevin Moore, Johan Frankelius, Laurie Bagley, Mike Rappaport, Dawa Gelje Sherpa, Ang Mingma Sherpa, Dawa Nuru Sherpa, Lhakpa Sherpa, Brad Clement, Ali Bushnaq, Dudu Yifrah, Micha Yaniv, Tonya Riggs, Selebelo Sclamolela, and Gautam Patil.

Duncan Chessell has proven an excellent expedition organizer, an honest source, and a good friend. Jamie McGuinness was an exceptional leader, with an encyclopedic knowledge of Nepal, Tibet, and the Himalaya. Luis Benitez, Guy Cotter, and the Adventure Consultants crew; Ellie Henke, Dave Morton, Vern Tejas, and Willi Pritie at the Alpine Ascents camp; and Dr. Luanne Freer and Lakpa Sherpa were all gracious hosts on Everest. In Kathmandu, Billi Bierling, Elizabeth Hawley, and Wanda Vivequin were invaluable assistants to my research.

I can't possibly thank all of the climbers from other camps on Everest who assisted me, but I would like to mention Serena Brocklebank, John Whittle, Paul Moores, Dave Pritt, the members of the Italian EV/K2 expedition, Dan Mazur, Arnold Coster, and the rest of the SummitClimb expedition in 2004, and Russell Brice and his Himalayan Experience teams in 2004 and 2006. My work in Bolivia and Argentina would not have been possible without the help of Irene Meninato, Emilio Gonzalez Turu, Carlo Clerucci, and Gaby Burgoa.

Among the climbers I have tied in with throughout my climbing career, I would like to thank Joe Vitti, Dave Fasulo, Dave Raymond, Rob Lemire, and Will and Chris Tacy for their guidance and friendship.

But most of all, I must thank my wife, Carolyn. This book is as much hers as mine.

Bibliography

Barcott, Bruce. "Everest Profile: The Toddfather: The most imposing figure on Everest has been told to stay home. But don't count Henry Todd out yet." *Outside* (April 2001).

Benegas, Willie. "The Crystal Snake: Overlooking the Everest circus and yet a world away, a rivulet of water ice plunges down the huge north face of Nuptse, Nepal." *The American Alpine Journal,* Issue 78, Vol. 46 (2004): pp. 14–23.

Benitez, Luis. "The Rescue." MountainZone.com (May 25, 2003).

Bishop, Brent, and Naumann, Chris. "Mount Everest: Reclamation of the World's Highest Junkyard," *Mountain Research and Development,* Vol. 16, Number 3 (August 1996): pp. 323–327.

Boukreev, Anatoli, and Dewalt, G. Weston. *The Climb: Tragic Ambitions on Everest.* New York: St. Martin's Press, 1997.

Breed, Allen G., and Gurubacharya, Binaj. "Everest Remains a Deadly Draw for Climbers." Associated Press (July 15 and 16, 2006).

Brice, Russell. "Reflections on Everest 2006." Himalayan Experience, himex.com (2006).

Campbell-Johnston, Rachel. "In Memoriam: The Foolish and the Brave." *The Times* (April 18, 2003): pp. 2, 4.

Cowell, Alan. " 'Dead' Climber's Survival Impugns Mount Everest Ethics." *The New York Times* (May 28, 2006): p. 10.

Douglas, Ed. "Everest Mystery: Death Zone: The youngest Briton to climb Earth's tallest mountain never made it back. Now his family and the guides who led him there are locked in a bitter dispute, reports Ed Douglas." *The Observer* (November 11, 2001): p. 22.

———. "Everest: Return to Thin Air: Over the Top." *Outside,* Vol. 31, Number 9 (September 2006): pp. 72–76, 118–121.

English, Rebecca. "Why Our Son Need Not Have Died on Everest." *Daily Mail* (May 31, 2003): p. 40.

"Everest Expedition Hopes to Conquer Summit and Trash." Environmental News Network, March 31, 2000.

Fedarko, Kevin. "Masters of the Khumbu: They are called the 'Ice Doctors' of Everest, and they forge the most dangerous route to the summit. But at what cost?" *Men's Journal,* Vol. 16, Number 4 (May 2007): pp. 144–151, 258, 259.

Fielding, Nick. "Disappeared into Thin Air." *Sunday Times* (June 18, 2000).

———. "Family Launches Lawsuit over Everest Death." *Sunday Times* (June 2, 2002).

"Guias Peruanos sobreviven a la tragedia del Alpamayo," Peru eListas.net, Noticias Sobre Rescates, July 24, 2003.

Harding, Mike. *Yorkshire Transvestite Found Dead on Everest.* Kirkby Stephen, Cumbria: Hayloft Publishing Limited, 2005.

Heil, Nick. "Left to Die on Everest: No one came to David Sharp's aid on Everest. What happened?" *Men's Journal* (August 2006).

Inglis, Mark. *Legs on Everest: The Full Story of His Most Remarkable Adventure Yet.* Auckland, New Zealand: Random House, 2006.

Jones, Finn-Olaf. "Into Finn Air: Mayhem erupts on Mt. Everest as an e-mail goes astray. 'It's all bullshit on Everest these days.'—Sir Edmund Hillary." Forbes.com, 2001.

Kennedy, Dominic, and Pavia, Will. "Briton Sues Over Son Lost on Everest." London: Times Online (December 23, 2005).

Krakauer, Jon. *Into Thin Air: A Personal Account of the Mount Everest Disaster.* New York: Villard Books, 1997.

Leahy, Michael. "The Dark Side of the Mountain: When a doctor reached the peak of Everest, he celebrated with his guide and crew. So why was he left to die?" *The Washington Post Magazine* (November 28, 2004): pp. W12–17, 22–29.

Lee, Dick, and Pratt, Colin. *Operation Julie: How the Undercover Police Team Smashed the World's Greatest Drugs Ring.* London: W. H. Allen, 1978.

Pierce, Andrew. "Death Writ Threatens Mt. Everest Exhibition." *The Times* (July 4, 2002): p. 7.

Roberts, David. *Great Exploration Hoaxes.* New York: Modern Library Exploration, 2001.

———. "The Everest Decade 1996–2006: The Mad Season." *National Geographic Adventure,* Vol. 8, Number 7 (September 2006): pp. 54–57, 91–94.

Rose, David. "Why Was a Young Man Who Paid GBP 25,000 to Climb Everest Left to Die Alone at the Summit?" *Mail on Sunday* (May 7, 2000): pp. 58, 59.

Schoenberg, Shira. "Israeli Victims of Peru Avalanche Were Adventurous Nature Lovers." *The Jerusalem Post,* July 24, 2003, p. 4.

Scully, Lizzy. "Oh Brothers! When the Benegas Twins Meet the Mountains, It's Double Trouble." *Rock and Ice,* Issue 147 (January 2006): p. 74.

Sjogren, Tina. "Sale of the Century: Ten years after the 1996 Everest disaster, business is booming at the top of the world." *Rock and Ice,* Issue 154 (October 2006).

Index

Fred Beckham

Michael Kodas is an award-winning journalist whose work has been published by the *New York Times*, the *Los Angeles Times*, the *Washington Post*, the *Boston Globe*, the *Chicago Tribune*, *Newsweek*, *GEO* magazine, *Outside* online, and many other publications around the world. He was a member of the team of journalists at the *Hartford Courant* awarded the Pulitzer Prize for breaking news coverage in 1999. He lives in Hartford, Connecticut, with his wife, Carolyn Moreau.